GoLang

Go, also known as GoLang, is a Google-developed open-source, compiled, and statically typed computer language. Go is a general purpose programming language with a straightforward syntax and a large standard library. The building of highly accessible and scalable web apps is one of the primary areas where GoLang is widely used. It may also be used to develop command-line programs, desktop applications, and even mobile apps.

Go was designed from the ground up for networking and infrastructure-related applications. It was developed as a replacement for popular server-side languages like Java and C++. The Go programming language aims to combine the efficiency and safety of a statically typed, compiled language with the simplicity of programming of an interpreted, dynamically typed language. It also aspires to be cutting-edge, with networked and multicore computer capabilities.

Why Should You Learn GoLang?

GoLang is becoming one of the most popular languages, which means that learning it can open up new doors of opportunity and even help you land a job at various companies that use Go extensively.

Ease of writing concurrent programs, fast compilation, simple syntax, and static linking are some of the features that make Go an ideal candidate for developing various applications.

Features:

- Step-by-step approach to problem solving and skill development
- A quick run-through of the basic concepts, in the form of a "Crash Course"

- Advanced, hands-on core concepts, with a focus on real-world problems

- Industry-level coding paradigm, practice-oriented explanatory approach

- Special emphasis on writing clean and optimized code, with additional chapters focused on coding methodology

GoLang
The Ultimate Guide

Edited by
Sufyan bin Uzayr

CRC Press
Taylor & Francis Group
Boca Raton London New York

CRC Press is an imprint of the
Taylor & Francis Group, an **informa** business

First edition published 2023
by CRC Press
6000 Broken Sound Parkway NW, Suite 300, Boca Raton, FL 33487-2742

and by CRC Press
4 Park Square, Milton Park, Abingdon, Oxon, OX14 4RN

CRC Press is an imprint of Taylor & Francis Group, LLC

© 2023 Sufyan bin Uzayr

Library of Congress Cataloging-in-Publication Data

Names: Bin Uzayr, Sufyan, author.
Title: GoLang : the ultimate guide / Sufyan bin Uzayr.
Description: First edition. | Boca Raton : CRC Press, 2023. | Includes
bibliographical references and index.
Identifiers: LCCN 2022025681 (print) | LCCN 2022025682 (ebook) |
ISBN 9781032312323 (hardback) | ISBN 9781032312316 (paperback) |
ISBN 9781003309055 (ebook)
Subjects: LCSH: Go (Computer program language)
Classification: LCC QA76.73.G63 B56 2023 (print) | LCC QA76.73.G63
(ebook) | DDC 005.13/3--dc23/eng/20220919
LC record available at https://lccn.loc.gov/2022025681
LC ebook record available at https://lccn.loc.gov/2022025682

ISBN: 9781032312323 (hbk)
ISBN: 9781032312316 (pbk)
ISBN: 9781003309055 (ebk)

DOI: 10.1201/9781003309055

Typeset in Minion
by KnowledgeWorks Global Ltd.

Contents

Acknowledgments

There are many people who deserve to be on this page, for this book would not have come into existence without their support. That said, some names deserve a special mention, and I am genuinely grateful to:

- My parents, for everything they have done for me.

- My siblings, for helping with things back home.

- The Parakozm team, especially Divya Sachdeva, Jaskiran Kaur, and Vartika, for offering great amounts of help and assistance during the book-writing process.

- The CRC team, especially Sean Connelly and Danielle Zarfati, for ensuring that the book's content, layout, formatting, and everything else remain perfect throughout.

- Reviewers of this book, for going through the manuscript and providing their insight and feedback.

- Typesetters, cover designers, printers, and all other helpers in the development of this book.

- All the folks associated with Zeba Academy, either directly or indirectly, for their help and support.

- The programming community in general, and the web development community in particular, for all their hard work and efforts.

Sufyan bin Uzayr

About the Author

Sufyan bin Uzayr is a writer, coder, and entrepreneur with over a decade of experience in the industry. He has authored several books in the past, pertaining to a diverse range of topics, ranging from History to Computers/IT.

Sufyan is the Director of Parakozm, a multinational IT company specializing in EdTech solutions. He also runs Zeba Academy, an online learning and teaching vertical with a focus on STEM fields.

Sufyan specializes in a wide variety of technologies, such as JavaScript, Dart, WordPress, Drupal, Linux, and Python. He holds multiple degrees, including ones in Management, IT, Literature, and Political Science.

Sufyan is a digital nomad, dividing his time between four countries. He has lived and taught in universities and educational institutions around the globe. Sufyan takes a keen interest in technology, politics, literature, history, and sports, and in his spare time, he enjoys teaching coding and English to young students.

Learn more at sufyanism.com.

CHAPTER 1

Crash Course in GoLang

IN THIS CHAPTER

➤ What is GoLang?

➤ Major concepts

➤ Advantages and disadvantages

➤ Syntax and code basics

➤ Additional info

Go Language is an open-source computer language that emphasizes simplicity, dependability, and efficiency.

In 2007, Google created the Go programming language. At the time, Google was rapidly expanding, and the code used to run its infrastructure was also expanding in both size and complexity. Some Google cloud developers began to suspect that the massive and complicated codebase slowed their work. As a consequence, they determined that a new programming language focused on simplicity and speed was required. Go was created by Robert Griesemer, Rob Pike, and Ken Thompson.

In 2012, Go became an open-source project and was made available to the public. It swiftly grew in popularity and has since become one of the significant modern programming languages.

DOI: 10.1201/9781003309055-1

IS IT REFERRED TO AS Go OR GoLang?

Is the language known as Go or GoLang? Google takes it from the horse's mouth: the language is called "Go."

According to Google, the name "GoLang" originates from the URL GoLang.org, which was chosen since "go.org was not available to us." As a result, some individuals use the terms "GoLang" and "Go" interchangeably when referring to the programming language.

To be fair, GoLang is far more Google-able than Go, which may refer to either the strategic game or the cult-classic Doug Liman film. GoLang is also the Twitter hashtag for Go, #GoLang.

WHAT IS THE PURPOSE OF GoLang?

Go was initially designed for networking and infrastructure-related programming. It was designed to replace popular high-performance server-side languages, such as Java and C++. Go is now used for a wide range of purposes, including:

- Go is a popular programming language for cloud-based or server-side applications.

- Go is also widely used in DevOps and site reliability automation.

- Go is used to write a large number of command-line utilities.

- Go is widely used in artificial intelligence and data science.

- Some people use Go in microcontroller programming, robotics, and video games.

However, Go shines the brightest when it comes to infrastructure. Some of today's most popular infrastructure tools, such as Kubernetes, Docker, and Prometheus, are developed in Go.

WHY IS Go SO POPULAR?

There may be as many viewpoints on this as there are Go programmers, but two stand out:

- **The ease of use of programming languages:** To begin with, Go is easy to learn and comprehend. According to a common Go aphorism, the whole Go specification can be read and digested in an afternoon. Many developers who have dived into Go say that it is simple to learn compared to other languages.

- **Applications with high performance:** Second, when it comes to performance, Go is unrivaled. Because it was developed for large-scale automation, Go makes it very simple to create high-performance applications.

Other Programming Languages vs. Go

According to the Stack Overflow Developer Survey, Go is one of the most popular programming languages among its users. Go's own 2020 developer poll, which received a 92% satisfaction rating among Go users, agrees.

Python vs. Go

Python has been for more than 30 years, yet its popularity continues to rise. The language's design has withstood the test of time (despite some rough spots along the way). Python and Go are two of the most popular and user-friendly programming languages available today.

Python is an excellent object-oriented programming language, but it is also possible to develop programs with a functional programming approach. Python language is perhaps the most widely used programming language among non-programmers. Python's versatility is one of the reasons it is so popular. Use for anything from cleaning out files on your computer to developing online apps, serverless projects, teaching programming to children, working on animation, etc.

But How Does Go Stack Up against Python?

Python and Go have a straightforward syntax and are supported by all major cloud providers first-party.

Both Go and Python are simple to learn and straightforward to get started with for novices. Which is more manageable is debatable. Go is a more straightforward language that can be taught more quickly, but some people find it more challenging to get started than Python, which takes longer to master since there is more to understand.

SHOULD WE STUDY Go?

So, why should you study Go? It's simple to go. Many developers feel that Go is simple to learn. And its code is quite simple to grasp. Learning Go has a significant return in terms of power and variety.

Go is a versatile programming language that can handle everything from infrastructure to the web to data processing.

Go is popular on cloud systems. As a significant language, Amazon Web Services, Microsoft Azure, and Google Cloud Platform (GCP) provide first-class support for Go. So, if we're looking to program on the cloud, Go is a terrific option.

Go has a thriving and active open-source community that creates modules and libraries, mentors newcomers, and contributes to the overall Go project.

According to the Stack Overflow Developer Survey, the median income for Go developers in the United States is $140,000 per year.

So, consider Go if we're looking for a programming language that can accomplish a lot, has a wonderful community, and is simple to learn.

Go PROGRAMMING FEATURES

- **Language Design:** The language designers deliberately decided to keep the language basic and easy to grasp. The complete details are contained inside a few pages, and several intriguing design decisions were made using the language's object-oriented capabilities. The language is opinionated, promoting a conversational approach to problem-solving. Inheritance is favored over composition. "Do More with Less" is the Go Language slogan.

  Go includes contemporary development procedures for dealing with open-source projects into handling external packages. A series of simple commands allows us to fetch external packages and publish our own packages straight from the tools.

  Go features a rich standard library, which is supplied in packages.

- **Static Typing:** Go is a statically typed language. Consequently, this compiler works to build code properly and assures type conversions and compatibility. Because of this characteristic, Go avoids all of our problems with dynamically typed languages.

- **Testing Support:** By default, Go contains unit testing capabilities, including an easy framework for developing unit tests in tandem with our code, allowing us to understand code coverage through our tests. We can simply utilize this to produce code descriptions, for instance.

- **Platform Freedom:** Like the Java programming language, the Go programming language allows platform independence. Because of its modular architecture and flexibility, the code is compiled and transformed into the smallest binary form feasible, requiring no dependencies. We can compile them on any platform, server, or app.

WHAT MAKES GoLang SUPERIOR TO OTHER COMPUTER LANGUAGES?

In the field of programming languages, there is no respite for advancements and discoveries. Developers always search for a more simple, sophisticated, and project-friendly language. GoLang evolved as a fantastic new programming language with an abundance of options. Since its inception, GoLang has taken the programming world by surprise.

Many of the mysteries that set this language apart from the rest will be disclosed here.

GoLang's Core Capability

While looking for a code compilation project, Google developers purportedly came up with the GoLang. As a result, GoLang is the only language that encompasses all three desirable characteristics, namely simplicity of coding, efficient code compilation, and efficient execution. Combining these characteristics in a single language differentiates GoLang from other computer languages.

Go, often known as GoLang, is a powerful system-level programming language for massive network servers and huge distributed systems. GoLang evolved as an alternative to C++ and Java for app developers due to what Google needs for its network servers and distributed systems. The language was created to reduce the sluggishness and challenges of programming for big, scalable servers and software systems. Go came to Google to deliver the answers listed below to be more explicit.

- Compilation and execution in the blink of an eye.

- Remove the necessity to deal with many language subsets for a single project.

- Code readability and documentation have been improved.

- Providing an utterly consistent language.

- Allows for easy software versioning.

- The capacity to develop in a variety of languages.

- Making dependency management easier.

Multithreading and Concurrency

Manufacturers add cores to the system to boost performance as hardware grows more complex over time. The system must handle database connections via microservices, queues, and caches when dealing with many cores. As a result, today's hardware necessitates a programming language capable of supporting concurrency and scaling up performance as the number of cores rises over time.

Most programming languages restrict concurrent execution when dealing with several threads, which typically slows down the pace of programming, compilation, and execution. Go appears as the most plausible alternative for handling both multithreading and concurrency in this case.

Go as a computer language emerged when multicore processors were commonly available on powerful hardware. Naturally, the architects of Go prioritize concurrency. Go employs goroutines rather than threads to manage several tasks simultaneously.

From within, Go Empowers Hardware

Because hardware processors only comprehend binaries, any Java or JVM program is translated into binaries. This hardware-level interpretation lengthens the execution duration. This is why compiled languages, such as C/C++, may boost efficiency and implementation speed by eliminating the step of comprehension.

However, extracting and allocating variables in C/C++ is time-consuming and complicated. Go emerges as the ultimate option here, combining the best of both worlds. Go, like C/C++, is a programming technique that accounts for its speed. On the other hand, it employs garbage collection and object removal for variable allocation, much like Java. As a result, Go is an excellent programming language for working with any hardware system.

Unmatched Simplicity of Go

One of the key advantages of using Go is its simplicity. Despite being a very advanced language with a robust feature set, Go stands out from the crowd owing to its ease of use and fundamental approach.

- **No Generics:** Generics or patterns, which have long been a feature of several programming languages, frequently add to the ambiguity and difficulty of comprehension. The designers simplified things by choosing against them.

- **No Dynamic Libraries:** To keep the language basic, Go opted to omit any dynamic libraries. Users can, however, upload dynamic libraries through plug-in packages in the newest Go 1.10 version. This was merely inserted as an afterthought.

- **Single Executable:** GoLang does not come with a runtime library. It can produce a single executable file that may be released simply by copying. This eliminates any worry about making mistakes due to dependencies or version incompatibilities.

Built-in Testing and Profiling Framework

Many of us have met the complexity of picking a testing framework through a series of assessments when designing a JavaScript application. The fact that we seldom use more than 20% of the chosen framework is accurate most of the time. When excellent profiling is necessary for evaluation, a similar difficulty emerges.

Go has an in-built testing and profiling tool to help us test the application fast and efficiently. The tool may be used for testing and profiling purposes and offer ready-to-execute code samples.

Easy Learning Curve

One significant advantage of Go is its short learning curve. We shouldn't be astonished if we can learn all of GoLang's features in a matter of hours.

After learning the foundations, we'll need to know the best programming approaches for unique purposes and the standard library. A two- to three-hour session, on the other hand, is enough to acquire the language.

BEGINNING WITH Go

Numerous online IDEs, like The Go Playground, repl.it, and many others, can run Go applications without requiring any installation.

We need the following two pieces of software to install Go on our PCs or laptops: Text editor and Compiler.

Text Editor

We can write our source code on a text editor's platform. Below are some text editors:

- Brief
- OS Edit command
- Epsilon
- Windows notepad
- VS Code
- Emacs
- vm or vi

Finding a Go Compiler

The Go distribution is provided as a binary installer for FreeBSD, Mac OS X, Linux, and Windows with 32-bit (386) and 64-bit (amd64) x86 CPU architectures.

INSTALL Go ON WINDOWS

We must first install GoLang on our machine before we can proceed. We need a personal understanding of the Go Language and what it can achieve. Go is an open-source, statically typed language developed by Google's Robert Griesemer, Rob Pike, and Ken Thompson in 2007 but only published in 2009. It is also known as GoLang, and it supports the procedural programming language. Initially, it intended to increase programming efficiency on big codebases, multicore, and networked devices.

GoLang programs are simple to create. They may be written in any plain text editor, such as notepad++ or anything similar. To make creating and working on GoLang code easier, one can utilize an online IDE or install one on their machine. The best part is that the IDE makes writing GoLang code easier because IDEs have numerous capabilities such as an intuitive code editor, debugger, compiler, etc.

First, install the Go Language on the system to develop GoLang Codes and conduct different exciting and beneficial tasks.

How Can We Know Which Go Language Version Is Preinstalled?

Before installing Go, let's determine whether it's already installed on our machine. Go to the command line to test if our device has GoLang preinstalled for Windows, search for cmd in the Run dialog (+ R).

Execute the following command:

```
go version
```

If GoLang has been installed on our PC, it will create a message with all the GoLang version's data; otherwise, an error reading "Bad command or file name" will occur.

Downloading and Installing Go

We first must install it before we can begin the installation process. All Windows versions may download at https://go.dev/dl/.

Download GoLang for our system architecture, then follow the GoLang installation instructions:

- **Step 1:** After we've downloaded the archive file, unzip it. We'll discover a go folder in our current working directory after unzipping.

- **Step 2:** Copy/paste the extracted folder to anywhere we want it to go. In this situation, we'll install it on the C drive.

- **Step 3:** Configure the environment variables now. Right-click My Computer and choose Properties. Select Advanced System Settings from left menu, followed by Environment Variables.

- **Step 4:** Choose Path and then Modify from the system variables. Then, choose New and type in the Path with bin directory where we placed the Go folder. We'll update the path to C:gobiC:\go\bin and click OK.

- **Step 5:** Make a new user variable that informs the Go command where to find the GoLang libraries. To do so, navigate to User Variables and click New.

For the Variable name, enter GOROOT, and for the Variable value, enter the path to our GoLang folder. As a result, the Variable value in this example is C:\go\. Click OK once we've completed filling out the form.

Then, under Environment Variables, click OK, and our configuration is finished. Now, use the command prompt to check the GoLang version by entering the Go version.

Following the download, any text editor or IDE may use to write GoLang Codes, which can launch on the IDE or the Command prompt with the following command:

```
go run filename.go
```

WRITING THE FIRST Go PROGRAM

```
package main
import "fmt"
func main() {
    // print
    fmt.Println("Hello-everyone")
}
```

Explanation of the Go program syntax:

- **Line 1:** It comprises the core package of the software and its general content.
  It is the program's beginning point. Hence, it must be written.

- **Line 2:** It includes the preprocessor instruction import "fmt," which informs the compiler to include the files in the package.

- **Line 3:** It is the main function; this is where the program's execution begins.

- **Line 4:** It is fmt.

Println() is a standard library function that allows us to print something to the screen.

The fmt package has sent the Println method, which shows the output in this scenario.

Comment: Comments, like those used in Java, C, and C++, are used to clarify code. Compilers ignore and do not execute comment items. Comments can be of one or more lines long.

- **SingleLine comment**

  Syntax:

  ```
  // singleline-comment
  ```

- **Multiline comment**

  Syntax:

  ```
  /* multi-line comment */
  ```

  Example:

  ```
  package main
  import "fmt"
  func main() {
      fmt.Println("3 + 3 =", 3 + 3)
  }
  ```

- **The preceding program's explanation:** The following program uses the identical package line, import line, function declaration, and Println function as the prior GO program. We print 3 + 3 = followed by the result of equation 3 + 3 instead of the text "Hello, everyone." This expression comprises three parts: int numeric literal 3, + operator (which indicates addition), and another int numeric literal 3.

Why Is There a "Go Language"?

Because Go attempts to integrate the programming easiness of an interpreted language with the safety of a statically typed, dynamically typed language, and the performance of a compiled language, it also strives to be cutting-edge, with support for networked and multicore computing.

What Is Missing in Go That the Other Languages Have?

- Go strives to minimize typing in both senses of the term. Throughout the design phase, developers worked hard to reduce clutter and complexity to a minimum.

- There seem to be no forward declarations or header files, and everything is defined just once.

- Stuttering is reduced by utilizing the := declare-and-initialize construct for simple type derivation.

- There is no type hierarchy: types just exist; their connections are not needed to be announced.

Hardware Restrictions

Over a decade, we've seen hardware and processor configurations change rapidly. The P4 had a clock speed of 3.0 GHz in 2004. The Macbook Pro has a clock speed of about in 2018. (2.3 GHz vs. 2.66 GHz). Additional processors are used to speed up functionality. However, the expense of utilizing more processors grows as well. Consequently, we employ fewer processors, and with fewer processors, we have a heavy programming language whose threading uses more memory and slows down the speed of our system.

To resolve this challenge, GoLang was intended to utilize goroutine instead of threading, which is comparable to threading but consumes considerably less memory. Because threading requires 1 MB of memory and goroutines consume 2 KB, it is simple to activate millions of goroutines simultaneously. As a result of the above arguments, GoLang is a powerful language that manages concurrency in the same manner as C++ and Java.

The Upsides and Downsides of the Go Language

Upsides:

- **Adaptable:** It is adaptable because it is concise, direct, and easy to comprehend.

- **Concurrency:** It enables numerous processes to execute simultaneously and effectively.

- **Fast compilation:** It has a short compilation time.

- **Library:** It comes with an extensive standard library.

- Garbage collection is an essential aspect of Go. Go excels at giving you much control over memory allocation, and the garbage collector's latency has been drastically decreased in recent versions.

- It examines interface and type embedding.

Downsides:

- Despite several talks, it does not support generics.

- Although the packages bundled with this computer language are pretty helpful, Go is not an object-oriented programming language in the classic sense.

Some libraries are lacking, most notably a UI toolkit.

Among the most prominent Go Language applications are:

- **Docker:** It is a suite of tools used to manage and deploy Linux containers.

- **Red Hat:** Openshift is a platform as a service for cloud computing.

- **Kubernetes:** The Next Generation of Seamless Automated Deployment.

- **Dropbox:** It switches several essential components from Python to Go.

- **Netflix:** For two features of its server design.

- **InfluxDB:** It is an open-source time-series database created by InfluxData.

- **GoLang:** It is a language built-in Go.

TERMINAL

GoLang has a terminal emulator, allowing us to communicate with our command-line shell within the IDE. It can run Git commands, change file permissions, and do other command-line tasks without using specific terminal software.

The terminal emulator starts with our default system shell, but it also supports Windows PowerShell, Command Prompt cmd.exe, sh, bash, zsh, csh, and other shells.

The Open Terminal Tool Window

Select the View | Tool Windows | Terminal from the main menu or press Alt+F12.

By default, the terminal emulator executes with the current working directory set to the current project's root directory.

However, we may right-click any file (for instance, in the Project tool window and any open tab) and select Open in Terminal from the dialog box to open the Terminal tool window with a new session in the directory of the file.

Start the New Session

To establish a new session in a new tab on the toolbar, click the Add button.

Right-click tab and select Split Right or Split Down from the menu bar to run several sessions within it.

The terminal saves tabs and sessions when we finish this project or GoLand. The current working directory, tab names, and shell history are kept.

Use the terminal toolbar's Close button or right-click the tab and select Close Tab from the context menu to close a tab.

Press Alt+Right and Alt+Left to switch between active tabs. We may also use Alt+Down to display a list of all terminal tabs.

Right-click and choose Rename Session from the context menu to rename a tab.

In a Terminal session, Ctrl+F will search for a specified string. This searches the text of the whole session, including the prompt, commands, and results.

Set up the terminal emulator as follows:

To access the IDE settings, use Ctrl+Alt+S, then Tools | Terminal.

INSTALL Go ON Mac

We should first install GoLang on our machine before we proceed. We need a personal understanding of the Go Language and what it can achieve. Go is an open-source, statically typed language developed by Google's Robert Griesemer, Rob Pike, and Ken Thompson in 2007, but only published in 2009. It is also known as GoLang, and it enables the procedural computer program. It was created to increase programming efficiency on huge code-bases, multicore, and networked devices.

GoLang applications are written with any plain text editor, including TextEdit, Sublime Text, etc. To make creating and working on GoLang code easier, one can utilize an online IDE or install one on their machine. Using an IDE for simplicity makes writing GoLang code easier since IDEs provide various capabilities such as an intuitive code editor, debugger, compiler, etc.

The procedures for installing GoLang on MacOS are as follows:

- **Step 1:** Check to see if Go is installed. Before installing, let's determine whether it's already installed on our machine. To test if our device has GoLang preloaded, open the Terminal and enter the following command:

```
go version
```

   If GoLang is already installed on our computer, it will create a message containing all accessible GoLang version data; otherwise, it will return an error.

- **Step 2:** We must first download it before beginning the setup process. As a result, all Go for MacOS versions are now accessible for download at https://go.dev/dl/.

   Download GoLang, which is built on our system design. We obtained go1.13.1drawin-amd64.pkg for the system.

- **Step 3:** After downloading the package, install it on our PC.

- **Step 4:** After the installation operations have been completed. To check if Go is properly installed, use Terminal (MacOS' command-line interface) and use the GoLang version command. It displays the GoLang version information, showing that Go has been installed successfully on our machine.

After successfully installing Go on our machine, we will configure the Go workspace. A Go workspace is a folder on our PC where we will save all of our Go code.

- **Step 1:** In our documents, create a Go folder (or wherever we want in our system).

- **Step 2:** Inform the Go tools of the location of this folder. To begin, type the following command to go to our home directory:

```
cd ~
```

   Then, use the command to set the path to the folder:

```
echo "export GOPATH=/Users/anki/Documents/go"
>> .bash_profile
```

We add export "OPATH=/Users/anki/Documents/go to .bash profile" in this example. When we connect to our Mac account, the. bash profile file is immediately imported and contains all of our command-line interface startup parameters and preferences (CLI).

- **Step 3:** To verify that our .bash profile has the following path, run the following command:

```
cat .bash_profile
```

- **Step 4:** We'll now use the following command to validate our go route. If we choose, we may skip this step.

```
echo $GOPATH
```

Making Our First Program

- **Step 1:** Download and install our preferred text editor. After installation, create a folder in Documents named go (or whatever name we like) (or wherever we want in our system). Create a new folder named source in this folder and a new folder called welcome in this folder. This is where all of our Go programs are saved.

- **Step 2:** Create our first Go program. Open a text editor and paste the Go program into it.

- **Step 3:** After we've finished writing the Go program, save it with the extension. go.

- **Step 4:** Run our first Go program from the terminal.

- **Step 5:** Change the location of our program's files.

- **Step 6:** After changing directories, run the Go program using the following command:

```
go run name_ofthe_program.go
```

Implement a Go Program

Let's save the source code to a file, compile it, and run the program. Please follow the following steps:

- Copy and paste the preceding code into a text editor.

- Save the file as "heyy. go."

- Activate the command prompt.

- Navigate to the stored file's location.

- Enter go run "heyy."

- Go ahead and click enter to run our code.

- If our code is error-free, the message "Hello-Everyone" will appear on the screen.

```
$ go run heyy.go
```

Hello-Everyone

Check that the Go compiler is in our path but is executing in the directory containing the source file heyy.go.

Do Go Programs Interact with Programs Written in C/C++?

Although it is feasible to run C and Go in the same address space, it is not a natural match and may demand the deployment of special interface software. Furthermore, combining C and Go code compromises Go's memory safety and stack management features. When leveraging C libraries to address an issue, there is always an element of danger that is not there in pure Go code, so proceed cautiously.

If we utilize C with Go, the Go compiler implementation will define how we continue. The Go project supports three Go compiler implementations.

The default compiler is gc, followed by gccgo, which utilizes the GCC back end, and gollvm, which is significantly less mature and uses the LLVM infrastructure.

Gc cannot be called directly from C programs since it has a different calling convention and linker than C. The cgo program provides a "foreign function interface," enabling Go programs to contact C libraries securely. SWIG extends this feature to C++ libraries.

Gccgo and gollvm can also be used in combination with cgo and SWIG. Because they employ a standard API, code from these compilers may be safely linked with GCC/LLVM-compiled C or C++ applications. However, to do so securely, knowledge of all languages' calling protocols is required, as is caring for stack restrictions when calling C or C++ from Go.

HOW CAN WE CREATE AN EMPTY FILE IN GoLang?

The Go programming language allows us to create files like other computer languages. It provides the Create() function for creating a file, used to create or truncate the specified named file.

This function will truncate the given file if it already exists.

If the file supplied does not exist, this procedure will create it in mode 0666.

This operation will throw a *PathError exception if the given path is wrong.

This method returns a file descriptor, which may be read and written.

We must import the os package in our application to utilize the Create() function since it is provided in the os package.

Syntax:

```
func Create(filename string) (*File, error)
```

Example:

```
package main
import (
    "log"
    "os"
)
func main() {
    // creation of an empty file
    // Using the Create() method
    myfile, es := os.Create("heyy.txt")
    if es != nil {
        log.Fatal(es)
    }
    log.Println(myfile)
    myfile.Close()
}
```

In GoLang, we can determine whether or not a particular file exists: The Go programming language's IsNotExist() function allows us to detect whether or not a specified file exists. If the function mentioned above returns true, the error indicates that the provided file or directory does not already exist; if it returns false, the error indicates that the supplied file or directory does exist. This protocol is likewise satisfied by ErrNotExist and numerous syscall faults. We must import the os package in our code to utilize the IsNotExist() function since it is mentioned in the os package.

Syntax:

```
func IsNotExist(es error) bool
```

Example:

```
package main
import (
    "log"
    "os"
)
var (
    myfile *os.FileInfo
    es   error
)
func main() {
    // The Stat() method returns file information,
and if there is no file, it gives error.
    myfile, es := os.Stat("heyy.txt")
    if es != nil {
       // Using the IsNotExist() method to
determine whether a given file exists or not
        if os.IsNotExist(es) {
            log.Fatal("File was not found")
        }
    }
    log.Println("File-Exist")
    log.Println("File-Details:")
    log.Println("The Name is: ", myfile.Name())
    log.Println("The Size is: ", myfile.Size())
}
```

HOW TO MAKE A DIRECTORY IN Go

To construct a single directory in Go, use the os.Mkdir() function. To create a folder hierarchy, use os.MkdirAll() (nested directories). Both methods need a path and the folder's access bits as parameters.

Make a single directory:

```
package main
import (
    "log"
    "os"
)
```

```
func main() {
    if er := os.Mkdir("a", os.ModePerm); er != nil {
        log.Fatal(er)
    }
}
```

Make a directory hierarchy:

```
package main
import (
    "log"
    "os"
)
func main() {
    if er := os.MkdirAll("a/b/c/d", os.ModePerm); er
!= nil {
        log.Fatal(er)
    }
}
```

The os.Mkdir() method creates a new directory with the given name but does not enable subdirectories to be created.

HOW TO READ AND WRITE A Go PROGRAM

GoLang has an extensive built-in library to perform file read and write operations. The io/ioutil module is responsible for reading files from the local system. To store data in a file, use the io/ioutil module.

The fmt module provides techniques for taking input from stdin and outputting output to stdout to support formatted I/O. The log module is an implemented simple logging package.

It offers a Logger type with output formatting features. We can use native operating-system functions thanks to the os module. The bufio module implements buffered I/O, which aids in CPU performance.

- **os.Create():** This function generates a file with the given name. If another file with the same name previously exists, the make method deletes it and truncates it.

- **ioutil.ReadFile():** The path to the file to be read is the single parameter to the ioutil.ReadFile() method. This procedure either produces the contents of the file or an error.

- **ioutil.WriteFile():** It returns the ioutil. WriteFile() is a method that allows us to store data in a file. The WriteFile() function takes three parameters: the file's location, the data object, and the FileMode, which holds the file's mode and permission bits.log.

- **Fatalf:** After printing the log message, Fatalf will stop the program. It's equivalent to doing Printf() and then calling os.Exit (1).

- **log.Panicf:** Panic is comparable to an exception that might occur during runtime. Panicln is equivalent to Println() followed by panic(). The parameter passed to panic() is shown when the program terminates.

- **bufio.NewReader(os.Stdin):** This method creates a new Reader with the specified buffer size (4096 bytes).

- **inputReader.ReadString('n'):** This process utilizes user input from stdin until it encounters the first incidence of a delimiter and generates a string comprising the data up to and through the delimiter. An error before discovering a delimiter gives the data read before the problem and the error itself.

Example: Use the offline compiler for the optimal outcomes. Save the file as an a.go extension. To run the application, execute the command listed below.

```
go run file-name.go
```

```
// program for reading and writing files
package main
// importing-packages
import (
    "fmt"
    "io/ioutil"
    "log"
    "os"
)
func CreateFile() {
    // The fmt package provides formatted I/O and
includes functions such as Printf and Scanf
    fmt.Printf("Writing file in the Go lang\n")
    // If an error is thrown, it is received by
the err variable, and the Fatalf method of the
```

```go
    // log outputs the error message and terminates
program execution.
    file, er := os.Create("test.txt")
    if er != nil {
        log.Fatalf("failed the creating file: %s", er)
    }
    // Defer is used for cleaning reasons, such as
terminating a running file after the file has been
written, and the main function has finished
execution.
    defer file.Close()
    // The len variable stores the length of the
string written to the file.
    len, er := file.WriteString("Welcome
Everybody"+
            "Program displays reading and writing"+
                    " operations to file in
the GoLang.")
    if er != nil {
        log.Fatalf("failed writing to the file:
%s", er)
    }
    // The Name() function returns the name of the
file that was sent to the Create() method.
    fmt.Printf("\nFile-Name: %s", file.Name())
    fmt.Printf("\nLength is: %d bytes", len)
}
func ReadFile() {
    fmt.Printf("\n\nReading file in the GoLang\n")
    fileName := "test1.txt"
    // The ioutil package has built-in
// methods such as ReadFile, which reads a
filename and returns its contents.
    data, er := ioutil.ReadFile("test1.txt")
    if er != nil {
        log.Panicf("failed reading the data from
file: %s", er)
    }
    fmt.Printf("\nThe File Name is: %s", fileName)
    fmt.Printf("\nThe Size is: %d bytes", len(data))
    fmt.Printf("\nThe Data is: %s", data)
}
// the main function
```

```
func main() {
    CreateFile()
    ReadFile()
}
```

HOW DO WE RENAME AND TRANSFER A FILE IN GoLang?

The Go programming language's Rename() function allows us to rename and move an existing file to a new directory. This method is used to rename and move a file from one location to another.

This process will replace the supplied new path if it already exists and is not in a directory. However, OS-specific constraints may apply if the provided old and new paths are in different directories.

If the given path is incorrect, the error *LinkError will be thrown.

We must import the os package in our program to utilize the Remove() function because it is provided in the os package.

Syntax:

```
func Rename(oldpath, newpath string) error
```

Example:

```
// A program that demonstrates how to rename and
delete files in a new directory.
package main
import (
    "log"
    "os"
)
func main() {
    // File Rename and Remove
// Using the Rename() method
    OriginalPath := "/Users/anki/Documents/new_
folder/heyy.txt"
    NewPath := "/Users/anki/Documents/new_folder/
myfolder/xyz.txt"
    es := os.Rename(OriginalPath, NewPath)
    if es != nil {
        log.Fatal(es)
    }
}
```

HOW TO READ A FILE LINE BY LINE AND CONVERT IT TO A STRING

Scanner, a bufio package, is used to read a file line by line. Let's call the text file samples.txt, and the contents are as follows.

The GO programming language is a statically built, open-source programming language. It was built at Google by Rob Pike, Ken Thompson, and Robert Grieserner. It is also known as GoLang. The Go computer language is a general-purpose scripting language built for large-scale, complex software development.

```go
package main
import (
    "bufio"
    "fmt"
    "log"
    "os"
)
func main() {
    // os.Open() open the specific file in
    // the read-only mode,
    // this return-pointer of type os.
    file, er := os.Open("samples.txt")

    if er != nil {
        log.Fatalf("it failed to open")
    }
//bufio. NewScanner()' function is called, and an
object os.File is passed as a parameter.
//This function returns an object bufio.Scanner which
is utilized on the
//bufio.Scanner.Split() method.
    scanner := bufio.NewScanner(file)
    // bufio.ScanLines is used as
    // the input to method bufio.Scanner.Split()
    // then scanning forwards to each new line
    // using bufio.Scanner.Scan() method.
    scanner.Split(bufio.ScanLines)
    var text []string
    for scanner.Scan() {
        text = append(text, scanner.Text())
    }
    // method os.File.Close() is called
    // on the os.File object to close
```

```
file.Close()
   // then a loop iterates through,
   // the prints each of slice values.
   for _, each_ln := range text {
       fmt.Println(each_ln)
   }
}
```

BASIC SYNTAX

Tokens

A Go program is made up of many tokens. Keywords, identifiers, constants, string literals, and symbols are examples of tokens. To illustrate, the preceding Go expression is composed of six tokens:

```
fmt.Println("Hey, Everyone")
```

The following are the individual tokens:

```
fmt
.
Println
(
   "Hey, Everyone"
)
```

Line Separator

The line separator key serves as a statement terminator in a Go program. In all the other languages, individual expressions do not necessitate using a specific separator, such as ";" in C. The Go compiler uses the statement terminator ";" to indicate the conclusion of one logical entity.

Consider the following statements, for example:

```
fmt.Println("Hey, Everyone")
fmt.Println("We are now engaged in the environment of
Go programming")
```

Comments

Comments are comparable to help messages in our Go program, which the compiler ignores. They commence with/* and end with the characters */as demonstrated below:

```
/* Our first Go program */
```

There may be no comments inside comments, nor can they be inside strings or literal characters.

Identifiers

A Go identifier identifies a variable, function, or another user-defined item. An identifier begins with a letter from A to Z, a to z, or an underscore. Underscores can accompany it, zero or more characters, or numerals.

```
identifier = letter { letter | unicode_digit }
```

Punctuation characters like @, $, and % are not allowed in identifiers in Go. Go is a case-sensitive programming language. Manpower and manpower are thus two unique identities in Go. Here are some examples of suitable identifiers:

```
harish        sharma     xyz      movename      x_123
myname40   _temp        j        x23b8             retVal
```

It is not allowed to use keywords as identifiers.

Identifier _ is a one-of-a-kind identifier, often known as a blank identifier.

Later, we'll find that all types, variables, constants, labels, package names, and package import names must include identifiers.

A Unicode upper case letter is used to start an exported identifier. The term exported may be rendered as public in many different languages. Identifiers that are not exported do not begin with a Unicode upper case letter. The phrase "non-exported" is translated as "private in various languages." Eastern characters are currently considered non-exportable letters. Non-exported identifiers are sometimes known as unexported identifiers.

Keywords

The following are the reserved words in Go. These reserved words may not be used as names for constants, variables, or other identifiers.

Chan	default	import	Interface	Struct
case	defer	Go	Map	select
Break	else	fallthrough	Package	Switch
Const	if	Goto	Range	Type
continue	for	func	Return	Var

They are grouped into six categories: const, func, import, package, type, and var are used in Go programs to declare distinct sorts of code components.

Components of certain composite type denotations include chan, interface, map, and struct.

Break, case, continue, default, else, fallthrough, for, goto, if, range, return, select, and switch govern code flow.

Flow terms are controlled by both defer and go, but distinct ways.

Whitespace

Blanks, tabs, newline characters, and comments are examples of whitespace in Go. A blank line contains only whitespace, maybe with a remark, and is entirely disregarded by the Go compiler.

Whitespaces separate one segment of a statement from the next, allowing the compiler to discern where one element, int, finishes and the next element, int, begins in a statement. As a consequence, the given statement is correct:

```
var ages int;
```

There must be at least one whitespace character for the compiler to differentiate between int and ages (typically a space). Take the following statement in contrast:

```
fruits = kiwi + apple;   // obtain the total quantity
of fruit
```

DATA TYPES IN Go

Data types specify the data types stored in a valid Go variable. The Go Language divides types into various categories, which are as follows:

- Basic types contain numbers, strings, and booleans.

- Aggregate types contain arrays and structs.

- Examples of reference types are pointers, slices, maps, functions, and channels.

- The interface type.

This section will go through the fundamental data types in the Go programming language. The Basic Data Types are even further split into three subcategories, as follows:

- Numbers

- Booleans

- Strings

Numbers

In Go, numbers are divided into three subcategories, which are as follows:

- **Integers:** The Go programming language supports both signed and unsigned numbers in four sizes, as shown in the table. Signed integers are indicated by int, whereas unsigned integers are denoted by uint.

Data Type	Description
int8	8-bit signed integer
int16	16-bit signed integer
int32	32-bit signed integer
int64	64-bit signed integer
uint8	8-bit unsigned integer
uint16	16-bit unsigned integer
uint32	32-bit unsigned integer
uint64	64-bit unsigned integer
Int	In and uint have the same size, either 32 or 64 bits.
Uint	In and uint have the same size, either 32 or 64 bits.
Rune	It is the same as int32 and represents Unicode code points.
Byte	It is an abbreviation for uint8.
Uintptr	It is an unsigned integer type. It does not have a defined width, but it can hold all of the bits of a pointer value.

Example:

```
// Integers are used in this program to
demonstrate their use
package main
import "fmt"
func main() {
```

```go
// 8bit unsigned int using
var X uint8 = 221
fmt.Println(X, X-3)
// Using the 16bit signed int
var Y int16 = 32676
fmt.Println(Y+2, Y-2)
}
```

- **Floating-point numbers:** Floating-point numbers in Go are categorized into two categories, as shown in the table:

Data Type	Description
float32	32 bit IEEE 754 floating-point number
float64	64 bit IEEE 754 floating-point number

Example:

```go
// illustrate the use of floating-point numbers
package main
import "fmt"
func main()
{
    c := 22.46
    d := 35.88
    // Subtract of two floating-point number
    e := d-c
    // Display the result
    fmt.Printf("The Result is: %f", e)
    // Display the type of c variable
    fmt.Printf("\nThe type of e is : %T", e)
}
```

- **Complex numbers:** The complex numbers are separated into two portions in the table. These complex integers also include float32 and float64. The built-in function generates a complex number from its imaginary and real components, while the built-in imaginary and real functions remove those components.

Data Type	Description
complex64	Complex numbers have float32 as both a real and an imaginary component.
complex128	Complex numbers have float64 as both a real and an imaginary component.

Example:

```
// Illustrate use of the complex numbers
package main
import "fmt"
func main() {
   var c complex128 = complex(17, 2)
   var d complex64 = complex(9, 2)
   fmt.Println(c)
   fmt.Println(d)
   // Display the type
   fmt.Printf("The type of c is %T and "+
           "the type of d is %T", c, d)
}
```

Booleans

The boolean data type only represents two values: true and false. Boolean values are neither inherently nor explicitly changed to any other type.

Example:

```
// A program that demonstrates the use of Boolean
package main
import "fmt"
func main() {
    // variables
    strng1 := "PiiksofPiiks"
    strng2:= "piiksofpiiks"
    strng3:= "PiiksofPiiks"
    result1:= strng1 == strng2
    result2:= strng1 == strng3
        // Display the result
    fmt.Println( result1)
    fmt.Println( result2)
    // Display type of the
    // result1 and result2
    fmt.Printf("The type of result1 is %T and "+
                "the type of result2 is %T",
                        result1, result2)
}
```

Strings

A string data type comprises a sequence of Unicode code points. In other words, a string is a collection of immutable bytes, which means that we cannot change it once it is produced. A string can contain any human-readable data, including zero-value bytes.

Example:

```
// A program that demonstrates the use of strings.
package main
import "fmt"
func main()
{
    // strng variable stores strings
    strng := "PiiksofPiiks"
    // Display length of the string
    fmt.Printf("The Length of the string is:%d",
                                  len(strng))
    // Display the string
    fmt.Printf("\nthe String is: %s", strng)
    // Display the type of strng variable
    fmt.Printf("\nType of strng is: %T", strng)
}
```

VARIABLES IN Go

A typical program uses several variables that might change during execution. Consider a code that performs different operations on the data user input. The values entered by one user may differ from those of another. As an outcome, variables are necessary. This is so another user may not use the same settings again.

When a person begins a new value in the operation process, which will be used later, they can temporarily store it in the computer's Random Access Memory. The values in this part of memory change throughout the execution, giving birth to another term for this, Variables. A variable is a placeholder for information that may change during runtime. Variables allow us to retrieve and manipulate stored data.

Variable naming guidelines:

- Begin the variable name with a letter or an underscore (_). Furthermore, the letters 'a-z' or 'A-Z' and the numerals 0-9, and the symbol '_' may occur in the names.
  Piiks piiks, _piiks24 // valid variable
  124Piiks, 24piiks // invalid variable

- Never use a number to begin a variable name.
  235piiks // illegal-variable

- The name of the variable is case-sensitive.
  piiks and Piiks are the two different variables

- The usage of keywords as variable names is not authorized.

- The variable's name can be any length; however, it is advised to be no more than 4–15 letters long.

Declaring a Variable

In the Go computer language, we may declare variables in two ways:

Employing the var Keyword
Variables in Go are defined using the var keyword of a specific type, given a name and an initial value.

Syntax:

```
var variablename type = expression
```

Important notes:

- In the above syntax, either the type or the = expression is removable in a variable's definition, but not both.

- If the type is removed, the value-initialize in the statement decides the variable's type.

Example:

```
// Explain the variable concept
package main
   import "fmt"
func main() {
// Variable-declared &
// initialized without the specified type
var my_variable1 = 40
var my_variable2 = "PiiksofPiiks"
var my_variable3 = 42.70
// Display the value and
```

```
// type of variables
fmt.Printf("The Value of my_variable1 is : %d\n",
                my_variable1)
fmt.Printf("The Type of my_variable1 is : %T\n",
                my_variable1)
fmt.Printf("The Value of my_variable2 is : %s\n",
                my_variable2)
fmt.Printf("Type of my_variable2 is : %T\n",
                my_variable2)
fmt.Printf("The Value of my_variable3 is : %f\n",
                my_variable3)
fmt.Printf("The Type of my_variable3 is : %T\n",
                my_variable3)
}
```

- If the expression is removed, the variable will have a value of zero for the type, like zero for integers, false for Booleans, "" for strings, and nil for interface and reference types. As a result, the Go scripting language has no concept of an uninitialized variable.

Example:

```
// Variables are used in this program to
demonstrate the concept of variable.
package main
import "fmt"
    func main() {
      // Variable-declared &
      // initialized without expression
      var my_variable1 int
      var my_variable2 string
      var my_variable3 float64
      // Display zero value of the variables
      fmt.Printf("Value of my_variable1 is : %d\n",
                      my_variable1)
      fmt.Printf("Value of my_variable2 is : %s\n",
                      my_variable2)
      fmt.Printf("Value of my_variable3 is : %f",
                      my_variable3)
}
```

- We may specify several variables with the same type in a single declaration when using type.

Example:

```
// Program to illustrate the concept of variable
package main
import "fmt"
func main() {
    // Multiple variables of the same kind
    // in a single line, variables are declared and
    initialized
        var my_variable1, my_variable2, my_variable3
    int = 14, 354, 98
    // Display the values of the variables
    fmt.Printf("Value of my_variable1 is : %d\n",
                        my_variable1)
    fmt.Printf("Value of my_variable2 is : %d\n",
                        my_variable2)
    fmt.Printf("Value of my_variable3 is : %d",
                        my_variable3)
}
```

- We may specify several variables of different kinds in a single declaration if we omit the type. The initialized values show the variable's type.

Example:

```
// Program to show the
// concept of variable
package main
import "fmt"
func main() {
// Multiple variables of the different types
// are declared and initialized in single line
var my_variable1, my_variable2, my_variable3 = 14,
"XYZ", 79.26
// Display the value &
// type of the variables
fmt.Printf("Value of my_variable1 is : %d\n",
                    my_variable1)
fmt.Printf("Type of my_variable1 is : %T\n",
                    my_variable1)
fmt.Printf("\nValue of the my_variable2 is : %s\n",
                    my_variable2)
```

```
fmt.Printf("Type of the my_variable2 is : %T\n",
                    my_variable2)

fmt.Printf("\nThe value of the my_variable3 is :
%f\n",
                    my_variable3)
fmt.Printf("Type of the my_variable3 is : %T\n",
                    my_variable3)
}
```

- We may initialize a group of variables using the calling function that returns multiple values.

Example:

```
// Here, os.Open function return
// a file in the c variable and an error
// in the d variable
var c, d = os.Open(name)
```

Using the Short Variable Declaration

A short variable definition is used in functions to define and initialize local variables.

Syntax:

```
variable-name:= expression
```

Important notes:

- The type of the expression determines the type of the variable in the previous expression.

Example:

```
// Program to show the
// concept of variable
package main
import "fmt"
func main()
{
// Using the short-variable declaration
```

```
my_var1 := 39
my_var2 := "PiiksofPiiks"
my_var3 := 32.63
// Display the value and type of the variables
fmt.Printf("Value of my_var1 is : %d\n", my_var1)
fmt.Printf("Type of my_var1 is : %T\n", my_var1)
fmt.Printf("\nValue of my_var2 is : %s\n",
my_var2)
fmt.Printf("Type of my_var2 is : %T\n", my_var2)
fmt.Printf("\nValue of my_var3 is : %f\n",
my_var3)
fmt.Printf("Type of my_var3 is : %T\n", my_var3)
}
```

- Because of their brevity and adaptability, many local variables are defined and initialized using short variable declarations.

- Variables with the var declaration are used for local variables that require an explicit type that varies from the initializer expression and variables whose values are assigned later, and the initialized value is unnecessary.

- When utilizing a short variable declaration, we can declare many variables in a single declaration.

Example:

```
// Program to illustrate
// the concept of variable
package main
import "fmt"
func main()
{
// Using the short variable declaration
// Multiple variables of same types
// are declared & initialized in the single line
my_var1, my_var2, my_var3 := 630, 34, 76
// Display the value and
// type of the variables
fmt.Printf("The Value of my_var1 is : %d\n",
my_var1)
fmt.Printf("The Type of my_var1 is : %T\n",
my_var1)
```

```
fmt.Printf("\nThe Value of my_var2 is : %d\n",
my_var2)
fmt.Printf("The Type of my_var2 is : %T\n",
my_var2)
fmt.Printf("\nThe Value of my_var3 is : %d\n",
my_var3)
fmt.Printf("The Type of my_var3 is : %T\n",
my_var3)
}
```

- In a short variable declaration, the caller function can initialize a collection of variables that return several values.

Example:

```
// os.Open function return a
// file in the c variable and an
// error in the d variable
c, d := os.Open(name)
```

- Only when referring to previously specified variables in the same lexical block does a short variable declaration function similarly to an assignment. Variable declarations in the outer block are not recognized. And, as illustrated in the following example, at least one variable is a new variable produced by combining these two variables.

```
// Program to show
// concept of the variable
package main
import "fmt"
func main() {
// Using short variable declaration
// short variable declaration acts as
// an assignment for the my_var2 variable
// because the same variable present in same
block
// so the value of my_var2 is changed from 56 to
100
my_var1, my_var2 := 39, 56
my_var3, my_var2 := 56, 100
// If we try to run the commented lines,
```

```
// the compiler will throw an error since
// these variables have already been defined.
// my_var1, my_var2 := 52, 56
// my_var2:= 230
// Display values of the variables
fmt.Printf("Value of my_var1 and my_var2 is : %d
%d\n",
                    my_var1, my_var2)
fmt.Printf("Value of my_var3 and my_var2 is : %d
%d\n",
                    my_var3, my_var2)
}
```

- Using a short variable declaration, we may specify several variables of diverse types in a single declaration. The expression determines the type of these variables.

Example:

```
// Program to show the
// concept of the variable
package main
import "fmt"
func main() {
// Using short-variable declaration
// Multiple variables of the different types
// are declared and initialized in the single line
my_var1, my_var2, my_var3 := 800, "Piiks", 58.26
// Display the value and type of variables
fmt.Printf("Value of my_var1 is : %d\n", my_var1)
fmt.Printf("Type of my_var1 is : %T\n", my_var1)
fmt.Printf("\nValue of my_var2 is : %s\n", my_var2)
fmt.Printf("Type of my_var2 is : %T\n", my_var2)
fmt.Printf("\nValue of my_var3 is : %f\n", my_var3)
fmt.Printf("Type of my_var3 is : %T\n", my_var3)
}
```

CONSTANTS

It is fixed, as the name CONSTANTS indicates; likewise, once the value of a constant is specified in a programming language, it cannot change further. Constants can be of any basic data type, including integer constants, floating constants, character constants, and literal strings.

How Should We Declare?

Constants are declared the same way as variables, except that the const keyword is used as a prefix to specify a constant of a specific type. The := syntax cannot be used to describe it.

Example:

```
package main
import "fmt"
const Pie = 3.14
func main()
{
    const POP = "PiiksofPiiks"
    fmt.Println("Hello", everyone)
    fmt.Println("Happy", Pie, "Day")
    const Correct= true
    fmt.Println("Go rules?", Correct)
}
```

Untyped and Typed Numeric Constants

Untyped constants operate like literals and interact with comparable variables, but typed constants behave as immutable variables and can only interact with variables of the same type. Specify constants in Go with or without a type. The following is an example of both named and unnamed typed and untyped numeric constants.

```
const untyped_Integer   = 421
const untyped_Floating typed   = 421.12
const typed_Integer   int   = 421
const typed_FloatingPoint   float64   = 421.12
```

The following is a list of Go Language constants:

- Numeric Constant (Integer constant, Floating constant, and Complex constant)

- String literals

- Boolean Constant

Numeric Constant

Numeric constants are quantities that have a high degree of accuracy. Operations that mix numeric types are not permitted in Go since it is a statically typed language. A float64 or even an int32 cannot be added to an int. It is, nevertheless, permissible to write 1e6*time. Second, consider mathematics. Exp(1) or even 1('t'+2.0). Constants, unlike variables, behave in Go like conventional numbers.

Numerical constants are classified into integer, floating-point, and complex.

Integer Constant

- A prefix specifies the base or radix: 0x or 0X for hexadecimal, 0 for octal, and nothing for the decimal.

- An integer literal can also include a suffix that combines U(upper case) and L(upper case), indicating whether it is unsigned or long.

- It can a decimal, octal, or hexadecimal constant.

- An int can only hold a 64-bit integer at most, and sometimes less.

Here are some instances of integer constant:

- 45   : decimal

- 0312   : octal

- 0x3b   : hexadecimal

- 20   : int

- 20u   : unsigned int

- 20l   : long

- 20ul   : unsigned long

- 232   : Legal

- 225u   : Legal

- 0xFeeL   : Legal

- 068   : Illegal: 8 is not an octal digit

- 042UU   : Illegal: cannot repeat a suffix

Complex Constant   Complex constants behave in a manner comparable to floating-point constants. It is a pair of ordered or real integer constants (or parameters) separated by a comma and enclosed in parentheses. The first constant denotes the actual component, whereas the second denotes the imaginary component. COMPLEX*8 is a complex constant that takes up 8 bytes of memory.

Example: (0.0, 0.0) (−123.456E+30, 987.654E-29)

Floating Type Constant   An integer piece, a decimal point, a fractional part, and an exponent part compose a floating type constant.

Floating constants can be expressed as decimal or exponential values.

When expressing in decimal form, we should include the decimal point, the exponent, or both.

Furthermore, the integer, fractional, or both components must be included using the exponential form.

Here are a few examples of floating type constants:

- 3.14149   : Legal

- 314149E-5L   : Legal

- 520E   : Illegal : incomplete exponent

- 220f   : Illegal : no decimal or exponent

- .e56   : Illegal: missing integer or fraction

String Literals
Go offers two types of string literals: " " (double-quote style) and ' '(back-quote).

Strings can be concatenated using the + and += operators.

They are plain characters, escape sequences, and universal characters, characters in a string are similar to character literals.

This is an example of untyped.

String types with zero values are blank strings, which can be represented in literal by "or".

Strings of all kinds can be compared using operators like ==,!=, and (for comparing of same types).

Syntax:

```
type _string struct
{
    elements *byte // underlying-bytes
    len    int    //number of bytes
}
```

First example:

```
"hello, piiksofpiiks"
"hello, \
piiksofpiiks"
"hello " "piiks" "ofpiiks"
```

Second example:

```
package main
import "fmt"
func main()
{
    const C = "POP"
    var D = "PiiksofPiiks"
    // Concat the strings.
    var helloEveryone = C+ " " + D
    helloEveryone += "!"
    fmt.Println(helloEveryone)
    // Compare the strings.
    fmt.Println(C == "POP")
    fmt.Println(D < C)
}
```

Boolean Constant

Constants of both types are string constants and Boolean constants. It complies with the same rules as a string constant. The primary distinction is that it includes two untyped constants: true and false.

Example:

```
package main
import "fmt"
const Pie = 3.14
```

```
func main()
{
    const trueConst = true
    // Type definition using type keyword
    type my_Bool bool
    var default_Bool = trueConst // allowed
    var custom_Bool my_Bool = trueConst // allowed
    //  default_Bool = custom_Bool // not-allowed
    fmt.Println(default_Bool)
    fmt.Println(custom_Bool)
}
```

VARIABLE SCOPE IN Go

The scope of a variable may be defined as the area of the program where a given variable is available. Declare a variable in a class, method, loop, or other structure. All identifiers in GoLang, like those in C/C++, are lexically (or statically) scoped, which implies that the variable's scope is determined at compilation time. On the other hand, a variable may only be called from inside the code block in which it is defined.

Variable scope rules in GoLang are divided into two categories depending on where the variables are declared:

- Local Variables
- Global Variables

Local Variables

- Variables defined within a function or a block are local variables. These are unreachable outside of the function or block.

- These variables can also declare within for, while, and similar expressions in a function.

- On the other hand, retrieve these variables through nested code blocks within a function.

- These variables are also known as block variables.

- A compile-time error will occur if these variables are declared twice with the same name in the same scope.

- These variables are no longer present when the function's execution is complete.

- The variable defined outside the loop is accessible from within the nested loops. It denotes that a global variable is accessible to all functions and loops. The function's loop and function will access the local variable.

- A variable declared within a loop body is invisible to the outside world.

Example:

```
// Example of a program to demonstrate local
variables
package main
import "fmt"
// the main function
func main() { // the local level scope of the main
function begins here.
 // inside the main function, local variables
 var my_variable1, my_variable2 int = 90, 47
// Variable values are displayed
fmt.Printf("Value of my_variable1 is : %d\n",
                 my_variable1)
fmt.Printf("Value of my_variable2 is : %d\n",
                 my_variable2)
} // the main function's local level scope
terminates here.
```

Global Variables

- Global variables are those defined outside of a function or a block.

- These are only available for the length of the program.

- These are declared at the program's top, outside any functions or blocks.

- We can access these from any point in the program.

Example:

```
// To demonstrate the global variables, write a
program
package main
```

```
import "fmt"
// global-variable declaration
var my_variable1 int = 120
func main() { // from here the local level scope
begins
// the local variables inside main function
var my_variable2 int = 220
// Display the value of global variable
fmt.Printf("The Value of Global my_variable1 is :
%d\n",
                                  my_variable1)
// Display value of the local variable
fmt.Printf("The Value of Local my_variable2 is :
%d\n",
                                  my_variable2)
// calling the function
display()
} // local level scope ends
// taking function
func display() { // the local level begins
// Display the value of global variable
fmt.Printf("The Value of Global my_variable1 is :
%d\n",
                                     my_variable1)
} // the local scope terminates here
```

Note: What happens if a function has a local variable with the same name as a global variable?

The solution is simple: The compiler will prefer the local variable. The compiler issues a compile-time error typically when two variables with similar names are defined. The compiler will, however, accept variables provided in different scopes. When a local variable with the same name as a global variable is defined, the compiler will prioritize the local variable.

The output is shown in the example below. As my_variable1 in function, main has a value of 220. As a result, a local variable has a high preference over a global variable.

```
// Program to demonstrate the compiler preferring
// a local variable over a global variable.
package main
import "fmt"
// global-variable declaration
```

```
var my_variable1 int = 120
func main() { // from here the local-level scope
begins
// local variables inside the main function
// it is same as global variable
var my_variable1 int = 220
// Display the value
fmt.Printf("Value of my_variable1 is : %d\n",
                    my_variable1)
} // here the local level scope terminates
```

DECLARATION OF MULTIPLE VARIABLES

We can declare many variables in a single sentence.

The syntax for declaring multiple variables is var name1, name2 type = initialvalue1, initialvalue2.

Example:

```
package main
import "fmt"
func main() {
    var width, height int = 220, 60 //declaring
multiple-variables
    fmt.Println("width :", width, "height :",
height)
}
```

Suppose the variables have an initial value, then remove the type. The int type may delete because the variables in the previous program have starting values.

Example:

```
package main
import "fmt"
func main() {
    var width, height = 220, 60 //"int" is dropped
    fmt.Println("width :", width, "height :",
height)
}
```

For example, the above program will produce a width of 220 and a height of 60.

We should have figured that if no initial value for width and height is specified, we will set them to 0.

Example:

```
package main
import "fmt"
func main() {
    var width, height int
    fmt.Println("width :", width, "height :",
height)
    width = 220
    height = 60
    fmt.Println("new width :", width, "new height :",
height)
}
```

There may times when we need to specify many variables in a single statement. The syntax for doing so is as follows:

```
var (
        nme1 = initialvalue1
        nme2 = initialvalue2
)
```

Using the syntax explained above, the following program defines variables of various types.

```
package main
import "fmt"
func main() {
    var (
        name   = "harshita"
        age    = 23
        height int
    )
    fmt.Println("my name :", name, ", age :", age,
"and height :", height)
}
```

SHORTHAND DECLARATION

Go also includes a more condensed method of defining variables. This is known as a shorthand statement, and it uses the := operator.

Name := initialvalue is the shorthand for defining a variable.

Using the shorthand syntax, the following program declares a variable count with a value of 12. Because count began with the integer value 12, Go infers that it is of the type int.

```
package main
import "fmt"
func main() {
    count := 14
    fmt.Println("Count =",count)
}
```

Using shorthand syntax, several variables can also be specified on a single line.

```
package main
import "fmt"
func main() {
    name, age := "harshita", 23 //short-hand
declaration
    fmt.Println("my name :", name, "age :", age)
}
```

The given code declares two variables of the types string and int.

If we run the software mentioned above, we will see my name, harshita, and my age, 23, printed.

The assignment of initial values to all variables on the left side of the assignment is required by shorthand declaration. The following program will generate an assignment mismatch error since it has two variables but only one value. This is since age has not been assigned a monetary value.

```
package main
import "fmt"
func main() {
    name, age := "harshita" //error
    fmt.Println("my name :", name, "age :", age)
}
```

Shorthand syntax may be used only when at least one of the variables on the left side of := is newly declared. Consider the following program:

```
package main
import "fmt"
func main() {
    c, d := 40, 20 // declare variables c and d
    fmt.Println("c is", c, "d is", d)
    c, d := 60, 30 // d is already declared but e is new
    fmt.Println("d is", d, "e is", e)
    d, e = 20, 70 // assign new values to already
declared variables d and e
    fmt.Println("changed d is", d, "e is", e)
}
```

In comparison, if we run the following program,

```
package main
import "fmt"
func main() {
    c, d := 30, 40 //x and y declared
    fmt.Println("c is", c, "d is", d)
    c, d := 30, 40 //error, no new variables
}
```

It will output the error message.

OPERATORS IN Go

Operators are the fundamental building elements of all programming languages. Consequently, the Go Language's functionality is inadequate without the use of operators. Operators enable us to perform a variety of operations on operands. In the Go programming language, operators are categorized depending on their capabilities:

- Arithmetic Operators

- Misc Operators

- Relational Operators

- Bitwise Operators

- Logical Operators

- Assignment Operators

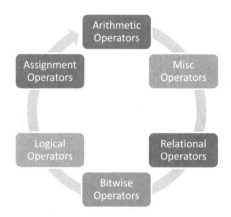

Operators in Go.

Arithmetic Operators

These are used in Go to perform arithmetic/mathematical operations on operands:

- **Addition:** The "+" operator connects two operands. For example, c+d.

- **Subtraction:** The "−" operator adds two operands together. For example, c−d.

- **Multiplication:** The asterisk (*) is used to multiply the two operands. For example, c*d.

- **Division:** The "/" operator splits the first and second operands. Consider the ratio c/d.

- **Modulus:** The remainder of the "percent" operator is returned when the first operand is divided by the second. For example, c percent d.

Example:

```
// A program to demonstrate the usage of
arithmetic operators.
```

```go
package main
import "fmt"
func main()
{
    c:= 47
    d:= 72
    // Addition
    result1:= c + d
    fmt.Printf("The Result of c + d = %d", result1)
    // Subtraction
    result2:= c - d
    fmt.Printf("\n The Result of c - d = %d", result2)
    // Multiplication
    result3:= c * d
    fmt.Printf("\n The Result of c * d = %d", result3)
    // Division
    result4:= c / d
    fmt.Printf("\n The Result of c / d = %d", result4)
    // Modulus
    result5:= c % d
    fmt.Printf("\n The Result of c %% d = %d", result5)
}
```

Relational Operators

Relational operators in Go are used to compare two values. Let's take a sneak peek at some of them:

- The operator '==' (Equal To) detects whether or not the two operands are equal. If this is the case, the function then returns true. If it does not, it returns false. For example, 9==9 will yield true.

- The '!=' operator determines if the two operands supplied are equal. It returns true if it does not. If it does not, it returns false. It is the boolean counterpart of the equals sign. For example, 9!=9 will yield false.

- If the first operand is greater than the second in the code, the '>'(Greater Than)operator is used. If this is the case, the function then returns true. If it does not, it returns false. 9>6, for example, will return true.

- The (Less Than)operator detects if the first operand is less than the second operand. If this is the case, the function then returns true. If it does not, it returns false. 64, for example, will get a misleading result.

- The '>=' (Greater Than or Equal To)operator returns true if the first operand is greater than or equal to the second operand. If it does not, it returns false. For example, 9>=9 will yield true.

- If the first operand is less than or equal to the second operand, the '<=' (Least Than or Equal To)operator returns true. If it does not, it returns false. For example, 9<=9 will likewise yield true.

Example:

```go
// Program to show the use of the relational
operators
package main
import "fmt"
func main() {
    c:= 38
    d:= 25
    // '=='(Equal To)
    result1:= c == d
    fmt.Println(result1)
    // '!='(Not Equal To)
    result2:= c != d
    fmt.Println(result2)
    // '<'(Less Than)
    result3:= c < d
    fmt.Println(result3)
    // '>'(Greater Than)
    result4:= c > d
    fmt.Println(result4)
    // '>='(Greater Than Equal To)
    result5:= c >= d
    fmt.Println(result5)
    // '<='(Less Than Equal To)
    result6:= c <= d
    fmt.Println(result6)
}
```

Logical Operators

Logical operators in Go are used to combine two or more conditions or enhance the original state's evaluation.

- **Logical AND:** When both requirements are met, the && operator returns true. If it does not, it returns false. For example, c && d returns true when both c and d are true (i.e., non-zero).

- **Logical OR:** The '||' operator returns true when one or both of the prerequisites are satisfied. If it does not, it returns false. c || d, for example, returns true if either c or d is true (i.e., non-zero). It returns true if both c and d are true.

- If the condition is not fulfilled, the '!' operator returns true. If it does not, it returns false. !c For example, returns true if it is false, i.e., when c=0.

Example:

```
// Program to show the use of logical operators
package main
import "fmt"
func main() {
    var c int = 46
    var d int = 85
    if(x!=y && x<=y){
        fmt.Println("True")
    }
    if(c!=d || c<=d){
        fmt.Println("True")
    }
    if(!(c==d)){
        fmt.Println("True")
    }
}
```

Bitwise Operators

Six bitwise operators function at the bit level or perform bit-by-bit operations in the Go programming. The bitwise operators are as follows:

- **& (bitwise AND):** Takes two operands and applies the AND operator to each bit of the two integers. AND only returns 1 if both bits are 1.

- **| (bitwise OR):** Takes two operands and applies the OR operator on each bit of the two numbers. If either of the two bits is 1 OR produces a result of 1.

- ^ **(bitwise XOR):** Takes two operands and applies the XOR function on each bit of the two integers. If two bits are not the same, the outcome of XOR is 1.

- << **(left shift):** The first operand's bits are left-shifted, while the second operand specifies the number of places to shift.

- >> **(right shift):** Takes two integers, shifts the first operand's bit to the right, and the second operand determines the number of places to shift.

- &^ **(AND NOT):** This is an easy-to-understand operator.

Example:

```
// A program that demonstrates the usage of
bitwise operators.
package main
import "fmt"
func main() {
    c:= 46
    d:= 85
    // & (bitwise AND)
    result1:= c & d
    fmt.Printf("Result of c & d = %d", result1)
    // | (bitwise OR)
    result2:= c | d
    fmt.Printf("\nResult of c | d = %d", result2)
    // ^ (bitwise XOR)
    result3:= c ^ d
    fmt.Printf("\nResult of c ^ d = %d", result3)
    // << (left shift)
    result4:= c << 1
    fmt.Printf("\nResult of c << 1 = %d", result4)
    // >> (right shift)
    result5:= c >> 1
    fmt.Printf("\nResult of c >> 1 = %d", result5)
    // &^ (AND NOT)
    result6:= c &^ d
    fmt.Printf("\nResult of c &^ d = %d", result6)
}
```

Assignment Operators

Assignment operators are used to assigning a value to a variable. The left operand of the assignment operator is a variable, whereas the right operand is a value. The right value must be of the same data type as the variable on the left, or the compiler will raise an error. Assignment operators include the following:

- **"=" (Simple Assignment):** The most fundamental assignment operator. Using this operator, the value on the right is assigned to the variable on the left.

- **"+="(Add Assignment):** A mix of the '+' and '=' operators. This operator first adds the current value of the variable on the left to the variable on the right and then assigns the result to the variable on the left.

- **"-="(Subtract Assignment):** A mixture of the '−' and '=' operators. This operator subtracts the current value of the variable on the left from the value on the right and assigns the result to the variable on the left.

- **"*=" (Multiply Assignment):** The '*' and '=' operators combined. This operator multiplies the variable on the left by the variable on the right and then assigns the result to the variable on the left.

- **"/=" (Division Assignment):** A mixture of the '/' and '=' operators. This operator in Go divides the current value of the variable on the left by the value on the right and then assigns the result to the variable on the left.

- **"%=" (Modulus Assignment):** This operator combines the '%' and '=' operators. This operator in Go multiplies the current value of the variable on the left by the value on the right and then assigns the result to the variable on the left.

- **"&="(Bitwise AND Assignment):** A mixture of the operators '&' and '='. Before assigning the result to the left variable, this operator "Bitwise AND" the current value to the left variable to the right.

- **"^="(Bitwise Exclusive OR):** A mix of the '^' and '=' operators. Before assigning the result to the left variable, this operator "Bitwise Exclusive OR" the current value of the left variable to the right.

- **"|="(Bitwise Inclusive OR):** The '|' and '=' operators are combined. Before assigning the result to the left variable, this operator "Bitwise Inclusive OR" the current value of the left variable to the right.

Example:

```go
// Program to demonstrate the usage of assignment
operators
package main
import "fmt"
func main()
{
    var c int = 46
     var d int = 85
    // "="(Simple Assignment)
    c= d
    fmt.Println(c)
    // "+="(Add Assignment)
     c += d
    fmt.Println(c)
    //"-="(Subtract Assignment)
    c-=d
    fmt.Println(c)
    // "*="(Multiply Assignment)
    c*= d
    fmt.Println(c)
    // "/="(Division Assignment)
     c /= d
    fmt.Println(c)
     // "%="(Modulus Assignment)
     c %= d
    fmt.Println(c)
}
```

Misc Operators

- **&:** This operator returns the address of the variable.

- ***:** This operator returns the address of the variable.

- **<-:** The name of this operator is received. Its purpose is to obtain a value from the channel.

Example:

```go
// Program to show the use of Misc Operators
package main
import "fmt"
```

```
func main() {
  c := 6
  // Using address of operator(&) and
  // pointer indirection(*) operator
  d := &c
  fmt.Println(*d)
  *d = 7
  fmt.Println(c)
}
```

CONTROL STATEMENTS

The developer must declare one or more conditions that the code will evaluate or test, statements executed if the condition is true, and optionally, further statements that will execute if the condition is false.

The Go programming language supports the following decision-making statements.

Sr. No	Statement & Description
1	if statement In an, if statement, a boolean expression is followed by one or more statements.
2	if...else statement When the boolean expression is false, the if an optional else statement follows statement.
3	nested if statements If or else if statements can be used within other if or else if statements.
4	switch statement A switch statement compares a variable against a collection of values for equality.
5	select statement A select statement is similar to a switch statement, but case statements interact with channel communications.

if Statement

This is the most direct decision-making statement. It is used to determine whether or not a specific statement or block of statements will be executed; for example, if a specified condition is true, then a block of statements is run; otherwise, it is not.

Syntax:

```
if(condition)
{
  // Statement to execute if condition is true
}
```

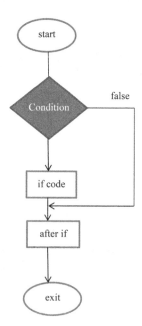

Statement of if.

Example:

```
// A program to demonstrate the use of the if
statement
package main
import "fmt"
func main() {
    // taking the local variable
    var d int = 600
    // using if statement for checking the condition
    if(d < 1000) {
        // print following if
        // condition evaluates to true
        fmt.Printf("d is less than 1000\n")
    }
    fmt.Printf("Value of d is : %d\n", d)
}
```

if...else Statement

If the condition is true, the if statement will execute a block of statements; if the condition is false, the block of statements will not run. But what if the condition is false and we want to do something different? This is when the else statement comes into effect. When the condition is false, we may run a code block using the else statement in conjunction with the if statement.

Syntax:

```
if (condition)
{
    // executes this block if the
    // condition true
} else {
    // executes this block if the
    // condition false
}
```

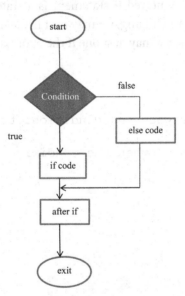

Statement of if-else.

Example:

```
// Program to show the use of if...else statement
package main
import "fmt"
func main() {
    // taking local variable
    var d int = 3200
    // using the if statement for
    // checking condition
```

```
if (d < 1000) {
    // print the following if
    // the condition evaluates to true
    fmt.Printf("d is less than 1000\n")
} else {
    // print the following if
    // the condition evaluates to true
    fmt.Printf("d is greater than 1000\n")
}
}
```

Nested if Statement

A nested if statement in Go is an if statement that is the target of another if or else expression. A nested if statement is a statement nestled inside another if statement. In GoLang, we may nest if statements within if statements. In other words, we may nest one if the expression is inside another.

Syntax:

```
if (condition1) {
    // executes when the condition1 true
    if (condition2) {
        // executes when the condition2 true
    }
}
```

Statement of nested-if.

Example:

```
// Program to show the use of nested if statement
package main
import "fmt"
func main() {
    // taking two local-variable
    var d1 int = 700
    var d2 int = 300
    // using if statement
    if( d1 == 700 ) {
        // if condition is true then
        // check the following
        if( d2 == 800 )  {
            // if the condition is true
            // then display following
            fmt.Printf("Value of d1 is 700 and d2 is
300\n" );
        }
    }
}
```

if..else..if Ladder

A user can choose from many options here. The if statements are executed in the order specified. The statement linked with that if is performed when one of the criteria is fulfilled, and the rest of the ladder is skipped. If none of the conditions are satisfied, the final else statement is executed.

Important notes:

- The if statement can be either zero or one, and it must come after any other if statements.

- The else if statement in an if statement can include zero to many other if statements and must come before the otherwise clause.

- If an else if statement succeeds, there is no need to test other if or else statements.

Syntax:

```
if(condition_1) {
        // this block will execute when condition_1 true
} else if(condition_2) {
```

```
        // this block will execute when condition2 true
}
....
else {
        // this block will execute when none
        // of the condition is true
}
```

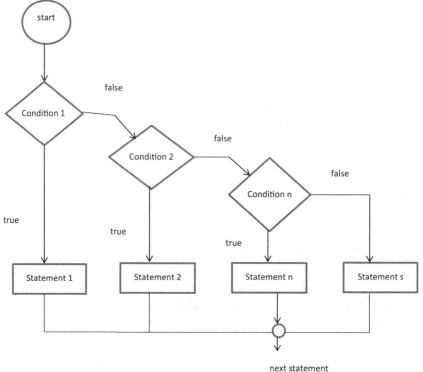

Statement of if-else-if.

Example:

```
// Program to demonstrate
// the use of if..else..if ladder
package main
import "fmt"
func main() {
        // taking local-variable
    var d1 int = 700
```

```
      // checking condition
   if (d1 == 220) {
      // if condition is true then
      // display following */
      fmt.Printf("Value of d1 is 220\n")
   } else if (d1 == 350) {
      fmt.Printf("Value of d1 is 350\n")
   } else if (d1 == 410) {
      fmt.Printf("Value of d1 is 410\n")
   } else {
      // if none of the conditions is true
      fmt.Printf("The None of values is
matching\n")
   }
}
```

SWITCH STATEMENT

A switch statement illustrates a multiway branch statement. It provides an efficient mechanism for moving execution to other code sections based on the value of the expression. There are two kinds of switch statements in the Go programming language:

- Expression Switch

- Type Switch

Expression Switch

The switch expression is similar to the switch statement in C, C++, and Java. It enables us to conveniently redirect execution to different portions of code dependent on the expression's value.

Syntax:

```
switch optstatement; optexpression{
case exp1: Statement
case exp2: Statement
...
default: Statement
}
```

Example:

```go
// Program to demonstrate the notion of the
Expression switch statement
package main
import "fmt"
func main() {
    // switch statement with the both
    // optional statement, i.e, day:=3
    // and the expression, i.e, day
    switch day:=3; day{
        case 1:
        fmt.Println("Sunday")
        case 2:
        fmt.Println("Monday")
        case 3:
        fmt.Println("Tuesday")
        case 4:
        fmt.Println("Wednesday")
        case 5:
        fmt.Println("Thursday")
        case 6:
        fmt.Println("Friday")
        case 7:
        fmt.Println("Saturday")
        default:
        fmt.Println("Invalid")
    }
}
```

Type Switch

A type switch is used when comparing types. The type that will compare to the type in the switch expression is included in the case in this switch.

Syntax:

```go
switch optstatement; typeswitchexpression{
case typelist 1: Statement
case typelist 2: Statement
...
default: Statement
}
```

Example:

```
// A program that demonstrates the concept of a
type switch statement.
package main
import "fmt"
func main() {
    var value interface{}
    switch d:= value.(type) {
        case bool:
        fmt.Println("Value is of boolean type")
        case float64:
        fmt.Println("Value is of float64 type")
        case int:
        fmt.Println("Value is of int type")
        default:
        fmt.Printf("Value is of type: %T", d)
    }
}
```

ARRAYS

Arrays in the GoLang scripting language are comparable to those in other languages. We may need to retain a collection of data of the same type in the program, such as a list of students' grades. In a program, this type of collection is held by an Array. An array is a fixed-length sequence used in memory to store similar elements. Because of their restricted length, an array is not as popular in the Go Language as Slice.

An array can store zero or more than zero items. The array items are indexed with the [] index operator and their zero-based positioning; thus, the index of the first element is array[0], and the index of the last element is array[len(array)−1].

Creating and Using an Array

In the Go programming, arrays are created using one of two methods:

Using var Keyword
The var keyword in Go is used to construct an array of a specified type with a name, size, and elements.

Syntax:

```
var array_name[length]Typle{item1, item2, item3,
...itemN}
```

or

```
Var array_name [length] Type
```

Example:

```
// Program to demonstrate how to
// build an array with the var keyword
// and access array elements with their index
value.
package main
import "fmt"
func main() {
// Creation of array of string type
// Using var keyword
var myarr [3] string
// The elements are assigned using index
myarr [0] = "HEW"
myarr [1] = "Heyevryoneoworld"
myarr [2] = "Hey"
// accessing the elements of array
// Using index value
fmt.Println("The Elements of Array:")
fmt.Println("The Element 1 is: ", myarr [0])
fmt.Println("The Element 2 is: ", myarr [1])
fmt.Println("The Element 3 is: ", myarr [2])
}
```

Using a Shorthand Declaration

In Go, arrays may also be defined using a shorthand declaration. It is more adaptable than the first assertion.

Syntax:

```
array_name := [length] Type{item1, item2, item3,...
itemN}
```

Example:

```
// A program to demonstrate how to build an array
using a shorthand declaration
// and how to retrieve the array's elements using
a for loop.
```

```
package main
import "fmt"
func main() {
// the shorthand declaration of array
arr:= [4]string{"hey", "hew", "Hey1431",
"Heyeveryoneworld"}
// Accessing the elements of
// array Using for loop
fmt.Println("Elements of the array:")
for d:= 0; d < 3; d++{
fmt.Println(arr[d])
}
}
```

Multidimensional Array

Although we are already aware that arrays are one-dimensional, we can make a multidimensional array. Multidimensional arrays are arrays of the same kind. In Go, we may create a multidimensional array by using the following syntax:

```
array_name [Length1] [Length2] .. [LengthN] Type
```

As seen in the code below, we may use the Var keyword or a shorthand declaration to create a multidimensional array.

Example:
```
// program to demonstrate the concept of
multidimension arrays.
package main
import "fmt"
func main() {
// Creation and initializing
// two-dimensional-array
// Using shorthand-declaration
// (,) Comma is necessary
arry:= [3] [3]string{{"C#", "C", "Scala"},
                {"HTML", "C++", "PHP"},
                {"Ruby", "C#", "Go"},}
// Accessing the values of
// array Using the for loop
fmt.Println("The Elements of Array 1")
```

```
for c:= 0; c < 3; c++{
for d:= 0; d < 3; d++{
fmt.Println(arry[c][d])
}
}
// Creation of a two-dimensional
// array using var keyword
// and initializing multi
// -dimensional array using the index
var arry1 [2][2] int
arry1[0][0] = 400
arry1[0][1] = 300
arry1[1][0] = 900
arry1[1][1] = 100
// Accessing the values of array
fmt.Println("The Elements of the array 2")
for c:= 0; d<2; c++{
for d:= 0; d<2; d++{
fmt.Println(arry1[c][d])
}
}
}
```

How Do You Copy an Array into Another Array?

Arrays in the GoLang scripting language are comparable to those in other languages. We may need to retain a collection of data of the same type in the software, such as a list of student grades. In a program, this type of collection is held by an Array. An array is a fixed-length sequence used in memory to store similar elements. There is no built-in function in GoLang for replicating one array into another. We may clone an array by assigning a specific array by value or reference to a new variable.

If we make a duplicate of an array by value and update the values of the original array, in the replicate of that array, the changes are reflected. And if we construct a copy of an array by reference and update the values in the original array, the changes are reflected in the replica of that array. As shown in the following examples:

Syntax:

```
// creation of a copy of an array by value
arry := arr1
```

```
// Creation of a copy of an array by reference
arry := &arr1
```

Example:

```
// program that demonstrates how to copy an array
by value.
package main
import "fmt"
func main() {
    // Creating, initializing array
    // Using shorthand-declaration
    my_arry1 := [5]string{"C++", "Go", "Ruby", "
Scala ", "C"}
    // Copying array into the new variable
    // elements are passed by value
    my_arry2 := my_arry1
    fmt.Println("Array_1: ", my_arry1)
    fmt.Println("Array_2:", my_arry2)
    my_arry1[0] = "C"
    // when we copy an array into
    // the another array by value then changes
made in the original
    // array don't reflect in the copy of that array
    fmt.Println("\nThe Array_1 is: ", my_arry1)
    fmt.Println("The Array_2 is: ", my_arry2)
}
```

How Can We Pass an Array to a Function?

Arrays in the GoLang programming language are comparable to those in other languages. We may need to retain a collection of data of the same type in the software, such as a list of student grades. In a program, this type of collection is held by an Array. An array is a fixed-length sequence used in memory to store similar elements.

In the Go programming language, we may pass an array as an argument to a function. To send an array as an argument to a function, first define a formal parameter using the following syntax:

```
// For sized-array
func function_name(variable_name [size]type){
// Code..
}
```

We may provide one or more dimensional arrays to the function using this approach. Let us use an example here to demonstrate this point:

```
// A program that demonstrates how to pass an array as
an argument to a function.
package main
 import "fmt"
// This function accept an
// array as argument
func myfun(c [5]int, size int) int {
    var c, val, d int
    for c = 0; c < size; c++ {
        val += c[x]
    }
    d = val / size
    return d
}
// main-function
func main() {
    // Creating, initializing array
    var arr = [5]int{37, 99, 29, 45, 24}
    var rest int
    // Passing array as an argument
    rest = myfun(arr, 5)
    fmt.Printf("The Final result is: %d ", rest)
}
```

SLICES

Slice is a more efficient, adaptable, and accessible Go data structure than an array. Multiple components cannot be placed in the same slice because it is a variable-length sequence of items of the same type. It is similar to an array in that it has a length and an index value. Unlike an array, though, the size of the slice is extended. A slice and an array are connected internally; a slice refers to an underlying array. The slice may include duplicate components. The first index point in a slice is always 0, and the last is (length of slice − 1).

Slice Declaration

A slice is described in the same way as an array, except it does not specify the size of the slice. As a result, it may grow and compress as needed.

Syntax:

```
[]D
```

or

```
[]D{}
```

or

```
[]D{value1, value2, value3, ...value n}
```

D denotes the element type in this case. As an illustration:

```
var myslice[]int
```

Slice Components

A slice is composed of three parts:

- **Pointer:** The pointer points to the first array element accessible through the slice. In this scenario, the indicated element doesn't need to be the first element of the array.

- **Length:** An array's length is the total number of elements in the array.

- **Capacity:** The capacity represents the maximum size to which it may extend.

Example:

```
//program that demonstrates how the slice
components function.
package main
import "fmt"
func main() {
    // Array-Creation
    arry := [7]string{"This", "is", "instance",
                        "of", "Go", "language"}
    // Display-array
    fmt.Println("Array:", arry)
    // Creation of a slice
```

```
    myslice := arry[1:6]
    // Display-slice
    fmt.Println("Slice:", myslice)
    // Display length of the slice
    fmt.Printf("The Length of the slice is: %d",
len(myslice))
    // Display capacity of the slice
    fmt.Printf("\nThe Capacity of the slice is: %d",
cap(myslice))
}
```

How Do We Create and Begin a Slice?

In Go, a slice may be created and begin in the following ways:

Using Slice Literal

To make a slice, use the slice literal. A slice literal is constructed similarly to an array literal, with the distinction that you are not authorized to declare the size of the slice in the square brackets[]. In the illustration below, the slice literal is shown on the right-hand side of the expression.

```
var my_slice1 = []string{"Hey", "from", "Everyone"}
```

Example:

```
// program to demonstrate how to use a slice
literal to create a slice.
package main
import "fmt"
func main() {
    // Creation of slice using var keyword
    var myslice1 = []string{"Hey", "from",
"Everyone"}
    fmt.Println("My Slice 1 is:", myslice1)
    // Creation of a slice
    //using shorthand-declaration
    myslice2 := []int{34, 25, 67, 59, 31, 14, 75}
    fmt.Println("My Slice 2 is:", myslice2)
}
```

Using an Array

We can construct a slice from the provided array since the slice is the array's reference. To make a slice from a given array, define the lower and upper boundaries, implying that the slice can receive elements from the array starting with the lower bound and ending with the upper bound. It excludes the things in the upper bound mentioned above. As shown in the following cases:

Syntax:

```
arrayname[low:high]
```

Example:

```
// program to demonstrate how to create array
slices
package main
import "fmt"
func main() {
    // Array-Creation
    arry := [4]string{"Hey", "from", "Creator",
"HFC"}
    // Creating slices from the given array
    var myslice1 = aryr[1:2]
    myslice2 := arry[0:]
    myslice3 := arry[:2]
    myslice4 := arry[:]
    // Display-result
    fmt.Println("My Array is: ", arry)
    fmt.Println("My Slice 1 is : ", myslice1)
    fmt.Println("My Slice 2 is: ", myslice2)
    fmt.Println("My Slice 3 is: ", myslice3)
    fmt.Println("My Slice 4 is: ", myslice4)
}
```

Using an Existing Slice

We can use the provided slice to generate a new slice. To make a new slice from the current slice, first define the lower and upper bound, which show that the slice can take components from the given slice, starting with the lower bound and moving up. It excludes the things in the upper bound mentioned above. As shown in the following example:

Syntax:

```
slicename[low:high]
```

Example:

```
// Program to show how to create slices from slice
package main
import "fmt"
func main() {
    // Creating-slice
    oRignAl_slice := []int{60, 10, 40, 80,
        52, 39, 61}
    // Creating slices from the given slice
    var myslice1 = oRignAl_slice[1:5]
    myslice2 := oRignAl_slice[0:]
    myslice3 := oRignAl_slice[:6]
    myslice4 := oRignAl_slice[:]
    myslice5 := myslice3[2:4]
    // Display-result
    fmt.Println("Original Slice is:",
oRignAl_slice)
    fmt.Println("New Slice 1 is:", myslice1)
    fmt.Println("New Slice 2 is:", myslice2)
    fmt.Println("New Slice 3 is:", myslice3)
    fmt.Println("New Slice 4 is:", myslice4)
    fmt.Println("New Slice 5 is:", myslice5)
}
```

Using the make() Function

Alternatively, we may utilize the go library's make() method to construct a slice. This function takes three arguments as input: type, length, and capacity. In this scenario, the capacity value is optional. It returns a slice that refers to the underlying array and assigns an underlying array with the provided capacity size. The make() function returns an empty slice most of the time. Empty slices have an empty array reference in this situation.

Syntax:

```
func make([]T, len, cap) []T
```

Example:

```
// Program to show how to create slices
// Using make-function
package main
```

```
import "fmt"
func main() {
    // Creating array of  the size 8 and slice
this array till 3
    // and return the reference of slice
    // Using make function
   var myslice1 = make([]int, 3, 8)
    fmt.Printf("Slice 1 = %v, \nlength = %d,
\ncapacity = %d\n",
                    myslice1, len(myslice1),
cap(myslice1))
    // Creating another array of the size 8
    // and return the reference of slice
    // Using make-function
   var myslice2 = make([]int, 9)
    fmt.Printf("Slice 2 = %v, \nlength = %d,
\ncapacity = %d\n",
                    myslice2, len(myslice2),
cap(myslice2))
    }
```

How to Iterate over a Slice

It is possible to iterate over slices like follows:

Using the for Loop

It is the simplest way for iterating slice, as seen in the following cases:

Example:

```
// program to show
// iterating over a slice using the for loop
package main
import "fmt"
func main() {
    // Creating-slice
    myslice := []string{"This", "is", "the",
"instance",
        "of", "Go", "programing"}
    // Iterate using for-loop
    for d := 0; d < len(myslice); d++ {
        fmt.Println(myslice[d])
    }
}
```

Using Range in a for Loop

In Go, we can iterate through a slice by using a range for a loop. The index and element value may be acquired using a range in a for loop, as seen in the following example:

```
// Program to show the iterating over a slice using a
range in the for loop
package main
import "fmt"
func main() {
    // Creating-slice
    myslice := []string{"This", "is", "the",
"instance",
                                "of", "Go", "language"}
    // Iterate slice using range in the for loop
    for index, ele := range myslice {
        fmt.Printf("Index = %d and element = %s\n",
index+3, ele)
    }
}
```

Using a Blank Identifier in a for Loop

If we don't want to get the index value of the elements in the range for loop, we may replace the index variable with blank space(_), as shown in the following example:

```
// program to show the iterating over a slice using a
range in the for loop without an index
package main
import "fmt"
func main() {
    // Creating-slice
    myslice := []string{"This", "is", "the",
        "instance", "of", "Go", "language"}
    // Iterate-slice
    // using range in the for loop without index
    for _, ele := range myslice {
        fmt.Printf("Element = %s\n", ele)
    }
}
```

Slice Composite Literal

The two terms are Slice and Composite Literal. Like an array, a slice is a composite data type containing objects of the same data type. The key contrast between an array and a slice is that the size of a slice may change dynamically, but the size of an array cannot.

Composite literals create values for arrays, structs, slices, and maps. A new value is generated each time they are evaluated. They are composed of the literal's type containing a list of things brace-bound. After reading this, we will comprehend what a composite literal is, and we will be astonished that we already know.

Example:

```go
// Program to demonstrate slice composite literal
package main
import "fmt"
func main() {
    // Slice with composite literal
    // Slice allows to group together
    // values of the same type
    // here the type of values is int
    st1 := []int{33, 46, 29, 74}
    // displaying-values
    fmt.Println(st1)
}
```

We understand what the word "composite literal" means. As a result, composite literals assign values to arrays, slices, etc. These are frequently used to combine a set of values of similar types.

How to Sort a Slice of ints

Slice is a Go data model that is more flexible, efficient, and user-friendly than an array. The slice is a variable-length sequence that only contains items of the same kind; different components cannot be kept in the same slice.

The Go programming language enables us to sort the objects in the slice by type. Consequently, an int-type slice is sorted using the functions as shown below. Because these methods are defined in the sort package, we must import them into our program to utilize them.

Ints

This method only sorts an int slice, and the components in the slice are sorted in ascending order.

Syntax:

```
func Ints(slc []int)
```

In this scenario, slc represents an int slice. Let us use an example here to demonstrate this point:

```
//program that demonstrates how to sort a slice of
integers
package main
import (
    "fmt"
    "sort"
)
// main-function
func main() {
    // Creating and initializing the slices
    // Using shorthand-declaration
    scl1 := []int{400, 200, 100, 700, 300, 600, 800}
    scl2 := []int{-14, 167, -44, 79, 0, 32, -4}
    // Displaying-slices
    fmt.Println("Slices(Before):")
    fmt.Println("Slice 1 is: ", scl1)
    fmt.Println("Slice 2 is: ", scl2)
    // Sortingslice of ints
    // Using the Ints function
    sort.Ints (scl1)
    sort.Ints (scl2)
    // Displaying-result
    fmt.Println("\nSlices(After):")
    fmt.Println("Slice 1 is: ", scl1)
    fmt.Println("Slice 2 is: ",scl2)
}
```

IntsAreSorted

This function determines if the provided slice of ints is sorted or not (in increasing order). This method then returns true if the slice is sorted; else, it returns false.

Syntax:

```
func IntsAreSorted(scl []int) bool
```

In this scenario, scl represents an int slice. Let us use an example here to demonstrate this point:

```go
// program that demonstrates
// how to determine whether a given
// slice of ints is in sorted form or not.
package main
import (
    "fmt"
    "sort"
)
// main-function
func main() {
    // Creating and initializing the slices
    // Using shorthand-declaration
    scl1 := []int{400, 200, 100, 700, 300, 600, 800}
    scl2 := []int{-14, 167, -44, 79, 0, 32, -4}
    // Displaying-slices
    fmt.Println("Slices:")
    fmt.Println("Slice 1 is: ", scl1)
    fmt.Println("Slice 2 is: ", scl2)
    // Checking the slice is in the sorted form or not
    // Using the IntsAreSorted function
    rest1 := sort.IntsAreSorted(scl1)
    rest2 := sort.IntsAreSorted(scl2)
    // Displaying-result
    fmt.Println("\nResult:")
    fmt.Println("Is Slice1 is sorted?: ", rest1)
    fmt.Println("Is Slice2 is sorted?: ", rest2)
}
```

How Do We Trim a Slice of Bytes in GoLang?

Slice is a Go data model that is more adaptable, effective, and user-friendly than an array. The slice is a variable-length sequence that only contains items of the same kind; different components cannot be kept in the same slice.

Trim() in the Go slice of bytes method allows us to remove all UTF-8-encoded code points from the supplied slice.

This function creates a subslice of the original slice by deleting all preceding and trailing UTF-8-encoded code points from the input text. This function returns the original slice with no modifications if the bytes slice does not contain the necessary string. We must import the bytes package in our program to utilize the Trim function because it is provided in the bytes package.

Syntax:

```
func Trim(ori_slice[]byte, cut_string string) []byte
```

ori_slice is the original slice of bytes, and cut_string indicates a string that we want to trim in the provided slice. Let's dig deep using the example given:

```
// program to demonstrate the concept of trim in a
byte slice
package main
import (
    "bytes"
    "fmt"
)
func main() {
    // Creating and initializing
    // the slice of bytes
    // Using shorthand-declaration
    slice_1 := []byte{'!', '!', 'H', 'e', 'y', 'y',
'f', 'r',
                      'o', 'm', 'W', 'o', 'r', 'l', 'd',
'#', '#'}
    slice_2 := []byte{'*', '*', 'L', 'i', 'c', 'h',
'i', '^', '^'}
    slice_3 := []byte{'%', 'h', 'e', 'l', 'l', 'o',
'%'}
    // Displaying slices
    fmt.Println("Original-Slice:")
    fmt.Printf("Slice 1 is: %s", slice_1)
    fmt.Printf("\nSlice 2 is: %s", slice_2)
    fmt.Printf("\nSlice 3 is: %s", slice_3)
    // Trimming specified leading
    // and trailing the Unicodes points
    // from the given slice of bytes
```

```
    // Using the Trim function
    rest1 := bytes.Trim(slice_1, "!#")
    rest2 := bytes.Trim(slice_2, "*^")
    rest3 := bytes.Trim(slice_3, "@")
    // Display-results
    fmt.Printf("New Slice:\n")
    fmt.Printf("\nSlice 1 is: %s", rest1)
    fmt.Printf("\nSlice 2 is: %s", rest2)
    fmt.Printf("\nSlice 3 is: %s", rest3)
}
```

How Do We Split a Slice of Bytes?

The slice is a variable-length sequence that only contains items of the same kind; different components cannot be kept in the same slice.

We may use the Split() function to split the specified slice of bytes in Go. This function separates a byte slice into all subslices separated by the separator specified and returns a slice containing all of these subslices. We must import the bytes package in our code to utilize the Split function because it is provided in the bytes package.

Syntax:

```
func Split(o_slice, sep []byte) [] []byte
```

Example:

```
// Program to demonstrate the concept of splitting
a slice of bytes
package main
import (
    "bytes"
    "fmt"
)
func main() {
    // Creating and initializing slice of bytes
    // Using shorthand-declaration
    slice_1 := []byte{'!', '!', 'H', 'e', 'y',
'y', 'f',
        'r', 'o', 'm', 'W', 'o', 'r', 'l', 'd',
'#', '#'}
    slice_2 := []byte{'L', 'i', 'c', 'h', 'i'}
```

```
        slice_3 := []byte{'%', 'h', '%', 'e', '%', 'l',
                            '%', 'l', '%', 'o', '%'}
        // Displaying-slices
        fmt.Println("Original-Slice:")
        fmt.Printf("Slice 1 is: %s", slice_1)
        fmt.Printf("\nSlice 2 is: %s", slice_2)
        fmt.Printf("\nSlice 3 is: %s", slice_3)
        // Splitting the slice of bytes
        // Using Split function
        rest1 := bytes.Split(slice_1, []byte("iik"))
        rest2 := bytes.Split(slice_2, []byte(""))
        rest3 := bytes.Split(slice_3, []byte("%"))
        // Display results
        fmt.Printf("\n\nAfter-splitting:")
        fmt.Printf("\nSlice 1 is: %s", rest1)
        fmt.Printf("\nSlice 2 is: %s", rest2)
        fmt.Printf("\nSlice 3 is: %s", rest3)
}
```

STRING

Strings in Go are distinct from those in other languages, such as Java, C++, Python, etc. It's a string of variable-width characters, each represented by one or more UTF-8-encoded bytes. Strings are either an immutable chain of arbitrary bytes or a read-only slice of bytes whose bytes may be represented in Unicode text using UTF-8 encoding.

Because of UTF-8 encoding, a GoLang string may include material mash-up of every language globally without generating confusion or restricting the page. Strings are typically enclosed in double-quotes "", as shown in the given an example:

```
// Program to show how to create strings
package main
import "fmt"
func main() {
    // Creating and initializing the
    // variable with string
    // Using shorthand-declaration
    My_value_1:= "Welcome Home"
    // Using var-keyword
    var My_value_2 string
    My_value_2 = "World"
```

```
    // Displaying the strings
    fmt.Println("String 1 is: ", My_value_1)
    fmt.Println("String 2 is: ", My_value_2)
}
```

String Literals

In the Go programming language, string literals are created in two ways:

Using Double Quotes ("")

Double quotes ("") are used to create string literals in this scenario. As shown in the following table, this string type can contain escape characters, but it cannot span several lines. This type of string literal is often used in GoLang programming.

Escape Character	Description
\\	Backslash
\000	Unicode character with the given 3-digit 8-bit octal code point
\'	Single quote ('). It is allowed inside the character literal
\"	Double quote ("). It is allowed inside the interpreted string literal
\a	ASCII bell
\b	ASCII backspace
\f	ASCII formfeed
\n	ASCII linefeed
\r	ASCII carriage return
\t	ASCII tab
\uhhhh	Unicode character with the given 4-digit 16-bit hex code point
	Unicode character with the given 8-digit 32-bit hex code point
\v	ASCII vertical tab
\xhh	Unicode character with the given 2-digit 8-bit hex code point

Using Backticks(")

Backticks(") are used to form string literals, also known as raw literals. Raw literals do not support escape characters, span several lines, or include characters other than the backtick. It is frequently used to generate multi-line messages, regular expressions, and HTML.

Example:

```
    // Program to show string literals
    package main
```

```go
import "fmt"
func main() {
    // Creating, and initializing a
    // variable with the string literal
    // Using double-quote
    My_value_1 := "Welcome to Home"
    // Adding escape character
    My_value_2 := "Welcome!\nHome "
    // Using backticks
    My_value_3 := 'Hello!Everybody'
    // Adding escape-character
    // in the raw literals
    My_value_4 := 'Hello!\nPiiksforPiiks'
    // Displaying-strings
    fmt.Println("The String 1 is: ", My_value_1)
    fmt.Println("The String 2 is: ", My_value_2)
    fmt.Println("The String 3 is: ", My_value_3)
    fmt.Println("The String 4 is: ", My_value_4)
}
```

How Do We Trim a String?

Strings in Go differ from those in other languages, such as Java, C++, Python, etc. It's a series of variable-width characters, each represented by one or more UTF-8-encoded bytes. We can trim a string in various ways using the methods indicated below. We must import these functions into our application to utilize them because they are defined in the strings package.

Trim

This method trims the text by deleting all of the stored procedure leading and trailing Unicode code points.

Syntax:

```go
func Trim(str string, cutstr string) string
```

Example:

```go
// program that demonstrates how to trim string
package main
import (
```

```
        "fmt"
        "strings"
)
// main-method
func main() {
        // Creating and initializing the string
        // Using shorthand-declaration
        stry1 := "!!Welcome to Home!!"
        stry2 := "@@This is a example of GoLang$$"
        // Displaying -trings
        fmt.Println("Strings-before-trimming:")
        fmt.Println("String 1 is: ", stry1)
        fmt.Println("String 2 is:", stry2)
        // Trimming-given-strings
        // Using the Trim() function
        rest1 := strings.Trim(stry1, "!")
        rest2 := strings.Trim(stry2, "@$")
        // Displaying-results
        fmt.Println("\nStrings-after-trimming:")
        fmt.Println("Result 1 is: ", rest1)
        fmt.Println("Result 2 is:", rest2)
}
```

TrimLeft

TrimLeft is a function that trims the string's Unicode code points on the left side.

Syntax:

```
func TrimLeft(str string, cutstr string) string
```

Example:

```
// program to demonstrate how to trim the left-
hand side components of a string
package main
import (
        "fmt"
        "strings"
)
// main-method
func main() {
```

```
    // Creating, and initializing the string
    // Using shorthand-declaration
    stry1 := "!!Welcome to home **"
    stry2 := "@@This is a example of GoLang$$"
    // Displaying-strings
    fmt.Println("Strings-before-trimming:")
    fmt.Println("String 1 is: ", stry1)
    fmt.Println("String 2 is:", stry2)
    // Trimming-given-strings
    // Using-TrimLeft()-function
    rest1 := strings.TrimLeft(str1, "!*")
    rest2 := strings.TrimLeft(str2, "@")
      // Displaying-results
    fmt.Println("\nStrings after the trimming:")
    fmt.Println("Result 1 is: ", rest1)
    fmt.Println("Result 2 is:", rest2)
}
```

TrimRight

This method cuts the string's right-hand side Unicode code points (specified in the function).

Syntax:

```
func TrimRight(str string, cutstr string) string
```

Example:

```
// Program to show how to
// trim the right-hand side elements from the
string
package main
import (
    "fmt"
    "strings"
)
// main-method
func main() {
    // Creating, and initializing the string
    // using shorthand declaration
    stry1 := "!!Welcome to Home **"
    stry2 := "@@This is an example of GoLang$$"
```

```
    // Displaying-strings
    fmt.Println("Strings-before-trimming:")
    fmt.Println("String 1 is: ", stry1)
    fmt.Println("String 2 is:", stry2)
    // Trimming given strings
    // Using TrimRight() function
    rest1 := strings.TrimRight(stry1, "!*")
    rest2 := strings.TrimRight(stry2, "$")
    // Displaying-results
    fmt.Println("\nStrings after trimming:")
    fmt.Println("Result 1 is: ", rest1)
    fmt.Println("Result 2 is:", rest2)
}
```

TrimSpace
This method eliminates all white space from the provided string, including the leading and following white space.

Syntax:

```
func TrimSpace(str string) string
```

Example:

```
// Program to show how to trim
// the white space from the string
package main
import (
    "fmt"
    "strings"
)
// main-method
func main() {
    // Creating, and initializing the string
    // Using shorthand declaration
    stry1 := "   **Welcome to Home**   "
    stry2 := "   ##This is an example of
GoLang##   "
    // Displaying-strings
    fmt.Println("Strings-before-trimming:")
    fmt.Println(stry1, stry2)
    // Trimming white space from the given strings
```

```go
    // Using the TrimSpace() function
    rest1 := strings.TrimSpace(stry1)
    rest2 := strings.TrimSpace(stry2)
      // Displaying-results
    fmt.Println("\nStrings-after-trimming:")
    fmt.Println(rest1, rest2)
}
```

TrimSuffix

The trailing suffix of the string is removed using this procedure. If the given string does not include the requested suffix string, this function returns the original text without modification.

Syntax:

```go
func TrimSuffix(str, suffstr string) string
```

Example:

```go
// Program to show how to
// trim suffix string from the
// given string
package main
import (
    "fmt"
    "strings"
)
// main-method
func main() {
    // Creating, and initializing the string
    // Using-shorthand-declaration
    stry1 := "Welcome, Home"
    stry2 := "This is an example of GoLang"
    // Displaying-strings
    fmt.Println("Strings-before-trimming:")
    fmt.Println("String 1 is: ", stry1)
    fmt.Println("String 2 is:", stry2)
    // Trimming suffix string from the given
strings
    // Using-TrimSuffix()-function
    rest1 := strings.TrimSuffix(str1,
"Helloeveryone")
    rest2 := strings.TrimSuffix(str2, "Helloo")
```

```
    // Displaying the results
    fmt.Println("\nStrings after the trimming:")
    fmt.Println("Result 1 is: ", rest1)
    fmt.Println("Result 2 is:", rest2)
}
```

TrimPrefix

The leading prefix of the string is removed using this procedure. If the input string does not include the desired prefix string, this function returns the original string without modification.

Syntax:

```
func TrimPrefix(str, suffstr string) string
```

Example:

```
// program to demonstrate how to trim a prefix
string from a specified string.
package main
import (
    "fmt"
    "strings"
)
// Main-method
func main() {
    // Creating, and initializing the string
    // Using-shorthand-declaration
    stry1 := "Welcome, Home"
    stry2 := "This is an example of GoLang"
    // Displaying the strings
    fmt.Println("Strings-before-trimming:")
    fmt.Println("String 1 is: ", stry1)
    fmt.Println("String 2 is: ", stry2)
    // Trimming prefix string from the given strings
    // Using-TrimPrefix()-function
    rest1 := strings.TrimPrefix(str1, "Hello")
    rest2 := strings.TrimPrefix(str2, "Everyone")
    // Displaying-results
    fmt.Println("\nStrings-after-trimming:")
    fmt.Println("Result 1 is: ", rest1)
    fmt.Println("Result 2 is: ", rest2)
}
```

How to Split a String

Strings in Go are distinct from those in other languages like C++, Python, Java, etc. It's a string of variable-width characters, each indicated by one or more UTF-8-encoded bytes. We may divide a string into Go-strings slices using the following functions. Because these functions are defined in the strings package, we must import them into our application to utilize them:

Split

This function divides the text into all substrings separated by the provided separator and returns a slice holding these substrings.

Syntax:

```
func Split(str, sep string) []string
```

The string str is utilized here, as is the separator sep. If str does not include the specified sep and sep is not empty, it will produce a slice of length 1 containing only str. The code will divide after each UTF-8 sequence if the sep option is not specified. If both str and sep are empty, it will generate an empty slice.

Example:

```go
// Program to show how to split a string
package main
import (
    "fmt"
    "strings"
)
// main-function
func main() {
    // Creating, and initializing string
    stry1 := "Welcome, to, our channel,
Helloeverybody"
    stry2 := "My pet name is Bruno"
    stry3 := "I love to play cricket"
    // Displaying-strings
    fmt.Println("String 1 is: ", stry1)
    fmt.Println("String 2 is: ", stry2)
    fmt.Println("String 3 is: ", stry3)
    // Splitting the given strings
```

```
    // Using-Split()-function
    rest1 := strings.Split(stry1, ",")
    rest2 := strings.Split(stry2, "")
    rest3 := strings.Split(stry3, "!")
    rest4 := strings.Split("", "Helloeverybody,
hello")
    // Displaying result
    fmt.Println("\nResult 1 is: ", rest1)
    fmt.Println("Result 2 is: ", rest2)
    fmt.Println("Result 3 is: ", rest3)
    fmt.Println("Result 4 is: ", rest4)
}
```

SplitAfter
Splits a string into all substrings following each iteration of the given separator and returns a slice with these substrings.

Syntax:

```
func SplitAfter(str, sep string) []string
```

Example:

```
// Program to show how to split a string
package main
import (
    "fmt"
    "strings"
)
// main-function
func main() {
    // Creating, and initializing string
    stry1 := "Welcome, to online course,
Heyeveryone"
    stry2 := "My pet name is fluffy"
    stry3 := "I love to bake cake"
    // Displaying-strings
    fmt.Println("String 1 is: ", stry1)
    fmt.Println("String 2 is: ", stry2)
    fmt.Println("String 3 is: ", stry3)
    // Splitting the given strings
    // Using-SplitAfter()-function
```

```
    rest1 := strings.SplitAfter(str1, ",")
    rest2 := strings.SplitAfter(str2, "")
    rest3 := strings.SplitAfter(str3, "!")
    rest4 := strings.SplitAfter("", "Heyeveryone,
Hello")
    // Displaying-result
    fmt.Println("\nResult 1 is: ", rest1)
    fmt.Println("Result 2 is: ", rest2)
    fmt.Println("Result 3 is: ", rest3)
    fmt.Println("Result 4 is: ", rest4)
}
```

SplitAfterN

After each usage of the given separator, split a string into all substrings and provide a slice comprising these substrings.

Syntax:

```
func SplitAfterN(str, sep string, m int) []string
```

Example:

```
// Program that shows how to split a string
package main
import (
    "fmt"
    "strings"
)
// main-function
func main() {
    // Creating, and initializing string
    stry1 := "Welcome, to online session,
Heyeveryone"
    stry2 := "My pet name is fluffy"
    stry3 := "I love to bake cake"
    // Displaying-strings
    fmt.Println("String 1 is: ", stry1)
    fmt.Println("String 2 is: ", stry2)
    fmt.Println("String 3 is: ", stry3)
    // Splitting-given-strings
    // Using the SplitAfterN() function
    rest1 := strings.SplitAfterN(stry1, ",", 2)
```

```
    rest2 := strings.SplitAfterN(stry2, "", 4)
    rest3 := strings.SplitAfterN(stry3, "!", 1)
    rest4 := strings.SplitAfterN("", "Heyeveryone,
hello", 3)
    // Displaying-result
    fmt.Println("\nResult 1 is: ", rest1)
    fmt.Println("Result 2 is: ", rest2)
    fmt.Println("Result 3 is: ", rest3)
    fmt.Println("Result 4 is: ", rest4)
}
```

MAPS

A map is a powerful, innovative, and flexible data structure in the Go computer language. Maps in the GoLang programming language are a collection of unordered key-value pairs. It's popular because it provides speedy lookups and values that can be obtained, modified, or deleted using keys.

- It's a pointer to a hash table.

- Because of its reference type, it is cheap to pass; for example, on a 64-bit CPU, it costs 8 bytes, but on a 32-bit computer, it requires 4 bytes.

- A key in a map must be unique and always of the type that can be compared using the == operator or the type that can be evaluated using the != operator. Consequently, most built-in types, such as int, float64, rune, string, comparable array and structure, pointer, and so on, may be used as keys. Slice and noncomparable arrays and structs and custom data types that are not comparable are not utilized as map keys.

- Values in maps, unlike keys, are not unique and can be of any type, including int, float64, text, rune, pointer, reference type, map type, and so on.

- Values and keys must be of the same type; different keys and values in the same mappings are not allowed. The kind of key and type values, on the other hand, may differ.

- Other names for maps include a hash table, hash map, unordered map, dictionary, and associative array.

- After a map has been initialized, we can only add value to it. The compiler throws an error when adding a value to an uninitialized map.

How Do We Create and Initialize Maps?

There are two ways to construct and initialize maps in the Go programming language:

Simple

We may create and initialize a map in this manner without using the make() function:

- **Creating a Map:** We can simply construct a map by using the following syntax:

```
// Empty-map
map[KeyType]ValueType{}
// Map with keyvalue pair
map[KeyType]ValueType{key1: value1, ..., keyN:
valueN}
```

Example:

```
var mymap map[int]string
```

A map's zero value in maps is nil. Therefore, a nil map has no keys. The compiler will detect a runtime error by adding a key-value pair into the nil map.

- **Using map literals to initialize the map:** The easiest approach to populate a map with data is with map literals; separating the key-value pair by a colon and the last trailing colon is necessary; otherwise, the compiler will create an error.

Example:

```
// Program to show how to
// create, and initialize the maps
package main
import "fmt"
func main() {
    // Creating, and initializing the empty map
    // Using-var-keyword
    var map_1 map[int]int
    // Checking if the map is nil or not
    if map_1 == nil {
```

```
        fmt.Println("True")
    } else {
        fmt.Println("False")
    }
    // Creating, and initializing map
    // Using shorthand-declaration
    // and using map literals
    map_2 := map[int]string{
            90: "Hen",
            91: "Cow",
            92: "Goat",
            93: "Cat",
            94: "Bird",
    }
    fmt.Println("Map-2: ", map_2)
}
```

Using the make() Function
The make() method is used to generate a map. This is an inbuilt function, and we must supply the map type to it to return an initialized map.

Syntax:

```
make(map[KeyType]ValueType, initial_Capacity)
make(map[KeyType]ValueType)
```

Example:

```
// Program to show how to
// create, and initialize map
// and using make() function
package main
import "fmt"
func main() {
    // Creation of map
    // using make() function
    var Mymap = make(map[float64]string)
    fmt.Println(Mymap)
    // As we all know, the make() method always
returns a map that has been initialized
    // We can include values in it
    Mymap[1.3] = "Nidhi"
```

```
    Mymap[1.5] = "Sunidhi"
    fmt.Println(Mymap)
}
```

WHAT IS A BLANK IDENTIFIER (underscore)?

_(underscore) is known as the Blank Identifier in GoLang. Identifiers are user-defined names for software components that are used to identify them. GoLang has a feature that lets us define and use an unused variable using a Blank Identifier. Unused variables are those that the user defines throughout the program but never uses. Because of these variables, the program is practically incomprehensible. Because GoLang is a more concise and clear programming language, the programmer cannot declare an unnecessary variable; the compiler will generate an error if we do.

When a function returns several values, but we only need a few of them and discard some, we may use the Blank Identifier. It informs the compiler that this variable isn't needed and may disregard without causing an error. It conceals the values of the variables and makes the program intelligible. As a result, anytime we provide a value to Bank Identifier, it becomes useless.

Example:

```
// Program to show compiler throws
// an error if variable is declared but not used
package main
import "fmt"
// main -unction
func main() {
    // calling the function
    // function returns two values which
    // are assigned to mul and div identifier
    mul, div := mul_div(140,1 9)
    // using the mul variable only
    // compiler will give an error
    fmt.Println("140 x 19 = ", mul)
}
// function returning two
// values of the integer type
func mul_div(nm1 int, nm2 int) (int, int) {
    // returning-values
    return nm1 * nm2, nm1 / nm2
}
```

DEFER KEYWORD

In the Go programming language, defer instructions postpone the execution of a function, method, or anonymous method until the neighboring functions return. In other words, deferred function or method call arguments evaluate instantly but do not run until the nearby function returns. We may create a delayed method, function, or anonymous function using the defer keyword.

Syntax:

```
// Function
defer func func-name(parameter_list Type)
return_type{
// Code
}
// Method
defer func (receiver Type) method_name(parameter_
list){
// Code
}
defer func (parameter_list)(return_type){
// code
}()
```

Example:

```
// Program to show
// concept of defer statement
package main
import "fmt"
// Function
func mul(d1, d2 int) int {
    rest := d1 * d2
    fmt.Println("Result: ", rest)
    return 0
}
func show() {
    fmt.Println("Hello, Everybody")
}
// main-function
func main() {
```

```
// Calling mul() function
// Here mul function behaves
// like normal-function
mul(43, 25)
// Calling mul()function
// Using the defer keyword
// Here mul() function is defer-function
defer mul(27, 46)
// Calling the show() function
show()
}
```

PANIC IN GoLang

In the Go scripting language, panic, like an exception, happens during runtime. In other words, panic happens when an unforeseen condition arises in our Go program, resulting in the program's execution being terminated. When a specific circumstance exists, such as out-of-bounds array accesses, panic can occur during runtime, as shown in example.

Syntax:

```
func panic(v interface{})
```

Example:

```
// Program which illustrates concept of panic
package main
import "fmt"
// tmain-function
func main() {
    // Creating the array of string type
    // Using var-keyword
    var myarr [3]string
    // The elements are assigned using index
    myarr[0] = "HE"
    myarr[1] = "Heyyyeverybody"
    myarr[2] = "Hello"
    // Accessing elements of the array
    // Using index-value
    fmt.Println("Elements of Array is:")
    fmt.Println("Element 1 is: ", myarr[0])
    // Program panics because size of the array is 3
```

```
    // we try to access the
    // index 5 which is not
    // available in the current array,
    // it gives runtime error
    fmt.Println("Element 2 is: ", myarr[5])
}
```

RECOVER

The recover function in Go is used to manage panic in the same way that try/catch blocks capture exceptions in languages, such as Java, C#, and others. It is a built-in function defined in the built-in package of the Go programming language. This approach is mainly used to re-establish control of a panicked goroutine. In other words, it addresses the goroutine's frantic behavior.

Syntax:

```
func recover() interface{}
```

Example:

```
// program that demonstrates the concept of
recover
package main
import "fmt"
// function is created to handle the
 panic occurs in the entry function
// but it does not handle panic occurred in entry
function
// because it called in normal function
func handlepanic() {
    if a := recover(); a != nil {
        fmt.Println("RECOVER", a)
    }
}
// Function
func entry(lang *string, aname *string) {
    // Normal-function
    handlepanic()
    // When value of lang
    // is nil it will panic
    if lang == nil {
```

```go
        panic("Error: Language cannot be nil")
    }
    // When value of  the aname
    // is nil it will panic
    if aname == nil {
        panic("Error: Author name cannot be nil")
    }
    fmt.Printf("Author Language is: %s \n Author
Name: %s\n", *lang, *aname)
    fmt.Printf("Return successfully from the entry
function")
}
// main-function
func main() {
    A_lang := "GO Language"
    entry(&A_lang, nil)
    fmt.Printf("Return successfully from main
function")
}
```

CLOSURES

The Go scripting language has an anonymous function. An anonymous function can form a closure. A closure is anonymous function that refers to variables defined outside the function. It is similar to accessing global variables available before the function's declaration.

Example:

```go
// Program to show how to create Closure
package main
import "fmt"
func main() {
    // Declaring-variable
    HFW := 0
    // Assigning anonymous
    // function to a variable
    counter := func() int {
        HFW += 1
        return HFW
    }
    fmt.Println(counter())
    fmt.Println(counter())
}
```

RECURSION

Recursion is the process through which function, either implicitly or explicitly, calls itself, and the corresponding function is known as a recursive function. The anonymous function is unique to the Go programming language. It is a function without a name. It is used to create an inline function. It is also possible to specify and define anonymous recursive functions. Recursive anonymous functions, commonly known as recursive function literals, are a type of recursive function.

Syntax:

```
func(parameter-list)(return-type){
// code call same function
// within function for recursion
// Use return statement only
// if return-type are given.
return
}()
```

Example:

```
// Program to show
// how to create recursive Anonymous-function
package main
import "fmt"
func main() {
    // Anonymous-function
    var recursiveAnonymous func()
    recursiveAnonymous = func() {
        // Printing message to show the
        // function call and iteration
        fmt.Println("Anonymous functions could be
recursive.")
                    // Calling same function
recursively
        recursiveAnonymous()
    }
    // main calling of function
    recursiveAnonymous()
}
```

POINTERS

In the Go computer language or GoLang, pointers are variables that retain the memory address of another variable. In GoLang, pointers are known as special variables. Variables are used in the system to keep data at a specified memory address. Memory addresses are always written in hexadecimal (starting with 0x like 0xFFAAF, etc.).

What Are Points Used For?

To comprehend this need, we must first comprehend the concept of variables. Variables are the names given to memory regions that hold actual data. We need to know the address of that same memory region to access the stored data. Manually remembering all of the memory locations is a waste of time. We use variables to store data, and variables can be retrieved simply by using their name.

GoLang also allows us to use the literal expression to save a hexadecimal number into a variable, which means that any integer beginning with 0x is a hexadecimal number.

Example:

```
// Variables demonstration program
// storing hexadecimal values
package main
import "fmt"
func main() {
    // storing hexadecimal values in variables
    x := 0xFF
    y := 0x9C
    // Displaying values
    fmt.Printf("Type of variable x is %T\n", x)
    fmt.Printf("Value of x in hexadecimal is
%X\n", x)
    fmt.Printf("Value of x in decimal is %v\n", x)
    fmt.Printf("Type of variable y is %T\n", y)
    fmt.Printf("Value of y in hexadecimal is
%X\n", y)
    fmt.Printf("Value of y in decimal is %v\n", y)
}
```

Pointers Declaration and Initialization

Two important operators are used in pointers before we begin:

- The pointer variable operator, often known as the '*' dereferencing operator, declares a pointer variable and accesses the value stored in the address.

- The & operator also referred to as the address operator, is used to return the address of a variable or obtain the address of a variable via a pointer.

Declaring a Pointer

```
var pointer_name *Data_Type
```

Example: Consider the string pointer as shown below, which can only hold the memory locations of string variables.

```
var st *string
```

Pointer Initialization

To do this, use the address operator to establish a pointer with the memory address of another variable, as seen in the following example:

```
// normal variable-declaration
var c = 95
// Initialization of the pointer st with
// memory address of the variable c
var st *int = &c
```

Example:

```
// program to show declaration and initialization
package main
import "fmt"
func main() {
    // taking normal-variable
    var c int = 3998
    // declaration of the pointer
```

```
        var d *int
        // initialization of the pointer
        d = &c
        // displaying-result
        fmt.Println("Value stored in c = ", c)
        fmt.Println("Address of c = ", &c)
        fmt.Println("Value stored in variable d = ", d)
    }
```

Dereferencing a Pointer

The * operator is also known as the dereferencing operator. It is used to specify the pointer variable and to access the value of a variable to which the pointer points, a process known as indirecting or dereferencing. The value at the location is sometimes referred to as the * operator. Let's look at an example to help us comprehend this concept:

```
// Program to illustrate
// the concept of dereferencing a pointer
package main
import "fmt"
func main() {
    // using the var keyword
    // we are not defining any type with the variable
    var x = 328
    // taking pointer variable using
    // the var keyword without specifying the type
    var a = &x
    fmt.Println("The Value stored in x = ", x)
    fmt.Println("The Address of x = ", &x)
    fmt.Println("The Value stored in pointer variable
a = ", a)
    // this is dereferencing a pointer
    // using * operator before the pointer
    // variable to access value stored at the variable
at which it is pointing
    fmt.Println("The Value stored in y(*a) = ", *a)
}
```

Instead of assigning a new value to the variable, we can alter the value of the pointer or memory location.

Example:

```
// Program to illustrate the above mentioned concept
package main
import "fmt"
func main() {
    // using the var keyword
    // we are not defining any type with the variable
    var x = 458
    // taking pointer variable using
    // the var keyword without specifying the type
    var a = &x
    fmt.Println("The Value stored in y before
changing = ", x)
    fmt.Println("The Address of x = ", &x)
    fmt.Println("The Value stored in pointer
variable a = ", a)
    // this is dereferencing pointer
    // using the * operator before pointer
    // variable to access value stored at the
variable at which it is pointing
    fmt.Println("The Value stored in x(*a) Before
Changing = ", *a)
    // changing the value of x by assigning
    // the new value to the pointer
    *a = 500
     fmt.Println("Value stored in x(*a) after
Changing = ",x)
}
```

In GoLang, How Can We Instantiate a Struct Using the New Keyword?

A struct mainly serves as a container for all other data types. We can easily manipulate/access the data allocated to a struct by utilizing a reference to a struct. In GoLang, we may create Struct using the new keyword as well as the Pointer Address Operator.

Example: In this case, we can see that we are instantiating a Struct with the new keyword.

```
// Program to show how to instantiate Struct
// using a new keyword
package main
```

```go
import "fmt"
type emp struct {
    name    string
    empid   int
    salary int
}
func main() {
    // emp1 is a pointer to an instance of emp
    // using the new keyword
    emp1 := new(emp)
    emp1.name = "ABC"
    emp1.empid = 2325
    emp1.salary = 37000
    fmt.Println(emp1)
    // emp2 is an instance of emp
    var emp2 = new(emp)
    emp2.name = "XYZ"
    emp2.salary = 40000
    fmt.Println(emp2)
}
```

Pointers to a Function

Pointers are variables in the Go programming language, or GoLang used to hold the memory address of another variable. We may also pass pointers to the function in the same way variables are. There are two ways to accomplish this.

Create a Pointer and Pass It to the Function

In the following program, we use a function ptf with an integer type pointer parameter, instructing the function to accept only pointer type arguments. This function essentially modified the value of the variable y. At the start, y has the value of 200. However, following the function call, the value changed to 638, as seen in the output.

```go
// Program to create a pointer and
// passing it to the function
package main
import "fmt"
// taking function with integer
// the type pointer as an parameter
func ptf(b *int) {
```

```
        // dereferencing
        *b = 638
}
  // the main function
func main() {
        // taking normal variable
        var y = 200
            fmt.Printf("Value of y before function call
is: %d\n", y)
        // taking pointer variable and
        // assigning the address
        // of y to it
        var pb *int = &y
        // calling tfunction by
        // passing the pointer to function
        ptf(pb)

        fmt.Printf("Value of y after function call is:
%d\n", y)
}
```

Passing an Address of the Variable to Function Call
In the following program, we do not create a pointer to hold the address of the variable y, as we did in the previous program. We are directly passing the address of y to the function call, which works in the same way as the previously stated.

```
// Program to create a pointer and
// passing address of the variable to the function
package main
import "fmt"
// taking function with integer
// the type pointer as an parameter
func ptf(b *int) {
        // dereferencing
        *b = 638
}
// the main function
func main() {
        // taking normal variable
        var y = 200
        fmt.Printf("Value of y before function call is:
%d\n", y)
```

```
    // calling the function by
    // passing address of
    // the variable y
    ptf(&y)
    fmt.Printf("Value of y after function call is:
%d\n", y)
}
```

Note: The variables and pointers in the preceding programs can also be declared using the short declaration operator(:=).

Pointer to a Struct

A pointer is a variable that stores the memory address of another variable. Pointers are also known as special variables in GoLang. The variables are used to store data in the system at a specific memory address.

A pointer to a struct can also use. In GoLang, a struct is a user-defined type that allows us to group/combine elements of possibly diverse kinds into a single type. To utilize a pointer to a struct, use the & operator, also known as the address operator. GoLang allows programmers to use pointers to access the fields of a structure without explicitly dereferencing it.

Example: We will make an Employee structure that contains two variables. Create an instance of the struct, i.e., emp, in the main function. We may send the struct's address to the pointer, which represents the pointer to the struct idea. There is no need to explicitly use dereferencing because it will provide the same effect as shown in the following program.

```
// Program to illustrate
// the concept of the Pointer to struct
package main
import "fmt"
// taking structure
type Employee struct {

    // taking the variables
    name  string
    empid int
}
// the main Function
func main() {
    // creating instance of the Employee struct type
```

```
        emp := Employee{"XYZ", 17028}
        // Here, it is the pointer to struct
        pts := &emp
        fmt.Println(pts)
        // accessing struct fields using pointer
        // but here we are not using
        // the dereferencing explicitly
        fmt.Println(pts.name)
        // same as above by explicitly using the
        // dereferencing concept means
        // the result will be the same
        fmt.Println((*pts).name)
}
```

Pointer to Pointer in Go

In the Go programming language or GoLang, pointers are variables that retain the memory address of another variable. A pointer is a particular variable that may point to any variable, even another pointer. Essentially, this looks to be a pointer chain. When we define a pointer to a pointer, the address of the second pointer is stored in the first pointer. This notion is also known as double pointers.

How to Declare a Pointer to a Pointer

Declaring a pointer to a pointer is the same as declaring a pointer in Go. The distinction is that we must put an additional '*' before the pointer's name. This is usually done when we declare the pointer variable using the var keyword and the type. The example and illustration below will illustrate the concept much better.

Example: In the program below, the pointer pt2 saves the location of the pointer pt1. Dereferencing pt2, i.e., *pt2 returns the address of variable V or the value of pointer pt1. If we attempt **pt2, you will get the value of the variable V, which is 200.

```
// Program to illustrate
// the concept of the Pointer to Pointer
package main
import "fmt"
// the main Function
func main() {
        // taking variable
        // of the integer type
```

```
        var V int = 200
                // taking a pointer
        // of integer type
        var pt1 *int = &V
                // taking pointer to
        // pointer to pt1
        // storing the address
        // of pt1 into pt2
        var pt2 **int = &pt1
        fmt.Println("Value of Variable V is = ", V)
        fmt.Println("The Address of variable V is = ", &V)

        fmt.Println("Value of pt1 is = ", pt1)
        fmt.Println("The Address of pt1 is = ", &pt1)
            fmt.Println("Value of pt2 is = ", pt2)
        // Dereferencing pointer to pointer
        fmt.Println("The Value at the address of pt2
is or *pt2 = ", *pt2)
        // double pointer will give the value of
variable V
        fmt.Println("*(The Value at the address of pt2
is) or **pt2 = ", **pt2)
        }
```

Comparing Pointers

Pointers are variables in the Go scripting language, or GoLang, holding another variable's memory address. In GoLang, pointers are sometimes referred to as special variables. The variables are used to keep data in the system at a specified memory address. Memory addresses are always in hexadecimal format (starting with 0x like 0xFFAAF, etc.).

In the Go scripting language, we may compare two pointers. Two pointer values are only identical if they point to the same memory address or are nil. We may compare pointers using the == and != operators provided by the Go programming language.

== operator

If both pointers refer to the same variable, this function returns true. Return false if both pointers are pointing to separate variables.

Syntax:

```
pointer1 == pointer2
```

Example:

```go
// program to show the concept of comparing two
pointers
package main
import "fmt"
func main() {
    val1 := 6135
    val2 := 926
    // Creating, and initializing the pointers
    var p1 *int
    p1 = &val1
    p2 := &val2
    p3 := &val1
    // Comparing the pointers with each other
    // Using == operator
    res1 := &p1 == &p2
    fmt.Println("Is p1 pointer is equal to p2
pointer: ", res1)
    res2 := p1 == p2
    fmt.Println("Is p1 pointer is equal to p2
pointer: ", res2)
    res3 := p1 == p3
    fmt.Println("Is p1 pointer is equal to p3
pointer: ", res3)
    res4 := p2 == p3
    fmt.Println("Is p2 pointer is equal to p3
pointer: ", res4)
    res5 := &p3 == &p1
    fmt.Println("Is p3 pointer is equal to the p1
pointer: ", res5)
}
```

!= operator
This operator returns false if both pointers lead to the same variable. Return true instead if both pointers refer to different variables.

Syntax:

```go
pointer_1 != pointer_2
```

Example:

```
// Program to show the concept of comparing two
pointers
package main
import "fmt"
func main() {
    val1 := 12469
    val2 := 925
    // Creating, and initializing the pointers
    var p1 *int
    p1 = &val1
    p2 := &val2
    p3 := &val1
    // Comparing pointers with each other
    // Using != operator
    res1 := &p1 != &p2
    fmt.Println("Is p1 pointer not equal to the p2
pointer: ", res1)
    res2 := p1 != p2
    fmt.Println("Is p1 pointer not equal to the p2
pointer: ", res2)
    res3 := p1 != p3
    fmt.Println("Is p1 pointer not equal to the p3
pointer: ", res3)
    res4 := p2 != p3
    fmt.Println("Is p2 pointer not equal to the p3
pointer: ", res4)
    res5 := &p3 != &p1
    fmt.Println("Is p3 pointer not equal to p1
pointer: ", res5)
}
```

GoLang STRUCTURES

In GoLang, a structure, also known as a struct, is a user-defined type that allows us to group/combine parts of possibly divergent kinds into a single type. A struct is a set of properties/fields that may represent any real-world entity. This idea is related to classes in general in object-oriented programming. It's a straightforward class that doesn't enable inheritance but does allow for composition.

Declaring a structure:

```
type Address struct {
     name string
     streetno string
     city string
     state string
     Pin-code int
}
```

Example:

```
var x = Address{Name:"Harash",
streetno:"Sitanagar", state:"Punjab", Pin-code:
321429} //city:""

// Program to illustrate how to declare and define
struct
package main
import "fmt"
// Defining struct-type
type Address struct {
     Name     string
     city     string
     Pin-code int
}
func main() {
     // Declaring variable of the struct type
     // All struct fields are initialized with
     their zero-value
     var x Address
     fmt.Println(x)
     // Declaring and initializing struct using
struct literal
     x1 := Address{"Harshita", "Kolkatta", 9214271}
     fmt.Println("Address1: ", x1)
     // Naming the fields while initializing struct
     x2 := Address{Name: "Rishi", city: "Jakarta",
                              Pincode: 913011}
     fmt.Println("Address2: ", x2)
     // uninitialized fields are set to
     // their corresponding zerovalue
```

```
    x3 := Address{Name: "Ludhiana"}
    fmt.Println("Address3: ", x3)
}
```

Pointers to a Struct

Pointers are variables in the Go programming language, or GoLang, that store the memory address of another variable. We may also refer to a struct, as seen in the following example:

```
// Program to show a pointer to the struct
package main
import "fmt"
// defining-structure
type Employee struct {
    first-name, last-name string
    age, salary int
}
func main() {
    // passing address of struct-variable empy is a
pointer to Employee struct
    empy := &Employee{"Rakshit", "Shardh", 62, 8100}
    // (*empy).first-name is the syntax to access
first-name of the empy struct
    fmt.Println("First Name:", (*empy).first-name)
    fmt.Println("Age:", (*empy).age)
}
```

GoLang's NESTED STRUCTURE

A structure, also known as a struct in GoLang, is a user-defined type that allows us to group items of various kinds into a single unit. Any real-world object, which completes with attributes and fields, may be represented by a struct. The Go programming language supports nested structures. A nested structure acts as a field for another. A nested structure contains another structure.

Syntax:

```
type structname1 struct{
  // Fields..
}
type structname2 struct{
  variablename  structname1
}
```

Example:

```
// Program to show nested-structure
package main
import "fmt"
// Creating-structure
type Author struct {
    name    string
    branchno   string
    year    int
}
// Creating nested-structure
type HR struct {
    // structure as field
    details Author
}
func main() {
    // Initializing fields of the structure
    results := HR{
        details: Author{"Diksha", "CID", 2022},
    }
    // Display values
    fmt.Println("\nDetails of the Author")
    fmt.Println(results)
}
```

GoLang METHODS

With one exception, Go methods are equivalent to Go functions in implementation. A receiver parameter is included in the procedure. The receiver parameter allows the method to access the attributes of the receiver. In this case, the recipient might be either struct or non-struct. We must maintain the receiver and receiver type in the same package while writing code. Furthermore, we are not permitted to write a method whose receiver type has already been specified in another package, including built-in kinds, such as int, string, etc. If we attempt, the compiler will generate an error.

Syntax:

```
func(reciver-name Type) method-name(parameter-
list)(return-type){
// Code
}
```

Method with the Struct Type Receiver

We may define a method with a struct receiver in the Go programming language. As seen in the following example, this receiver is available within the method:

```go
// demonstrate the method using a struct type receiver
using this program
package main
import "fmt"
//authorstructure
type author struct {
    name        string
    branch      string
    particles   int
    salary      int
}
// Method with the receiver of author type
func (x author) show() {
    fmt.Println("The Author's Name is: ", x.name)
    fmt.Println("The Branch Name: ", x.branch)
    fmt.Println("The Published articles is: ",
x.particles)
    fmt.Println("The Salary is: ", x.salary)
}
// main-function
func main() {
    // Initializing-values of author structure
    rest := author{
        name:       "Diksha",
        branch:     "DFC",
        particles: 814,
        salary:     73000,
    }
    // Calling-method
    rest.show()
}
```

Method with the Non-Struct Type Receiver

In Go, we can define a method with a non-struct type receiver as long as the type and method declarations are in the same package. Because they are defined in many packages, the compiler will generate an error if found in multiple packages, such as int, string, etc.

Example:

```
// Program to show method with non-struct type
receiver
package main
import "fmt"
// Type-definition
type data int
// Defining method with the non-struct type
receiver
func (d1 data) multiply(d2 data) data {
    return d1 * d2
}
/*
// if we try to run code, compiler will throw
error
func(d1 int)multiply(d2 int)int{
return d1 * d2
}
*/
// the main-function
func main() {
    value1 := data(73)
    value2 := data(41)
    rest := value1.multiply(value2)
    fmt.Println("The Final result is: ", rest)
}
```

Methods with the Pointer Receiver

A method with a pointer recipient is permitted in the Go programming language. When a modification is made to a pointer receiver method, the caller is updated, which is not the case with value receiver methods.

Syntax:

```
func (p *Type) method-name(...Type) Type {
// Code
}
```

Example:

```
// Program to illustrate pointer receiver
package main
```

```go
import "fmt"
// authorstructure
type author struct {
    name        string
    branch      string
    particles int
}
// Method with the receiver of author type
func (d *author) show(abranch string) {
    (*d).branch = abranch
}
// main-function
func main() {
    // Initializing-values of author structure
    rest := author{
        name:    "Harsh",
        branch: "HRF",
    }
    fmt.Println("The Author's name is: ", rest.
name)
    fmt.Println("The Branch Name(Before) is: ",
rest.branch)
    // Creating-pointer
    p := &rest
    // Calling show-method
    p.show("KIH")
    fmt.Println("The Author's name is: ", rest.
name)
    fmt.Println("The Branch Name(After) is: ",
rest.branch)
}
```

INTERFACES

The Go Language's interfaces are distinct from those of other languages. In Go, an interface is a specific type that expresses a collection of one or more method signatures. Because the interface is abstract, we cannot create an instance of it. However, we are authorized to create an interface type variable that may be assigned with a concrete type value with the interface's needed methods. In other words, the interface is a collection of methods and a custom type.

How Do We Make an Interface?

We may define an interface in the Go programming language using the following syntax:

```
type interface_name interface{
// Method-signatures
}
```

Example:

```
// Creating-interface
type myinterface interface{
// Methods
func1() int
func2() float64
}
```

The type and interface keywords enclose the interface name, whereas curly brackets enclose the method signatures.

How to Implement Interfaces

To implement an interface in the Go programming language, all of the methods described in the interface are implemented. The Go programming language's interfaces are implemented implicitly. In addition, unlike other languages, it does not have a different name for implementing an interface.

Example:

```
// Program shows how
// to implement interface
package main
import "fmt"
// Creating-interface
type tank interface {
    // Methods
    Tarea() float64
    Volume() float64
}
type myvalue struct {
    radius float64
```

```go
    height float64
}
// Implementing methods of tank interface
func (m myvalue) Tarea() float64
{
    return 2*m.radius*m.height +
        2*3.14*m.radius*m.radius
}
func (m myvalue) Volume() float64
{
    return 3.14 * m.radius * m.radius * m.height
}
// the main-Method
func main() {
    // Accessing the elements of tank interface
    var tk tank
    tk = myvalue{10, 14}
    fmt.Println("The Area of tank :", tk.Tarea())
    fmt.Println("The Volume of tank:",
tk.Volume())
}
```

Why Are Go Interfaces Wonderful?

A "interface" explains what an object can do in object-oriented programming. This is usually in the form of a list of methods that an object must-have. C #, Java, and the Go programming language all offer interfaces, while Go's interfaces are especially simple to use.

We don't have to declare that a Go type (equivalent to a "class" in other languages) implements an interface, as we would in C# or Java. We just define the interface, and then any type with those methods is used anywhere that interface is necessary.

Redundant Functions

Assume we have a pet package (in other languages, a "package" is analogous to a "library") that contains Dogs and Cats types. Dogs use the Fetch method, cats use the Purr method, and the Walk and Sit both dogs and cats use techniques.

```go
package pets
import "fmt"
```

```
type Dogs struct {
    Name   string
    Breed string
}
func (d Dogs) Walk() {
    fmt.Println(d.Name, "walks across the hall")
}
func (d Dogs) Sit() {
    fmt.Println(d.Name, "sits-down")
}
func (d Dogs) Fetch() {
    fmt.Println(d.Name, "fetches-toy")
}
type Cats struct {
    Name   string
    Breed string
}
func (c Cats) Walk() {
    fmt.Println(c.Name, "walks across the hall")
}
func (c Cats) Sit() {
    fmt.Println(c.Name, "sits-down")
}
func (c Cats) Purr() {
    fmt.Println(c.Name, "purrss")
}
```

INHERITANCE

Inheritance, which entails inheriting the superclass's attributes into the base class, is one of the essential concepts in object-oriented programming. Because GoLang lacks classes, inheritance is achieved using struct embedding. We cannot extend structs directly but must instead utilize a concept known as composition, in which the struct is used to construct more objects. As a result, there is no idea of inheritance in GoLang.

Base structs can be embedded in a child struct in composition, and the base struct's methods can be called directly on the child struct, as seen in the following example:

```
// Program to demonstrate the concept of inheritance
package main
```

```go
import (
    "fmt"
)
// declaring-struct
type Comic struct{
    // declaring struct-variable
    Universe string
}
// function to return the universe of comic
func (comic Comic) ComicUniverse() string {
    // returns comic-universe
    return comic.Universe
}
// declaring struct
type Marvel struct{
    // anonymous field,
    // this is composition where the struct is
embedded
    Comic
}
// declaring-struct
type DC struct{
    // anonymous-field
    Comic
}
// main-function
func main() {

    // creating-instance
    cs1 := Marvel{
        // child struct can directly access base
struct variables
            Comic{
            Universe: "MCU",
            },
        }
    // child struct can directly access the base
struct methods printing base method using the child
        fmt.Println("Universe is:", cs1.
ComicUniverse())
            cs2 := DC{
        Comic{
```

```
        Universe : "DC",
    },
}
// printing the base method using child
fmt.Println("The Universe is:", cs2.
ComicUniverse())
}
```

POLYMORPHISM USING INTERFACES

The occurrence of several forms is referred to as polymorphism. Polymorphism, in other words, is the ability of a message to appear in several forms. Polymorphism, in technical terms, refers to the use of the same method name (but different signatures) for numerous types. A lady, for example, may exhibit many qualities at the same time. As an example, consider the following: mother, wife, sister, employee, etc. As a result, the same person behaves differently in different situations. This is referred to as polymorphism.

We can't establish polymorphism in Go with classes since Go doesn't support them, but we can do it with interfaces. Interfaces, as previously noted, are implemented implicitly in Go. As a result, when we create an interface, and other types desire to implement it, those types use the interface by utilizing its methods without knowing the type. An interface type variable in an interface can hold any value that implements the interface. This property helps interfaces achieve polymorphism in the Go programming language. As an example, consider the following:

```
// Program to show the concept of polymorphism using
the interfaces
package main
import "fmt"
// Interface
type employee interface {
    develop() int
    name() string
}
// Structure-1
type team1 struct {
    totalapp_1 int
    name_1      string
}
// Methods of employee interface are implemented by
the team1 structure
```

```go
func (tm1 team1) develop() int {
    return tm1.totalapp_1
}
func (tm1 team1) name() string {
    return tm1.name_1
}
// Structure-2
type team2 struct {
    totalapp_2 int
    name_2      string
}
// Methods of the employee interface are implemented
by team2 structure
func (tm2 team2) develop() int {
    return tm2.totalapp_2
}
func (tm2 team2) name() string {
    return tm2.name_2
}
func finaldevelop(i []employee) {
    totalproject := 0
    for _, ele := range i {
        fmt.Printf("\nProject environment = %s\n ",
ele.name())
        fmt.Printf("Total number of project %d\n ",
ele.develop())
        totalproject += ele.develop()
    }
    fmt.Printf("\nTotal projects completed by "+
        "the company = %d", totalproject)
}
  // main-function
func main() {
    res1 := team1{totalapp_1: 20,
        name_1: "IOS"}
    res2 := team2{totalapp_2: 35,
        name_2: "Android"}
    final := []employee{res1, res2}
    finaldevelop(final)
}
```

This chapter covered a crash course in GoLang, including its definition, benefits, installation, and fundamental syntax for all topics with examples.

CHAPTER 2

Test-Driven Development

IN THIS CHAPTER

➤ Refactoring

➤ Error handling

➤ Writing tests

In the previous chapter, we covered all the basic concepts of GoLang. This chapter will discuss Test-Driven Development (TDD) with Go, where we covered error handling, refactoring, and writing tests.

First, let's talk about the procedure. TDD is a programming paradigm that isn't specific to Go but is quite popular among Go developers.

When developing a program to perform anything (say, multiply two integers), one must first write a test.

A test is also a program, but it is designed to run another program with various inputs and examine the outcome. The test ensures that the software behaves as expected.

What's remarkable about the TDD methodology is that we create the test first before the code is tested (this is frequently referred to as test-first development). So, why are we doing this?

By developing the test first, we are forced to think explicitly about how the program should behave and describe those requirements as executable code with great precision.

Because we'll be calling our program from the test, we'll also need to create its API. So, contrary to its name, TDD isn't actually about testing. Instead,

DOI: 10.1201/9781003309055-2

it's a tool for thinking, a method for creating well-structured systems with decent APIs. Because we are our own first users, we can quickly identify when the code isn't convenient or comfortable to use, and we can improve it.

Let's examine how we may use that method now that we've begun working on our calculator app.

DEVELOPING A NEW PROJECT

Every Go project requires two things: a folder on the disc to store the source code and a go.mod file that specifies the module or project name.

If we don't already have one, we recommend making a new folder on our computer to house our Go projects (this can be in any location we like). Then, within this folder, make a calculator subdirectory.

Begin a shell session with our terminal program (for example, the macOS Terminal app) or code editor. Using the cd command, change our working directory to the project folder (for example, cd ~/go/calculator).

Next, type the following command in the shell to create a new Go module in this folder:

```
go mod init calculator

go: creating new go.mod: module calculator
```

MAKING Go FILES

A friendly colleague from Texio Instronics has provided us with some Go code that implements some of the calculator's functionality and a test for it, so we don't have to start from blank. We'll add that code to our project folder in this section.

First, create a calculator file with our code editor in the calculator folder. Then copy and paste the code in the below part:

```go
// Package calculator provides a library for
// simple calculations in the Go.
package calculator

// Add takes two numbers and returns result
// of adding them together.
func Add(c, d float64) float64 {
    return c + d
}
```

Don't worry about knowing all of the code at this point; we'll go over it in depth later. For the time being, simply enter this code into the calculator. Go ahead and save it.

Create a new file called calculator_test.go together with the following:

```
package calculator_test

import (
    "calculator"
    "testing"
)

func TestAdd(t *testing.T) {
    t.Parallel()
    var want float64 = 6
    got := calculator.Add(3, 3)
    if want != got {
        t.Errorf("want %f, got %f", want, got)
    }
}
```

RUN TESTS

Run the following command while still in the calculator folder:

```
go test
```

If everything is in order, we should see the following output:

```
PASS
ok calculator 0.234s
```

A TEST THAT FAILED

Now that our development environment is complete, someone requires our assistance. They have been trying to get the calculator to subtract numbers, but there's a problem: the test is failing.

Copy and paste the following code then into the calculator test.go file (after the TestAdd function):

```
func TestSubtract(t *testing.T) {
    t.Parallel()
    var want float64 = 3
```

```
    got := calculator.Subtract(6, 3)
    if want != got {
        t.Errorf("want %f, got %f", want, got)
    }
}
```

Here is the (wrong) code for implementing the Subtract function; paste it into the calculator .go file, following the Add function:

```
// Subtract takes two numbers c and d, and
// returns the result of subtracting d from c.
func Subtract(c, d float64) float64 {
    return d - c
}
```

Save this file and perform the following tests:

```
go test

--- FAIL: TestSubtract (0.01s)
    calculator_test.go:22: want 2.000000, got -2.000000
FAIL
exit status 1
FAIL    calculator    0.128s
```

This test failure indicates the specific position of the problem:

```
calculator_test.go:22
```

It also explains what the issue was:

```
want 2.000000, got -2.000000
```

To begin, the t.Parallel() sentence is a common test prelude: it instructs Go to execute this test concurrently with other tests, saving time.

The following sentence declares a variable named wish to represent what it expects from executing the method under test (Subtract):

```
var want float64 = 2
```

Then it invokes the Subtract function with the numbers 6, 3 and saves the result in another variable obtained:

```
got := calculator.Subtract(6, 3)
```

After obtaining this pair of variables, the goal is to compare wish to get and discover if they vary. If they are, the Subtract function is not functioning properly, and the test fails:

```
if want != got {
    t.Errorf("want %f, got %f", want, got)
}
```

THE FUNCTION BEING TESTED

So, let's have a look at the Subtract function code (in calculator.go). Here's what it is:

```
func Subtract(c, d float64) float64 {
    return d - c
}
```

If we find an error in the Subtract function, try modifying the code to solve it. Rerun the go test to ensure we got it properly. If we're experiencing problems, try modifying the numbers that Subtract is called with to see if we can figure out what's going wrong.

We can proceed once the exam has been passed.

WRITING A TEST-FIRST FUNCTION

Outstanding effort. We now have a calculator that can add and subtract (properly). That's a fantastic start. Let's move on to multiplication.

We've been running existing tests and altering existing code up to this point. We're going to write the test and the function it's testing for the first time.

GOAL: Create a test for the Multiply function, which, like Add and Subtract, accepts two integers as arguments and returns a single number reflecting the outcome.

Where should we begin? Because this is a test, begin in the calculator_test.go file. In Go, test functions must have a name that begins with

Test (otherwise, Go will not call them when we execute the go test). So TestMultiply is a wonderful name, isn't it? Let's add the new test after TestSubtract at the end of the file.

Except for the precise inputs and the anticipated return value, TestAdd and TestSubtract appear remarkably similar. So, to begin, clone one of those functions, rename it TestMultiply and make the necessary adjustments.

Only the name of the test, the function being called (Multiply instead of Add, for example), maybe the inputs to it, and the anticipated result of desire will need to be changed.

Something like this will suffice:

```
func TestMultiply(t *testing.T) {
    t.Parallel()
    var want float64 = 6
    got := calculator.Multiply(3, 2)
    if want != got {
        t.Errorf("want %f, got %f", want, got)
    }
}
```

When we're finished, running the tests should result in the following compilation error:

```
undefined: calculator.Multiply
```

This makes sense because we haven't yet built that function.

We're now ready to go to the next phase to get to a failed test. This will necessitate fixing the compilation problem, which will necessitate putting some code in the calculator package. But maybe not as much code as we think!

GOAL: Write the bare minimum of code required to build and fail the test.

What is the bare minimum of code required to compile? In the calculator package, we must define a Multiply function. Because it doesn't need to perform anything yet, the simplest method to get this program to compile is to make the function return zero:

```
func Multiply(c, d float64) float64 {
    return 0
}
```

Before we do anything else, double-check that the test is correct. Because we know that 0 is the incorrect answer, the test should fail, shouldn't it? If not, there is an issue with the test.

```
--- FAIL: TestMultiply (0.01s)
    calculator_test.go:30: want 9.000000, got 0.000000
```

Perfect! Now we're ready to put Multiply into action for real. We'll know when we've nailed it when our failed test begins to pass. And then we may come to a halt!

REFACTORING Go WITH Go/ANALYSIS

Refactoring is a method of enhancing our source code without adding new functionality. Refactoring assists us in keeping our code robust, dry, and simple to maintain.

Invoke the Refactoring Command

Choose an item to refactor. In the Project tool window, we may pick a file/folder or an expression/symbol in the editor.[1]

Ctrl+Alt+Shift+T will bring up a selection of refactoring from which to choose.

We may also use a keyboard shortcut to perform a specific refactoring.

Ctrl+Z will allow us to undo our refactoring.

Conflicts Resolve

When GoLand detects issues with our refactoring, it displays a dialog with a list of conflicts and brief explanations.

Click Continue to dismiss the error and open the preview in the Find tool window.

To open the conflict items in the Find tool window and deal with them further, click Show Conflicts in View.

For example, we may try to exclude an entry from refactoring by pressing Delete, or we can cancel and return to the editor by clicking Cancel.

Configure the Refactoring Options

Select Editor | Code Editing from the Settings/Preferences menu (Ctrl+Alt+S).

---

[1] https://www.jetbrains.com/help/go/refactoring-source-code.html

Adjust the refactoring choices and click OK on the Code Editing page's Refactoring section.

My Top Four Go Refactoring Approaches

Refactoring is defined as "a modification made to the underlying structure of software to make it easier to understand and cheaper to alter without affecting its observable behavior."

Refactoring is a broad topic, and we believe they play an essential part in the software development process. Their importance is such that they are a fundamental component of the TDD life cycle.[2]

Because of their importance, we'd like to share four of the refactoring techniques we've used the most in my role as a software developer in this post. However, because applying refactoring techniques can be automated (i.e., some IDEs provide us with tools to apply refactoring and make our life easier with a couple of clicks and selections), we'll describe them manually for Go language and try to follow them as a reference guide. To be honest, and consider this a MUST sentence, our development team is aware that before using any refactoring approach, all observable functionality in source code should be covered with unit tests and passed.

Method of Extraction

This is an approach we commonly use in my programming. It entails removing a chunk of code that has been grouped by intention and moving it into a new method. We've discovered one compelling reason to use it: it allows us to divide a big method or function into shorter methods that group a piece of logic. In most cases, the name of the little method or function offers a clearer understanding of what that bit of logic is.

The following example displays the before and after effects of this refactoring method. My primary objective was to abstract complexity by breaking it down into distinct functions.

```
func StringCalculator(exp string) int {
    if exp == "" {
        return 0
    }

    var sum int
```

---

[2] https://wawand.co/blog/posts/four-most-refactoring-techniques-i-use/

```go
        for _, number := range strings.Split(exp, ",") {
            nm, err := strconv.Atoi(number)
            if err != nil {
                return 0
            }
            sum += nm
        }
        return sum
    }
    func StringCalculator(exp string) int {
        if exp == "" {
            return 0
        }
        return sumAllNumberInExpression(exp)
    }

    func sumAllNumberInExpression(exp string) int {
        var sum int
        for _, number := range strings.Split(exp, ",") {
            sum += toInt(number)
        }
        return sum
    }

    func toInt(exp string) int {
        nm, err := strconv.Atoi(exp)
        if err != nil {
            return 0
        }
        return nm
    }
```

The StringCalculator function proved to be simpler, but it adds complexity when two more methods are introduced. This is a risk I'm willing to accept with a calculated judgment. I use this as a guideline rather than a rule because understanding the outcome of a refactoring approach might help us decide whether to use it.

Method of Move

After using the extract method refactoring, I sometimes wonder if this function should belong to this struct or package. Move Method is a straightforward approach that involves (as the name says) transferring a method from one struct to another. One way I've discovered for determining if a method should belong to that struct is to see if it accesses the internals of another struct dependence more than its own. Consider the following example:

```
type Book struct {
    ID    int
    Title string
}

type Books []Book

type User struct {
    ID    int
    Names string
    Books Books
}

func (u User) Info() {
    fmt.Printf("ID:%d - Names:%s", u.ID, u.Names)
    fmt.Printf("Books:%d", len(u.Books))
    fmt.Printf("Books titles: %s", u.BooksTitles())
}

func (u User) BooksTitles() string {
    var titles []string
    for _, book := range u.Books {
        titles = append(titles, book.Title)
    }
    return strings.Join(titles, ",")
}
```

As we can see, the User's method, BooksTitles, makes greater use of internal attributes from books (i.e., Title) than the User's, indicating that this method should be held by Books rather than the User. Let's utilize this refactoring approach to convert this function to the Books type, which will subsequently be called by the user's Info method.

```
func (b Books) Titles() string {
    var titles []string
    for _, book := range b {
        titles = append(titles, book.Title)
    }
    return strings.Join(titles, ",")
}
```

```
func (u User) Info() {
    fmt.Printf("ID:%d - Names:%s", u.ID, u.Names)
    fmt.Printf("Books:%d", len(u.Books))
    fmt.Printf("Books titles: %s", u.Books.Titles())
}
```

The Books type obtains cohesiveness after using this technique since it is the only one that has control and access to its fields and internal attributes. Again, this mental process precedes a conscious action, understanding the repercussions of refactoring.

Create a Parameter Object

How often have we encountered a method like this with a long list of parameters?

```
func (om *OrderManager) Filter(startDate, endDate time.Time,
country, state, city, status string) (Orders, error) {
```

Even though we don't see the code within the function, we may imagine how many operations it does when we see many parameters like this.

Sometimes we notice that such parameters are significantly connected to one another and are utilized together afterward within the method where they were declared. This refactoring involves grouping those arguments into a struct, changing the method signature to use that object as a parameter, and using that object inside the function to handle that circumstance more object-oriented.

```
type OrderFilter struct {
    StartDate time.Time
    EndDate time.Time
    Country    string
    City       string
    State      string
    Status     string
}

func (om *OrderManager) Filter(of OrderFilter) (Orders,
error) {
    // use of.StartDate, of.EndDate, of.Country, of.city,
of. State, of.Status
```

That looks cleaner and provides more information about those parameters. Still, it would necessitate changing all references where this method is called and creating a new object of type OrderFilter as an argument before sending it to the function. Again, I try to be extremely deliberate and consider the consequences before doing this modification. When the amount of influence in our code is modest, I believe this strategy is quite effective.

Replace Symbolic Constant with Magic Number

This approach involves replacing a hard-coded value with a constant variable to give it intention and meaning.

```go
func Add(input string) int {
    if input == "" {
        return 0
    }

    if strings.Contains(input, ";") {
        nm1 := toNumber(input[:strings.Index(input, ";")])
        nm2 := toNumber(input[strings.Index(input, ";")+1:])

        return nm1 + nm2
    }

    return toNumber(input)
}

func toNumber(input string) int {
    nm, err := strconv.Atoi(input)
    if err != nil {
        return 0
    }
    return nm
}
```

What exactly does that symbol imply? If the response is too vague for us, we may create a temporary variable and set the value with the hard-coded character to give it identity and intent.

```go
func Add(input string) int {
    if input == "" {
        return 0
    }
```

```
    numberSeparator := ";"
    if strings.Contains(input, numberSeparator) {
        nm1 := toNumber(input[:strings.Index(input,
numberSeparator)])
        nm2 := toNumber(input[strings.Index(input,
numberSeparator)+1:])

        return nm1 + nm2
    }

    return toNumber(input)
}

func toNumber(input string) int {
    nm, err := strconv.Atoi(input)
    if err != nil {
        return 0
    }
    return nm
}
```

REFACTORING OUR FIRST Go CODE

Now we will go through it and refactor it. Begin by examining the primary function. It is, after all, the sole function of this project.

```
func main() {
    args := os.Args[1:]

    inFile := args[0]
    inHash := args[1]

    // keep check case insensitive
    inHash = strings.ToLower(inHash)

    file, err := os.Open(inFile)
    if err != nil {
        log.Fatal(err)
    }
    defer file.Close()

        // review: maybe change name to hasher
    hash := sha256.New()
    if _, err := io.Copy(hash, file); err != nil {
        log.Fatal(err)
    }
```

```
    hashToCheck := hex.EncodeToString(hash.Sum(nil))

        // review: introduce string formatting
    if inHash == hashToCheck {
        color.Green(inFile + " has SHA256 " + inHash)
    } else {
        color.Red(inFile + " does not match with " + inHash)
        color.Red("Correct hash is: " + hashToCheck)
    }
}
```

As a result, we've already discovered some issues. We'd also like to isolate the checking logic and develop tests for it.

Include a Parameter Check

We'll add a parameter count check at the top of the main function to enhance error handling. We're also putting a non-zero exit code here so we can see if the command was successful or not on our command line.

```
func main() {
    // check for the missing parameters
if len(os.Args) != 3 {
    fmt.Println("Error occured: missing-parameters")
    // emit non-zero exit code
    os.Exit(1)
}
    // continue..
}
```

Add String Formatting

Although, it is not a good idea to use string concatenation for command-line printing. It is, of course, preferable to print something using string formatting.

So, let's start with

```
color.Green(inFile + " has SHA256 " + inHash)
```

to that:

```
color.Green("%s has SHA256 %s", inFile, inHash)
```

Take Out the Code

We'd want to write a function that validates hashes for arbitrary streams rather than just files. One may consider verifying a hash when receiving files from an HTTP server, assuming the file is already in memory. As a result, I'm employing the io.Reader interface. It will also make the coding unit testable.

```go
// checkHash calculates hash using and io.Reader, so it's
now testable
func checkHash(reader io.Reader, hash string) (isValid
bool, calculatedHash string, err error) {
    // keep check case-insensitive
    hash = strings.ToLower(hash)

    hasher := sha256.New()
    if _, err := io.Copy(hasher, reader); err != nil {
        return false, "", err
    }

    calculatedHash = hex.EncodeToString(hasher.Sum(nil))
    return hash == calculatedHash, calculatedHash, nil
}
```

Write a Test

We must now develop tests for the code because it is testable.

```go
func TestCheckHash(t *testing.T) {
    d := []byte{0xbe, 0xef, 0x10, 0x10, 0xca, 0xfe}

    s := bytes.NewReader(d)

    isValid, calculatedHash, err := checkHash(s, "77efeeff
80507604bbd4c32b32ce44306879154f83f46afe8c15223932a6a4cb")

    if err != nil {
        t.Error(err)
    } else if !isValid {
        t.Error("hashes don't match", calculatedHash)
    }
}
```

So, in the above code, we generate a byte slice containing the hex codes 0xbeef1010cafe, an io.Reader from it and compute its hash.

GoLang ERROR HANDLING

Error handling.

Compared to other major languages, such as JavaScript, Java, and Python, error handling in GoLang is unusual. This can make it difficult for inexperienced programmers to understand GoLang's approach to error handling.

In this session, we'll look at how to handle failures using built-in GoLang capabilities, how to extract information from errors, and the best practices for doing so.

Errors in GoLang

Errors indicate that an undesirable circumstance is occurring in our application. Assume we wish to establish a temporary directory to store some files for our program.[3] However, the directory creation fails. Because this is an undesirable circumstance, it is represented with an error.

```
package main
import (
    "fmt"
    "ioutil"
)
```

---

[3] https://gabrieltanner.org/blog/GoLang-error-handling-definitive-guide

```
func main() {
    dir, err := ioutil.TempDir("", "temp")
        if err != nil {
            return fmt.Errorf("failed to create temp dir
is: %v", err)
        }
}
```

The built-in error type in GoLang is used to represent errors, which we shall look at in more detail in the next section. As illustrated in the above example, the error is frequently returned as a second parameter to the function. The TempDir method returns the directory name and an error variable in this case.

Creating Our Own Mistakes

Errors, as previously stated, are represented using the built-in error interface type, which has the definition:

```
type error interface {
    Error() string
}
```

The interface only has one method, Error(), which returns an error message as a string. Any type that implements the error interface can be utilized as an error. When displaying the error with techniques such as fmt. GoLang automatically calls the Error() function when it encounters an error.

In GoLang, there are several methods for constructing bespoke error messages, each with its own set of benefits and drawbacks.

Errors Caused by Strings

String-based errors are used for basic faults that only need to produce an error message and maybe constructed using two out-of-the-box GoLang options.

```
err := errors.New("math: divided by zero")
```

The errors.New() method is used to create new errors and takes the error message as its only argument.

```
err2 := fmt.Errorf("math: %g cannot divided by zero", x)
```

fmt.Errorf, on the other hand, allows us to format our error message as well. As seen above, a parameter can be given that will be included in the error message.

Data Custom Mistakes

We may create our own error type by implementing the Error() method supplied in the error interface on our struct. Here is an example:

```
type PathError struct {
    Path string
}

func (e *PathError) Error() string {
    return fmt.Sprintf("error in the path: %v", e.Path)
}
```

PathError implements the Error() method and hence conforms to the error interface. Implementing the Error() method now returns a string containing the PathError struct's path. We may now use PathError to throw an error anytime we wish.

Here is a simple example:

```
package main

import (
    "fmt"
)

type PathError struct {
    Path string
}

func (e *PathError) Error() string {
    return fmt.Sprintf("error in path: %v", e.Path)
}
```

```
func throwError() error {
    return &PathError{Path: "/test"}
}

func main() {
    err := throwError()

    if err != nil {
        fmt.Println(err)
    }
}
```

Handling Errors in Functions

Let's look at how to handle problems in functions now that we've learned everything on how to create custom errors and extract as much information as possible from failures.

Most errors are not handled directly in functions but are instead returned as a value. We can use the fact that GoLang allows multiple return values for a function here. As a result, we may provide our error with the function's ordinary result – errors are always returned as the final parameter, as seen below:

```
func divide(c, d float64) (float64, error) {
    if d == 0 {
        return 0.0, errors.New("can't divide through zero")
    }

    return c/d, nil
}
```

The function call will then appear as follows:

```
func main() {
    numb, err := divide(200, 0)
    if err != nil {
        fmt.Printf("error: %s", err.Error())
    } else {
        fmt.Println("Number: ", numb)
    }
}
```

If the returned error is not nil, it is clear that there is a problem, and we need to deal with it correctly. Depending on the situation, this may entail sending a log message to the user, retrying the function until it works, or closing the application entirely. The only downside is that GoLang does not need to process returned errors, so we may just ignore handling errors.

Consider the following code as an example:

```
package main

import (
    "errors"
    "fmt"
)

func main() {
    num2, _ := divide(100, 0)

    fmt.Println("Number: ", num2)
}
```

The blank identifier here is an anonymous placeholder, allowing us to ignore values in an assignment while avoiding compiler problems. However, keep in mind that using a blank identifier instead of dealing with difficulties is dangerous. It is recommended to avoid if at all feasible.

Defer

A defer statement is a technique for deferring a function by placing it on an executed stack after the function containing the defer statement has been completed, either generally by executing a return statement or abnormally by panicking. Deferred functions are then run in the reverse order that they were deferred.

As an example, consider the following function:

```
func processHTML(url string) error {
    resp, err := http.Get(url)
    if err != nil {
        return err
    }
    ct := resp.Header.Get("Content-Type")
```

```
        if ct != "text/html" && !strings.HasPrefix(ct,
"text/html;") {
                resp.Body.Close()
                return fmt.Errorf("%s has content type %s
which doesn't match text/html", url, ct)
        }

        doc, err := html.Parse(resp.Body)
        resp.Body.Close()
        // Process HTML
        return nil
}
```

The duplicated resp.Body.Close call, which guarantees that the response is correctly closed, may be seen here. As functions become more complicated and contain more mistakes that need to be handled, such duplications become increasingly challenging.

Because postponed calls are called once the function has finished, regardless of whether it succeeded or failed, they can be used to simplify such calls.

```
func processHTMLDefer(url string) error {
  resp, err := http.Get(url)
  if err != nil {
      return err
      }
  defer resp.Body.Close()
      ct := resp.Header.Get("Content-Type")
      if ct != "text/html" && !strings.HasPrefix(ct,
"text/html;") {
                return fmt.Errorf("%s has content type %s
which doesn't match text/html", url, ct)
      }
      doc, err := html.Parse(resp.Body)
      // Process HTML
      return nil
}
```

When the function completes, all delayed functions are run in the opposite order in which they were deferred.

```
package main
import (
        "fmt"
)
func main() {
        first()
}
func first() {
        defer fmt.Println("first")
        second()
}
func second() {
        defer fmt.Println("second")
        third()
}
func third() {
        defer fmt.Println("third")
}
```

The following is the output of executing the above program:

```
third
second
first
```

Panic

A panic statement informs GoLang that our code is unable to tackle the present problem and, as a result, the usual execution flow of our code is halted. When panic is triggered, all delayed functions are performed, and the program crashes with a log message including the panic values (typically an error message) and a stack trace.

GoLang, for example, will panic if an integer is split by zero.

```
package main
import "fmt"
func main() {
        divide(5)
}
func divide(x int) {
        fmt.Printf("divide(%d) \n", x+0/x)
        divide(x-1)
}
```

When the division function is invoked with a value of zero, the program panics, resulting in the results seen below.

```
panic: runtime error: integer divide by zero
goroutine 1 [running]:
main.divide(0x0)
        C:/Users/gabriel/articles/GoLang Error handling/
Code/panic/main.go:16 +0xe6
main.divide(0x1)
        C:/Users/gabriel/articles/GoLang Error handling/
Code/panic/main.go:17 +0xd6
main.divide(0x2)
        C:/Users/gabriel/articles/GoLang Error handling/
Code/panic/main.go:17 +0xd6
main.divide(0x3)
        C:/Users/gabriel/articles/GoLang Error handling/
Code/panic/main.go:17 +0xd6
main.divide(0x4)
        C:/Users/gabriel/articles/GoLang Error handling/
Code/panic/main.go:17 +0xd6
main.divide(0x5)
        C:/Users/gabriel/articles/GoLang Error handling/
Code/panic/main.go:17 +0xd6
main.main()
        C:/Users/gabriel/articles/GoLang Error handling/
Code/panic/main.go:11 +0x31
exit status 2
```

We may also panic in our own applications by using the built-in panic function. A panic should be used only when something unexpected occurs that the application is unable to manage.

```
func getArguments() {
        if len(os.Args) == 1 {
                panic("Not enough-arguments!")
        }
}
```

As previously stated, deferred functions will be executed before the application is terminated, as illustrated in the following example.

```
package main
import (
        "fmt"
)
func main() {
        accessSlice([]int{11,22,55,66,77,88}, 0)
}
func accessSlice(slice []int, index int) {
        fmt.Printf("item %d, value %d \n", index,
slice[index])
        defer fmt.Printf("defer %d \n", index)
        accessSlice(slice, index+1)
}
```

Here is the program's output:

```
item 0, value 1
item 1, value 2
item 2, value 5
item 3, value 6
item 4, value 7
item 5, value 8
defer 5
defer 4
defer 3
defer 2
defer 1
defer 0
panic: runtime error: index out of range [6] with length 6

goroutine 1 [running]:
main.accessSlice(0xc00011df48, 0x6, 0x6, 0x6)
        C:/Users/gabriel/articles/GoLang Error handling/
Code/panic/main.go:29 +0x250
main.accessSlice(0xc00011df48, 0x6, 0x6, 0x5)
        C:/Users/gabriel/articles/GoLang Error handling/
Code/panic/main.go:31 +0x1eb
main.accessSlice(0xc00011df48, 0x6, 0x6, 0x4)
        C:/Users/gabriel/articles/GoLang Error handling/
Code/panic/main.go:31 +0x1eb
main.accessSlice(0xc00011df48, 0x6, 0x6, 0x3)
        C:/Users/gabriel/articles/GoLang Error handling/
Code/panic/main.go:31 +0x1eb
main.accessSlice(0xc00011df48, 0x6, 0x6, 0x2)
        C:/Users/gabriel/articles/GoLang Error handling/
Code/panic/main.go:31 +0x1eb
```

```
main.accessSlice(0xc00011df48, 0x6, 0x6, 0x1)
        C:/Users/gabriel/articles/GoLang Error handling/
Code/panic/main.go:31 +0x1eb
main.accessSlice(0xc00011df48, 0x6, 0x6, 0x0)
        C:/Users/gabriel/articles/GoLang Error handling/
Code/panic/main.go:31 +0x1eb
main.main()
        C:/Users/gabriel/articles/GoLang Error handling/
Code/panic/main.go:9 +0x99
exit status 2
```

Recover

Panics should not terminate the program in some uncommon instances, but should instead be recovered. For example, if a socket server experiences an unexpected difficulty, it should notify the clients and subsequently disconnect all connections, rather than keeping the clients in the dark about what happened.

Recover panics by executing the built-in recover function within a delayed function within the panicking function. The current state of panic will then end, and the panic error value is returned.

```
package main
import "fmt"
func main(){
        accessSlice([]int{1,2,5,6,7,8}, 0)
}
func accessSlice(slice []int, index int) {
        defer func() {
                if p := recover(); p != nil {
                        fmt.Printf("internal error: %v", p)
                }
        }()
        fmt.Printf("item %d, value %d \n", index,
slice[index])
        defer fmt.Printf("defer %d \n", index)
        accessSlice(slice, index+1)
}
```

As we can see, after adding a recover function to the function we created above, the program no longer exists when the index is out of bounds.

Output:

```
item 0, value 1
item 1, value 2
item 2, value 5
item 3, value 6
item 4, value 7
item 5, value 8
internal error: runtime error: index out of range [6] with
length 6defer 5
defer 4
defer 3
defer 2
defer 1
defer 0
```

Recovering from panic attacks might be beneficial in specific situations, but we should avoid recovering from panic attacks as a general rule.

Error Wrapping

GoLang also allows errors to wrap up other errors, allowing us to provide additional context to our error messages. This is frequently used to offer complete details, such as where the issue occurred in our software.

As seen in the following example, we may produce wrapped errors by using the percent w (%w) option with the fmt.Errorf function.

```
package main
import (
        "errors"
        "fmt"
        "os"
)
func main() {
        err := openFile("non-existing")

        if err != nil {
                fmt.Printf("error running program: %s \n",
err.Error())
        }
}
func openFile(filename string) error {
        if _, err := os.Open(filename); err != nil {
```

```
              return fmt.Errorf("error opening %s: %w",
filename, err)
        }
        return nil
}
```

The application's output would now look something like this:

```
error running program: error opening non-existing: open
non-existing: no such file or directory
```

As we can see, the program outputs both the new error message generated by fmt.Errorf and the old error message supplied to the %w flag. GoLang also can recover a previous error message by unwrapping the error using errors.Unwrap.

```
package main
import (
        "errors"
        "fmt"
        "os"
)
func main() {
        err := openFile("nonexisting")
        if err != nil {
                fmt.Printf("error running-program: %s \n",
err.Error())
                // Unwrap error
                unwrappedErr := errors.Unwrap(err)
                fmt.Printf("unwrapped-error: %v \n",
unwrappedErr)
        }
}

func openFile(filename string) error {
        if _, err := os.Open(filename); err != nil {
                return fmt.Errorf("error opening %s: %w",
filename, err)
        }
        return nil
}
```

As can be seen, the output now includes the original mistake.

```
error running program: error opening non-existing: open
non-existing: no such file or directory
unwrapped error: open non-existing: no such file or directory
```

Errors can be wrapped and unwrapped several times, although wrapping them more than a few times is usually unnecessary.

Casting Errors

We'll need the means to cast between different error types from time to time, for example, to access unique information that only that type holds. The "errors.As" function makes this simple and safe by looking for the first error in the error chain that meets the error type's specifications. If there is no match, the method here returns false.

Let's have a look at the official errors.As To further understand what is going on, consider using the documentation example.

```
package main
import (
        "errors"
        "fmt"
        "io/fs"
        "os"
)
func main(){
        // Casting error
        if _, err := os.Open("non-existing"); err != nil {
                var pathError *os.PathError
                if errors.As(err, &pathError) {
                        fmt.Println("Failed at path:",
pathError.Path)
                } else {
                        fmt.Println(err)
                }
        }
}
```

Here, we attempt to cast our general error type to os.PathError to access the Path variable included in that specific issue.

Another essential feature is determining if a mistake is of a certain type. To do this, GoLang provides the "errors.Is" function. This section specifies our error and the specific error type we wish to verify. If the error is correct, the function will return true; otherwise, it will return false.

```go
package main
import (
        "errors"
        "fmt"
        "io/fs"
        "os"
)
func main(){
        // Check if error is specific type
        if _, err := os.Open("non-existing"); err != nil {
                if errors.Is(err, fs.ErrNotExist) {
                        fmt.Println("file doesn't exist")
                } else {
                        fmt.Println(err)
                }
        }
}
```

After we have checked, we may modify our error message accordingly.

WRITE UNIT TESTING IN Go

Unit testing is widely used in Go (GoLang) programs. Many of the applications for which Go is often used are relatively simple to develop decent unit tests for. However, we should know a few things whether we are new to the language or unit testing in general. This post will help us create unit tests and learn about some of the finest testing approaches.

If we're new to unit testing in general, we should read our post about the benefits of unit testing.

Beginning

Unlike most other languages I've dealt with, Go includes a built-in test runner and a foundation for standard language tools. The simplest approach to run unit tests for your project is from the command line using a command like go test. /... This program will find and execute any tests in your current directory or its subdirectories.

Tests must be written in files distinct from the main package code and must finish with the suffix_test.go. Starting with func Test identifies a test function. One of the most basic tests might look like this:

```
// hello.go - This is the code to test
package hello

func HelloEveryone() string {
    return "hello everyone"
}
// hello_test.go - This is unit test file
package hello_test

import (
    "fmt"
    "testing"
    "github.com/PullRequestInc/pkg/hello"
)

func TestHelloWorld(t *testing.T) {
    actual := hello.HelloEveryone()
    if actual != "hello everyone" {
        t.Errorf("expected 'hello everyone', got '%s'",
actual)
    }
}
```

The preceding test would pass as long as HelloEveryone() always returns the right string. However, if it fails, it will display the error message from t.Errorf.

Unique to Go

If we're used to creating unit tests in other languages, there are a few differences in writing unit tests in Go.

For one thing, we'll notice in the above example that the testing appears "crude," We execute the check ourselves and then return an error message. There are no helpers built-in for stuff like t.assertEquals (expected, actual). This is because Go errs on the side of minimalism, giving only the essentials required to do a task in one method. This allows the language to preserve backward compatibility for an extended time while also focusing on optimizing and enhancing these basic functions over time.

That being said, testify is a fantastic third-party package that is frequently used for executing various sorts of assertions. Testify includes the assert and need packages – the assert, like the built-in t.Fail will fail the test on the first failure it sees. Whereas t.Error will just report an error and continue the test; need will simply report an error and continue the test. We prefer using the assert package and believe it complements the built-in Go test tooling and infrastructure well. The fundamental structure of your tests will remain the same, except for certain assertion helpers that will result in significantly fewer lines of code. The above example would become:

```
assert.Equal(t, "hello everyone", hello.HelloEveryone())
```

Go tests are likewise designed to be comparable to how ordinary Go code is written. As a result, you may utilize and enhance our approaches for developing normal Go code while writing tests. Creating tests feels very different from writing ordinary code in many other languages. However, third-party frameworks such as Ginkgo are available if we wish to employ BDD testing. Although we are just getting started, I recommend avoiding huge third-party frameworks such as this because most teams and projects utilize the standard Go testing framework. Some components of the standard test framework, such as the concurrency testing mode, may not necessarily have as strong compatibility with these other frameworks.

Setup and Teardown

The Go tests are simple and just consist of a function. We may be familiar with many other test frameworks containing capabilities, such as setUp methods that run before each test and tearDown methods after each test. This is one of the reasons why some individuals may first persuade to use a third-party framework such as Ginkgo or others. However, Go tests can provide the same functionality.

In Go, this pattern is known as "table-driven testing." Here's how we'd accomplish a setUp and tearDown shared by several comparative tests.

```
// hello_test1.go
package hello_test1

import (
    "fmt"
    "testing"
    "github.com/PullRequestInc/pkg/hello"
)
```

```go
func TestHello(t *testing.T) {
    type test struct {
        input       string
        expected    string
    }

    tests := []test{
        {input: "world", expected: "hello everyone"},
        {input: "pullrequest", expected: "hello
pullrequest"},
    }

    for _, tc := range tests {
        // here perform setUp before each test
        t.Run(tc.input, func(t *testing.T) {
            actual := hello.Hello(tc.input)
            if actual != tc.expected {
                t.Errorf("expected '%s', got '%s'",
tc.expected, actual)
            }
            // perform tearDown after the each test here
        })
    }
}
```

This is just a simple example, and I'm not really utilizing the setUp or tearDown functions, but we can see where we can use such chores. On the other hand, these table-driven tests may be as complex as we want them to be. We may wish to pass a function as a parameter for some test scenarios and call distinct functions for tests with a shared setUp and tearDown.

Testing within the Same Package

There are two primary modularity choices for testing our Go package. We may either build a separate package for your test code or include it in the same package that we are testing.[4] Both methods will not include the code from our _test.go files in our binary since these files are disregarded during binary compilation. The fundamental distinction here is whether or not we require or desire access to the package's internal operations and data.

Using package hello or package hello test for our hello_test.go file will allow us to choose between these two testing methods.

---

4 https://www.pullrequest.com/blog/unit-testing-in-go/

Assume we have a package that looks like this:

```
package hello

func world() string {
    return "everyone"
}

func HelloEveryone() string {
    return "hello " + everyone()
}
```

If we wanted to test the world function independently of the HelloEveryone function, we could only do so if our test was in the same hello package. Since the world is an unexported method, you cannot access it outside of the package. If we try to test it from a hello_test1 package, we could get a compilation error saying that there is no symbol world.

If feasible, we recommend using a separate testing package and testing our publicly exported units. This results in more modular code, and we get to test our package in the same way that a consumer would. This might also assist us in understanding how the API reads. However, we would not export more internal functions merely to test the package in this manner, and testing within the same package is acceptable.

Five Basic Techniques and Strategies for Developing GoLang Unit Tests

TDD is an excellent technique to maintain good code quality while protecting yourself from regression and demonstrating to yourself and others that your code performs what it is designed to do.

Here are five test-improvement ideas and methods.

- **Put our tests in a separate package:** Except for "_test.go" files, Go demands that files in the same folder belong to the same package. By removing your test code from the package, we may write tests as if we were genuine users of the product. We can't mess with the internals; instead, we concentrate on the exposed interface and are always concerned about any noise you could introduce to our API.

- **Internal tests are kept in a separate file:** If you need to unit test specific internals, create a new file with the suffix "_internal test.go".

Internal tests will always be more brittle than interface tests. Still, they're a wonderful method to check internal components are working properly and are especially beneficial if we utilize TDD.

- **When we save, run all of our tests:** Go builds and runs rapidly, so there's little reason not to run our whole test suite every time we save.

  This may be accomplished in Sublime Text by installing GoSublime and pressing "Cmd+.,5" before adding the following configuration items:

```
"on_save": [{
  "cmd": "gs9o_run_many", "args": {
    "commands":[
      ["clear"],
      ["sh", "if [ -f onsave.sh ]; then. /onsave.sh;
else gofmt -s -w. / && go build. errors && go test -i
&& go test && go vet && golint ; fi"]
    ],
    "focus_view": false
  }
}],
"fmt_cmd": ["goimports"]
```

The preceding script first checks to see whether there is a "onsave.sh" file in the project, which it will use instead. This enables us to simply disable the auto-test capability for packages when it is not required.

- **Table-driven tests are written as:** Thanks to anonymous structs and composite literals, we can create prominent and easy table tests without relying on any external package.

  The code below enables us to build up a number of tests for an as-yet unwritten 'Fib' function:

```
var fibTest = []struct {
    nm       int // input
    expected int // expected-result
}{
    {1, 1},
    {2, 1},
    {3, 2},
    {4, 3},
    {5, 5},
    {6, 8},
    {7, 13},
}
```

Then, before declaring that the results are valid, our test function simply ranges through the slice, invoking the 'Fib' method for each 'n':

```
func TestFib(t *testing.T) {
    for _, tt := range fibTests {
        actual := Fib(tt.nm)
        if actual != tt.expected {
            t1.Errorf("Fib(%d): expected %d, actual %d",
tt.nm, tt.expected, actual)
        }
    }
}
```

- **Mock stuff up with Go code:** If we need to simulate something, our code depends on testing it effectively. It's probably a suitable candidate for an interface. Even if we're reliant on an external package that you can't modify, our code can still conform to an interface that the external types will fulfill.

   Assume we're importing the following external package:

```
package mailman
import "net/mail"
type MailMan struct{}
func (ml *MailMan) Send(subject, body string, to
...*mail.Address) {
  // some code
}
func New() *MailMan {
  return &MailMan{}
}
```

If the method under test requires a "MailMan" object, our test code can only call it by giving an actual "MailMan" instance.

```
func SendWelcomeEmail(ml *MailMan, to .....*mail.Address)
{...}
```

A genuine email might be sent every time we run our tests. Now think about it what would happen if we used the above-mentioned on-save functionality. We'd rapidly irritate our test users or rack up large service costs.

Another option is to incorporate the following primary interface into our code:

```
type EmailSender interface{
    Send(subject, body string, to ....*mail.Address)
}
```

Of course, because we removed the "Send" method signature from him in the first place, the "MailMan" already meets this interface, so we can still pass in "MailMan" objects as before.

However, we can now write a test email sender:

```
type testEmailSender struct{
    lastSubject string
    lastBody    string
    lastTo      []*mail.Address
}
// make sure it satisfies interface
var _ package.EmailSender = (*testEmailSender)(nil)
func (t *testEmailSender) Send(subject, body string, to
....*mail.Address) {
    t1.lastSubject = subject
    t1.lastBody = body
    t1.lastTo = to
}
```

Now we can change our "SendWelcomeEmail" method to accept the interface instead of the concrete type:

```
func SendWelcomeEmail(ml EmailSender, to ....*mail.Address)
{...}
```

In our test code, we may use a bogus sender and make assertions on the fields after calling the target function:

```
func TestSendWelcomeEmail(t *testing.T) {
    sender := &testEmailSender{}
```

```
    SendWelcomeEmail(sender, to1, to2)
    if sender.lastSubject != "Welcome" {
      t1.Error("The Subject line was wrong")
    }
    if sender.To[0] != to1 && sender.To[1] != to2 {
      t1.Error("Wrongrecipients")
    }
  }
```

This chapter discussed refactoring, error handling, and writing tests with relevant examples.

CHAPTER 3

Packaging in GoLang

IN THIS CHAPTER

➤ Working with packages

➤ Importing libraries and tools

➤ Dependency management

In the previous chapter, we discussed refactoring, error handling, and writing test units in GoLang. This chapter will cover working with packages and how to import libraries and tools. Moreover, we will also discuss dependency management.

PACKAGES IN GoLang

In this session, we'll look at packages in the Go programming language. When designing applications, it is vital to write maintainable and reusable code. Go provides modularity and code reusability through its package ecosystem. Go pushes us to package little bits of software and then utilize these small packages to assemble larger applications.

Workspace

While we go into Go packages, let's discuss Workspace structure code. Go programs are kept in a directory structure known as a workspace. A workspace is just the home directory for our Go programs. There are three subdirectories at the root of a workspace:

1. **src:** This directory contains source files organized as packages. We will write our Go applications in this directory.

2. **pkg:** This directory contains Go package objects.

3. **bin:** This directory includes executable applications.

Before we can begin developing Go programs, we must first establish the workspace's location. GOPATH is an environment variable that indicates where Go workspaces are located.

In Go, source files are grouped into system folders called packages, allowing code reuse among Go programs. The Go package naming convention utilizes the name of the system directory where we keep our Go source files. The package name remains the same for all source files included within that directory within a single folder. We create Go programs under the $GOPATH directory, where we organize source code files into packages as directories. All identifiers in Go packages are exported to other packages if the initial letter of the identifier name is in uppercase.

If we begin the identifier name with a lowercase letter, the functions and types will not export to other packages.

Go's standard library includes many helpful packages to construct real-world applications. The standard library, for example, has a "net/http" package that may use to create online applications and web services. The standard library packages may find in the GOROOT directory's "pkg" subfolder. When you install Go, an environment variable called GOROOT is added to our system to designate the Go installation path. The Go developer community is ecstatic about the prospect of creating third-party Go packages. These third-party Go packages can use for developing Go apps.

Main Package

When we create reusable code, you will create a package as a shared library. However, while creating executable applications, we will utilize the package "main" to convert the package into an executable program. The package "main" instructs the Go compiler to construct the package as an executable application rather than a shared library. The main function in package "main" will serve as the executable program's entry point. When you create shared libraries, there will be no main package or main function in the package.

Here's an example executable program that uses the package main, with the function main serving as the entry point.

```
package main
import (
```

```
"fmt"
)
func main(){
  fmt.Println("Hello, Everyone")
}
```

Import Packages

When importing a package into another package, "import" is used. We imported the package "fmt" into the sample program in Code to use the method Println. The "fmt" package is part of the Go standard library. When we import packages, the Go compiler searches for them in the locations indicated by the environment variables GOROOT and GOPATH. The GOROOT directory contains packages from the standard library. The GOPATH location contains packages that we have written and third-party packages that we have imported.

Install Third-Party Packages

We may get and install third-party Go packages by using the "Go get" command. The Go get command will retrieve the packages from the source repository and place them in the GOPATH location.

In the terminal, type and use the following command to install "mgo," a third-party Go driver package for MongoDB, into our GOPATH, which may be used across all projects in the GOPATH directory:

```
go get gopkg.in/mgo.v2
```

After installing the mgo, add the following import statement to our apps to reuse the code:

```
import (
        "gopkg.in/mgo.v2"
        "gopkg.in/mgo.v2/bson"
)
```

The MongoDB driver, mgo, provides two packages we have imported in the preceding import statement.

Init Function

When writing Go packages, we may include a function called "init" that is called at the start of the execution period. The init function is useful for adding initialization logic into a package.

```
package db
import (
        "gopkg.in/mgo.v2"
        "gopkg.in/mgo.v2/bson"
)
func init {
    // here initialization-code
}
```

In some instances, we may need to import a package to invoke its init function, and we do not need to call any of the package's other methods. If we import a package but do not use the package identification in the program, the Go compiler will complain. In this case, we may use a blank identifier (_) as the package alias name. The compiler will overlook the mistake of not utilizing the package identifier while still invoking the init function.

```
package main
import (
        _ "mywebapp/libs/mongodb/db"
  "fmt"
  "log"
)
func main() {
  //implementation-here
}
```

We imported a package called db into the sample program above. Assume we want to utilize this package to call the init function. The blank identifier will dodge the Go compiler error and execute the init function specified in the package.

To avoid package name ambiguity, we can use alias names for packages.

```
package main
import (
        mongo "mywebapp/libs/mongodb/db"
        mysql "mywebapp/libs/mysql/db"
)
```

```
func main() {
    mongodata :=mongo.Get() //calling the method of
package  "mywebapp/libs/mongodb/db"
    sqldata:=mysql.Get() //calling the method of
package "mywebapp/libs/mysql/db"
    fmt.Println(mongodata )
    fmt.Println(sqldata )
}
```

We're importing two separate packages from two different locations, but their names are identical. We may create an alias name for a single package and use it anytime we need to invoke a method in that package.

Important Considerations

1. **Import paths:** In the Go programming language, each package is specified by a unique string called an import path. We may import packages into our program using an import route. As an example:

   ```
   import "fmt"
   ```

   We are importing the fmt package into our program as stated in this sentence. Package import paths are unique on a global scale. To avoid conflicts with the paths of other packages than the standard library, the package path should begin with the Internet domain name of the entity that owns or hosts the package. As an example:

   ```
   import "geeksforgeeks.com/example/strings"
   ```

2. **Package declaration:** In the Go programming language, a package declaration is always included at the beginning of the source file. Its function is to set the default identifier for that package when another package imports it. As an example:

   ```
   package main
   ```

3. **Import declaration:** The import declaration follows the package declaration immediately. The Go source file has one or more import declarations, each of which gives the path to one or more packages in parentheses. As an example:

   ```
   // Importing the single package
   import "fmt"
   ```

```
// Importing the multiple packages
import(
"fmt"
"strings"
"bytes"
)
```

When we import a package into our program, we have access to the package's members. For example, we have a package called "sort," We can access sort when we import it into our program. Sort, Float64s() That package's SearchStrings() and other functionalities.

4. **Blank import:** In Go programming, there are occasions when we import specific packages but do not utilize them. When we execute programs that include unused packages, the compiler will generate an error. We use a blank identifier before the package name to circumvent this problem. As an example:

```
import _ "strings"
```

It's referred to as a blank import. It is used in several situations when the main program can enable the extra capabilities given by the blank importing additional packages at compile time.

5. **Nested packages:** In Go, we may construct a package within another package by simply establishing a subdirectory. And the nested package, like the root package, may import. As an example:

```
import "math/cmplx"
```

The math package is the primary package in this case, while the cmplx package is the nested package.

6. Although some packages may have the same name, the route to such packages is always distinct. For example, both the math and crypto packages have a rand-named package, but their paths are different, i.e., math/rand and crypto/rand.

7. In Go programming, why is the main package usually at the top of the program? Because the main package instructs the go build that the linker must enable to create an executable file.

Giving the Packages Names

When naming a package in Go, we must always keep the following criteria in mind:

- When constructing a package, we must keep the name brief and concise. Strings, time, flags, and so on are examples of standard library packages.

- The name of the package should be descriptive and clear.

- Always attempt to avoid using names already in use or those used for local relative variables.

- The package's name is usually written in the singular form. Several packages are named plural to prevent keyword conflicts, such as strings, bytes, buffers, etc.

- Always avoid package names with preexisting meanings. As an example:

```
// Program to illustrate
// the concept of packages
// Package declaration
package main
// Importing the multiple packages
import (
    "bytes"
    "fmt"
    "sort"
)
func main() {
    // Creating and initializing the slice
    // Using the shorthand declaration
    slice_1 := []byte{'*', 'H', 'e', 'l', 'l',
'o', 'f',
        'o', 'r', 'W', 'o', 'r', 'k', 's', '^',
'^'}
    slice_2 := []string{"hel", "lo", "for", "wor",
"ks"}
    // Displaying the slices
    fmt.Println("Original-Slice:")
    fmt.Printf("Slice 1 : %s", slice_1)
```

```
        fmt.Println("\nSlice 2: ", slice_2)
        // Trimming the specified leading
        // and trailing Unicode points
        // from given slice of bytes
        // Using the Trim function
        res := bytes.Trim(slice_1, "*^")
        fmt.Printf("\nNew Slice : %s", res)
        // Sorting the slice 2
        // Using the Strings function
        sort.Strings(slice_2)
        fmt.Println("\nSorted slice:", slice_2)
}
```

Code Exported

We might have noticed the declarations in the greet.go file we called were all uppercase. Go, unlike other languages, does not have the idea of public, private, or protected modifiers. Capitalization governs external visibility. Types, variables, functions, and that begin with a capital letter are publicly accessible outside of the current package. A symbol that can be seen outside of its container is termed exported.

If we add a new reset method to Octopus, we may call it from the welcome package but not from our main.go file, which is not part of the greet package:

```
package greet
import "fmt"
var Shark = "Rammy"
type Octopus struct {
        Name  string
        Color string
}
func (o Octopus) String() string {
        return fmt.Sprintf("Octopus's name is %q and
the color %s.", o.Name, o.Color)
}
func (o *Octopus) reset() {
        o.Name = ""
        o.Color = ""
}
func Hello() {
        fmt.Println("Hello, Everyone")
}
```

If we attempt to call reset from the main.go ahead and file:

```
package main
import (
        "fmt"
        "github.com/gopherguides/greet"
)
func main() {
        greet.Hello()
        fmt.Println(greet.Shark)
        oct := greet.Octopus{
                Name:   "Tessa",
                Color: "White",
        }
        fmt.Println(oct.String())
        oct.reset()
}
```

We'll receive the compilation error.
    To export Octopus' reset functionality, capitalize the R in reset:

```
package greet
import "fmt"
var Shark = "Rammy"
type Octopus struct {
        Name   string
        Color string
}
func (o Octopus) String() string {
        return fmt.Sprintf("The octopus's name is %q
and is the color %s.", o.Name, o.Color)
}
func (o *Octopus) Reset() {
        o.Name = ""
        o.Color = ""
}

func Hello() {
        fmt.Println("Hello, Everyone")
}
```

As a consequence, we may use Reset from another package without seeing an error:

```
package main
import (
        "fmt"
        "github.com/gopherguides/greet"
)
func main() {
        greet.Hello()
        fmt.Println(greet.Shark)
        oct := greet.Octopus{
                Name:   "Tessa",
                Color: "White",
        }
        fmt.Println(oct.String())
        oct.Reset()            .
        fmt.Println(oct.String())
}
```

Now, if we run the program:

```
$ go run main.go
```

Essential Go Packages and Libraries

Go is a fantastic language with a lot of momentum that focuses on simplicity. This approach is reflected in its standard library, which includes all of the necessities but not much else.

Fortunately, Go has a thriving community that builds and distributes many third-party libraries. We'll show you the top Go packages and libraries in this area. Some have restricted scope and may be added to any project, while others are gigantic projects that can integrate into massive, large-scale distributed systems.

Awesome Go

Before we get into the libraries, we'd like to introduce you to Awesome Go, a constantly updated and selected collection of Go libraries and other resources. We should check in every now and then to see what's new.

GoLang-Set

Go contains arrays, slices, and maps but no fixed data structure. Use a map of bools to simulate a set, but it's preferable to have a real data type with the appropriate methods and semantics. This is where GoLang-set comes in. Here's a simple example of establishing a new set, adding items, and testing membership:

```go
package main

import (
    "fmt"
    "github.com/deckarep/GoLang-set"
)

func main() {
    basicColors := mapset.NewSet()
    basicColors.Add("Yellow")
    basicColors.Add("White")
    basicColors.Add("Grey")

    if basicColors.Contains("Grey") {
        fmt.Println("Yay! 'Grey' is a basic color")
    } else {
        fmt.Println("What a disappointment! 'Grey' is not a
basic color")
    }

    if basicColors.Contains("Pink") {
        fmt.Println("Yay! 'Pink' is a basic color")
    } else {
        fmt.Println("What a disappointment! 'Pink' is not a
basic color")
    }
}

Output:

Yay! 'Grey' is a basic color
What a disappointment! 'Pink' is not a basic color.
```

It is worth noting that the package name is "mapset." Aside from the fundamentals, we may execute all set operations such as union, intersection, and difference. We may also iterate through the values we've chosen:

```go
package main

import (
    "fmt"
```

```
        "github.com/deckarep/GoLang-set"
    )


    func main() {
        basicColors := mapset.NewSet()
        basicColors.Add("White")
        basicColors.Add("Brown")
        basicColors.Add("Grey")

        otherColors := mapset.NewSetFromSlice([]interface{}
    {"Pink", "Black", "Indigo", "Blue"})
        rainbowColors := basicColors.Union(otherColors)

        for color := range rainbowColors.Iterator().C {
            fmt.Println(color)
        }
    }
```

Color

Let's keep the color scheme going. When designing command-line applications, use colors to emphasize important messages or distinguish between faults, successes, and warnings.

The color package allows you to add color to our applications easily. It employs ANSII escape codes and is also compatible with Windows! Here's a simple example:

```
package main

import (
    "github.com/fatih/color"
)

func main() {
    color.Red("Carrot is Orange ")
    color.Blue("Sky is blue")
}
```

The color package allows us to blend colors with backdrop colors, use styles like strong or italic, and splatter color over non-color output.

```
package main

import (
    "github.com/fatih/color"
    "fmt"
)

func main() {
    minion := color.New(color.FgBlack).Add(color.BgYellow).
Add(color.Bold)
    minion.Println("Minion says: banana!")

    m := minion.PrintlnFunc()
    m("We want another banana!")

    slantedRed := color.New(color.FgRed, color.BgWhite,
color.Italic).SprintFunc()
    fmt.Println("We've made a huge", slantedRed("mistake"))
}
```

Now

Now is a very basic package that acts as a wrapper for the standard time package, making it easy to interact with the various date and time constructions centered around the current time.

We can, for example, retrieve the start of the current minute or the end of the Sunday closest to the present time. Here's an example of how to utilize "now":

```
package main

import (
    "github.com/jinzhu/now"
    "fmt"
)

func main() {

    fmt.Println("All beginnings….")
    fmt.Println(now.BeginningOfMinute())
    fmt.Println(now.BeginningOfHour())
    fmt.Println(now.BeginningOfDay())
    fmt.Println(now.BeginningOfWeek())
    fmt.Println(now.BeginningOfMonth())
```

```
    fmt.Println(now.BeginningOfQuarter())
    fmt.Println(now.BeginningOfYear())

}

Output:

All the beginnings...
2017-06-04 16:59:00 -0700 PDT
2017-06-04 16:00:00 -0700 PDT
2017-06-04 00:00:00 -0700 PDT
2017-06-04 00:00:00 -0700 PDT
2017-06-01 00:00:00 -0700 PDT
2017-04-01 00:00:00 -0700 PDT
2016-12-31 23:00:00 -0800 PST
```

We may also parse dates and timings and even create our own forms (which will require updating the known formats). The Now type incorporates time. We have time so that you can utilize it all. Apply time methods directly to now objects.

Gen

The gen tool creates code for you, specifically type-aware code that attempts to bridge the gap left by Go's lack of templates and generics.

We add a specific comment to our types, and gen creates source files to include in our project. There is no runtime magic. Let's look at the following example, which is of the annotated type.

```
// +gen slice:"Where,Count,GroupBy[int]"
type Person struct {
  Names string
  Ages int
}
```

person_slice.go is generated by running gen (make sure it's on our path):

```
// Generated by: gen
// TypeWriter: slice
// Directive: +gen on the Person
```

```go
package main

// PersonSlice is a slice of type Person. Use it where we
would use [] Person.
type PersonSlice []Person

// Where returns new PersonSlice whose elements return true
for func. See: https://clipperhouse.github.io/gen/#Where
func (rcv PersonSlice) Where(fn func(Person) bool) (result
PersonSlice) {
    for _, v := range rcv {
        if fn(v) {
            result = append(result, v)
        }
    }
    return result
}

// Count gives number elements of PersonSlice that return
true for passed func. See: http://clipperhouse.github.io/
gen/#Count
func (rcv PersonSlice) Count(fn func(Person) bool) (result
int) {
    for _, v := range rcv {
        if fn(v) {
            result++
        }
    }
    return
}

// GroupByInt groups elements into map keyed by int. See:
http://clipperhouse.github.io/gen/#GroupBy
func (rcv PersonSlice) GroupByInt(fn func(Person) int)
map[int]PersonSlice {
    result := make(map[int]PersonSlice)
    for _, v := range rcv {
        key := fn(v)
        result[key] = append(result[key], v)
    }
    return result
}
```

The code includes LINQ-like methods for working with the PersonSlice type. It's straightforward to grasp and well-documented.

Here's how we put it to use. A PersonSlice is defined in the main function. The age() function chooses the age field from the Person parameter.

The produced GroupByInt() method takes the age() function and groups the persons in the slice by age.

```go
package main

import (
    "fmt"
)

// +gen slice:"Where,Count,GroupBy[int]"
type Person struct {
    Name string
    Age int
}

func age(p Person) int {
    return p.Age
}

func main() {
    people := PersonSlice {
        {"Jimy", 44},
        {"Hane", 28},
        {"Lyle", 21},
    }

    groupedByAge := people.GroupByInt(age)

    fmt.Println(groupedByAge)
}


Output:

map[44:[{Jimy 44}] 28:[{Hane 28} {Lyle 21}]]
```

Gorm

Go is noted for its austerity. Database programming is no exception. The majority of popular Go DB libraries are rather low-level. Gorm introduces the realm of object-relational mapping to Go by including the following features:

- Associations (Has One, Has Many, Belongs To, Many To Many, Polymorphism)

- Callbacks (before/after creating/saving/updating/deleting/finding)

- Preloading (eager loading)

- Transactions

- Composite The primary key

- Auto Migrations in SQL Builder

- Logger

- Write Plugins based on GORM callbacks to extend the functionality.

However, it does not cover everything. Don't expect SQLAlchemy to work its magic if we come from Python. We'll have to travel down a level to get more sophisticated items. Here's an example of how to utilize Gorm in conjunction with sqlite. Take note of the embedded Gorm. In the Product struct, create a model.

```go
package main

import (
    "github.com/jinzhu/gorm"
    _ "github.com/jinzhu/gorm/dialects/sqlite"
)

type Product struct {
  gorm.Model
  Code string
  Price uint
}

func main() {
  db, err := gorm.Open("sqlite3", "test.db")
  if err != nil {
    panic("failed to connect the database")
  }
  defer db.Close()

  // Migrate schema
  db.AutoMigrate(&Product{})

  // Create
  db.Create(&Product{Code: "L1212", Price: 1200})
```

```
// Read
var product Product
db.First(&product, 1) // find product with the id 1
db.First(&product, "code =? ", "L1212")

// Update - update-product's price to 2200
db.Model(&product).Update("Price", 2200)

// Delete - delete-product
db.Delete(&product)
```

Goose

Managing the schema is one of the most critical jobs when dealing with relational databases. Changing the database schema is seen as a "dangerous" modification in certain businesses. If necessary, the goose package allows us to perform schema modifications and even data migrations. We may go back and forth by goose up and goose down. But keep an eye on our data and make sure it doesn't get lost or damaged.

Goose works by versioning our schema and utilizing migration files for each schema. SQL commands or Go commands are used in the migration files. An example of a SQL migration file that adds a new table is shown below:

```
-- +goose Up
CREATE TABLE person (
    id int NOT NULL,
    names text,
    ages int,
    PRIMARY KEY(id)
);

-- +goose Down
DROP TABLE person;
```

Glide

Glide is a Go package manager. Many programs with conflicting dependencies may run under a single GOPATH. The answer is for each application to keep track of its own vendor directory of package dependencies. Glide assists with this task.

Glide has the following characteristics:

- Semantic Versioning 2.0.0 support is included in the versioning packages.

- Aliasing packages are supported (e.g., for working with GitHub forks).

- Remove the requirement for import statements to be munged.

- Work using all of the available tools.

- All of the VCS tools that Go offers are supported (git, bzr, hg, svn).

- Custom local and global plugins are supported.

- For optimal speed, use repository caching and data caching.

- Flatten dependencies, resolve version discrepancies, and prevent including a package more than once.

- In our version control system, we may manage and install dependencies on-demand or vendored.

Ginkgo

Ginkgo is a testing framework for Behavior Driven Development (BDD). It allows us to write your tests in a syntax similar to English, allowing less technical individuals to analyze the tests and ensure that they meet the business requirements.

This form of a test specification is also popular among developers. It connects with Go's built-in testing package and is frequently used in conjunction with Gomega. An example of a Ginkgo + Gomega test is as follows:

```
actual, err := foo()
Ω(err).Should(BeNil())
Ω(actual).ShouldNot(BeNil())
Ω(actual.result).Should(Equal(110))
```

Etcd

Etcd is a trustworthy distributed Key-Value store. The server is written in Go, and the Go client communicates with it through gRPC.

It focuses on the following aspects:

- **Simple:** a well-defined, user-friendly API (gRPC).

- TLS is used automatically, with optional client certificate authentication.

- **Fast:** 10,000 writes/sec benchmarked.

- Raft is a dependable distribution method.

Below is an illustration of connecting to a server, entering a value, and retrieving it, complete with timeouts and cleaning.

```
func test_get() {
    cli, err := clientv3.New(clientv3.Config{
        Endpoints:   endpoints,
        DialTimeout: dialTimeout,
    })
    if err != nil {
        log.Fatal(err)
    }
    defer cli.Close()

    _, err = cli.Put(context.TODO(), "fooo", "bar")
    if err != nil {
        log.Fatal(err)
    }

    ctx, cancel := context.WithTimeout(context.Background(),
                                       requestTimeout)
    resp, err := cli.Get(ctx, "fooo")
    cancel()
    if err != nil {
        log.Fatal(err)
    }
    for _, ev := range resp.Kvs {
        fmt.Printf("%s : %s\n", ev.Key, ev.Value)
    }
    // Output: fooo : bar
}
```

NSQ

NSQ is a fantastic distributed queue. It has served me well as the main building component for large-scale distributed systems. Here are some of its characteristics:

- Distributed topologies with no SPOF are supported.

- Horizontal scalability (no brokers, seamlessly add more nodes to the cluster).

- Push-based message delivery with low latency (performance).

- Message routing in a load-balanced and multicast fashion.

- Excel at both high-throughput streaming workloads and low-throughput job-oriented workloads.

- Mostly in-memory (beyond a high-water mark, messages are transparently kept on disk).

- Consumers can use a runtime discovery service to identify producers (nsqlookupd).

- The layer of protection for transport (TLS).

- Data formats are unimportant.

- Few dependencies (simple to deploy) and a reasonable, constrained default configuration.

- TCP protocol that is simple and supports client libraries in any language.

- HTTP interface for statistics, administrative activities, and producers (no client library needed to publish).

- For real-time instrumentation, it integrates with statsd.

- A powerful cluster administration interface (nsqadmin).

Here's an example how to send a message to NSQ:

```
package main

import (
  "github.com/bitly/go-nsq"
)

func main() {
  config := nsq.NewConfig()
  p, _ := nsq.NewProducer("127.0.0.1:4150", config)

  p.Publish("topic", []byte("messages"))
  p.Stop()
}
```

Docker

Docker is now a household name. We might be surprised to learn that Docker is built into Go. We don't usually use Docker in our work, but it's an important project that deserves to be acknowledged as a very successful and popular Go project.

Kubernetes

Kubernetes is a cloud-native container orchestration tool that is free source. It is another massively distributed system written in Go. We recently published a book, called *Mastering Kubernetes*, in which we go into great detail about the most advanced features of Kubernetes. Kubernetes is incredibly versatile from the standpoint of a Go developer, and it can be extended and customized via plugins.

DEPENDENCY MANAGEMENT

Go employs a unique approach to dependency management in that it is source-based rather than artifact-based. Packages in an artifact-based dependency management system are made up of artifacts created from source code and are kept in a repository system distinct from the source code. Many NodeJS packages, for example, utilize npmjs.org as a package repository and github.com as a source repository. Similarly, on the other hand, packages in Go are source code, and publishing a package does not require the creation of artifacts or establishing a separate repository. Go packages must be kept in a VCS server's version control repository. Dependencies are retrieved either directly from their VCS server or through an intermediate proxy, which retrieves them from their VCS server.

Versioning

Modules and first-class package versioning are added to the Go ecosystem with versioning Go 1.11. Previously, Go lacked a well-defined system for version control. While third-party version management solutions were available, the native Go experience did not allow versioning.

Semantic versioning is used in Go Modules. A module's versions are specified as version control system (VCS) tags that represent legitimate semantic versions prefixed with v. To release version 1.0.0 of gitlab.com/my/project, for example, the developer must generate the Git tag v1.0.0.

Other than 0 and 1, the module name is prefixed with/vX, where X is the major version. For example, gitlab.com/my/project/v2.0.0 must be titled and imported as gitlab.com/my/project/v2.[1]

---

[1] https://docs.gitlab.com/ee/development/go_guide/dependencies.html

Go employs "pseudo-versions," which are special semantic versions that correspond to a particular VCS commit. The semantic version's prerelease component must begin or finish with a timestamp and the first 12 characters of the commit identifier:

- vX.0.0-yyyymmddhhmmss-abcdefabcdef, if no previously tagged commit for X exists.

- vX.Y.Z-pre.0.yyyymmddhhmmss-abcdefabcdef, when most recent prior tag is vX.Y.Z-pre.

- vX.Y.(Z+1)-0.yyyymmddhhmmss-abcdefabcdef, when the most recent prior tag is vX.Y.Z.

- A VCS tag that fits one of these patterns is disregarded.

Modules

In GoLang, a module is a grouping of related packages versioned as one unit. We may use Go Modules to implement specific dependency needs and create repeatable builds for multiple environments. It dramatically simplifies dependency management in GoLang.

To begin utilizing Modules in your project, just run the following command (this is relevant if our project currently uses version control):

```
go mod init
```

Alternatively, we may start Go Modules by explicitly supplying the module import path. The path might be a module name, a project name, or the URL of the repository's code.

```
go mod init <module_path>
```

For instance, here's how you may begin utilizing modules in our project:

```
go mod init github.com/Alfrick/Go-Test
```

When we run the above command, it will create a go.mod module config file in the root directory of our project. The module and Go version information is included in the file.

```
module github.com/Alfrick/Go-Test

go 1.14
```

The file specifies the project's needs and includes all required dependencies, similar to the "package.json" file used in "Node.js" dependency management.

Installing Dependencies

We may now incorporate new dependencies into our codebase after starting our project to begin utilizing Go Modules.

To install dependencies in GoLang, use the go get command, automatically updating the go.mod file.

Here's an illustration:

```
go get github.com/lib/pq
```

We may also target a specific dependent branch:

```
go get github.com/lib/pq@master
```

Alternatively, here's a more specific version:

```
go get github.com/lib/pq@v1.8.0
```

After we execute the command, our go.mod file should look like this:

```
module github.com/Alfrick/Go-Test
    go 1.14
    require github.com/lib/pq v1.8.0 // indirect
```

The package is designated as indirect since it is not presently utilized else-where in the project. This statement might also exist on an indirect dependency package, which depends on another dependency.

The newly installed package may then be imported and used by specifying its import path and implementing one of its methods.

Here's an illustration:

```
// main.go
package main
import (
    "github.com/lib/pq"
)
func main() {
    pq.Load()
}
```

Dependencies Must Authenticate

Furthermore, installing a dependency will create a go.sum file at the root of our project. While it is not a lock file in the sense of package-lock.json in Node.js, it does include the expected cryptographic hashes of the content of specific module versions.

The go.sum file serves as a dependency checker, protecting your modules against unexpected or malicious modifications that might damage our whole codebase. In addition, if we cease utilizing a module, the stored checksum information will allow us to reuse it in the future.

Remove Unused Dependencies

To clear things up, type the following command into the terminal:

```
go mod tidy
```

When we execute the command above, it will remove any unneeded dependencies from our project and update the go.mod file.

Remember that even after we've deleted the package, the go.sum file will still contain the cryptographic hash of its contents.

It will also add any missing dependencies; such as if we imported an external package but did not initially retrieve it with the go get command.

Because the go.mod file includes all of the information required for repeatable builds, it's critical to execute the go mod tidy command after making any changes to our code. It will verify that your module file is correct and tidy, especially before each change.

Installing Dependencies That Are Missing

We may also use the go build or go test commands to install any missing dependencies automatically.

Assume we imported and utilized a third-party package in our project in the following manner:

```
// main.go
```

```
package main
import (
    "github.com/lib/pq"
    "github.com/subosito/gotenv"
)
func main() {
    pq.Load()
    log.Println(os.Getenv("APP_ID"))
}
```

The program will automatically retrieve the missing package and add it to our go.mod file before our project is constructed when we run go build.

The modified go.mod file is available here:

```
module github.com/Alfrick/Go-Test
    go 1.14
    require (
    github.com/lib/pq v1.8.0
    github.com/subosito/gotenv v1.2.0
    )
```

Updating the Versions of Dependencies

The Go Modules versions adhere to the Semantic Versioning (semver) standard, which is divided into three sections: major, minor, and patch. For example, if a package has a version number of 1.8.0, it signifies that 1 is a major version, 8 is a minor version, and 0 is a patch version.

There are numerous ways to change the version of a dependent in GoLang dependency management. First, if we know the version of a dependency that wants, just browse the go.mod file in our project and manually modify it to the required dependent version. Then, use the go get command to upgrade the go.sum file.

However, if we wish to upgrade to a major version, we must also change the import path. For example, to update from github.com/lib/pq v1.8.0 to v.2.2.3, alter the route from need github.com/lib/pq v1.8.0 to require github.com/lib/pq/v2 v2.2.3.

The Go Modules code opting standard uses a separate module path for each new major version mentioned. Beginning with the second version of a dependency, the path must conclude with the significant version number.

Alternatively, we may automatically use the go get command to update a dependency to the most recent version. Choosing this option will automatically upgrade the go.mod file, eliminating the need to change it manually.

For example, as previously demonstrated, we can use the following command to download and update to the latest dependent version ("latest" refers to the latest dependency version with a semver tag):

```
go get github.com/lib/pq
```

Alternatively, we can download and upgrade to a certain version:

```
go get github.com/lib/pq@v1.8.0
```

Additionally, we may update a dependent and all of its transitive dependencies to the most recent version by using the following command (the -u argument indicates that the most recent minor or patch releases are to be used):

```
go get -u github.com/lib/pq
```

If we wish to utilize the most recent patch release, do the following:

```
go get -u=patch github.com/lib/pq
```

Furthermore, additional operations, such as go build or go test, will automatically add new dependencies based on the requirements. As previously demonstrated, they may do this to meet import requirements, such as updating the go.mod file and installing the new dependencies.

Listing Dependencies

Run the below-given command to see a list of the current module (also known as the main module) and all its dependencies:

```
go list -m all
```

Run: to view a list of all available versions of a package.

```
go list -m -versions github.com/lib/pq
```

Module vs. Package

- A package is a directory that contains *.go files.

- A module is a directory that contains a go.mod file.

- A module is often accompanied by a package, which is a folder containing a go.mod file and *.go files.

- A module may contain subdirectories that are packages.

- Modules are often delivered in the form of a VCS repository (Git, SVN, Hg, and so on).

- Any subdirectories of a module that are modules themselves are unique, separate modules that are not included in the enclosing module.

- If a module repo has a go.mod file, then repo/sub and any files included within it are a distinct module and not a part of the repo.

Naming

Except for the standard library, the name of a module or package must be of the form (sub.)*domain.tld(/path)*. This is comparable to, but not the same as, a URL. The package name lacks a scheme (such as https://) and cannot include a port number. The name example.com:8443/my/package is invalid.

Fetching Packages

The following was the procedure for getting a package:

- Query https://{package name}?go-get=1.

- Look for the go-import meta tag in the answer.

- Using the specified VCS, get the repository provided by the meta tag.

- The meta tag should be of the following format: meta name= "go-import" content="{prefix} {vcs} {url}">. For example, gitlab.com/ my/project git https://gitlab.com/my/project.git specifies that Git should be used to fetch packages starting with gitlab.com/my/project from https://gitlab.com/my/project.git.

This chapter covered packages, working and installing packages, importing libraries and tools, and dependency management.

CHAPTER 4

Handling Concurrency

IN THIS CHAPTER

➤ Concurrency or parallelism

➤ Goroutines

➤ Shared resources

The previous chapter covered packages, where we discussed how to install and work with packages, import libraries, and dependency management. This chapter will cover concurrency, goroutines, and shared resources.

CONCURRENCY

Concurrency refers to a program's capacity to do numerous tasks simultaneously. This refers to a program with two or more jobs that simultaneously execute independently but are still part of the same program. Concurrency is critical in modern software because it allows separate sections of code to be executed as quickly as feasible without disrupting the overall flow of the program.

In GoLang language, concurrency refers to the ability for functions to operate independently of one another. A goroutine is a function that may execute in parallel with other functions. When you define a function as a goroutine, it is viewed as an independent unit of scheduled work and then runs on an available logical processor. The GoLang runtime scheduler handles all goroutines that are formed and need processor time. To run goroutines, the scheduler ties operating system threads to logical processors. Scheduler handles everything related to which goroutines are executing on which logical processors at any one time by sitting on top of the operating system.

Threads are used to provide concurrency in popular programming languages, such as Java and Python. Concurrency mechanisms provided into GoLang include goroutines and channels. Concurrency is cheap and simple in GoLang. Goroutines are lightweight, low-cost threads. Channels are the conduits that allow goroutines to communicate with one another.

Communicating Sequential Processes (CSP) is a term used to explain how systems having numerous concurrent models should communicate with one another. It is the underlying ethos of GoLang, and it often depends heavily on utilizing channels as a mechanism for sending messages between two or more concurrent processes.

- **Goroutines:** A goroutine is a function that operates independently of the function that initiated it.

- **Channels:** A channel is a data pipeline that sends and receives data. Channels allow one goroutine to transmit structured data to another.

Concurrency and parallelism come into play when looking for multitasking, and they are frequently used interchangeably; concurrent and parallel refer to similar but distinct aspects.

Concurrency is the ability to manage many tasks at the same time. This suggests we're attempting to manage many jobs at once in a short amount of time. We will, however, only be executing one activity at a time. This is common in programs where one job is waiting, and the software decides to drive another task during the idle period. It is a feature of the issue domain in which our application must handle several concurrent events.

Parallelism is the practice of performing many things at the same time. This implies that even if we have two processes running concurrently, there are no gaps in between. It is a feature of the solution domain in which we wish to speed up our program by processing separate parts of the issue in parallel.

A concurrent program contains many logical control threads. These threads may or may not run concurrently. A parallel program might theoretically run faster than a sequential program since it does various sections of the calculation simultaneously (in parallel). It may or may not contain more than one logical control thread.

Illustration of the Sleeping Barber Issue

The barbershop features one barber chair in the cutting section and a large waiting room with several chairs. When a barber has finished cutting a customer's hair, he dismisses the person and walks to the waiting room to see whether there are any other customers. He returns one of them to the chair and cuts their hair if there is any. If there aren't any, he returns to the chair and falls asleep in it. When a customer arrives, they glance to see what the barber is doing. If the barber is napping, the customer awakens him and takes his place on the cutting room chair.

When the barber starts cutting hair, the customer remains in the waiting area. If there is a free chair available in the waiting area, the consumer sits in it and waits their turn. If there are no available seats, the consumer departs.

```go
package main

import (
  "fmt"
  "sync"
  "time"
)

const (
  sleeping = iota
  checking
  cutting
)

var stateLog = map[int]string{
  0: "Sleeping",
  1: "Checking",
  2: "Cutting",
}
var wg *sync.WaitGroup // Amount of the potential customers

type Barber struct {
  name string
  sync.Mutex
  state    int // Sleeping, Checking, Cutting
  customer *Customer
}

type Customer struct {
  name string
}
```

```go
func (c1 *Customer) String() string {
  return fmt.Sprintf("%p", c1)[7:]
}
func NewBarber() (b1 *Barber) {
  return &Barber{
    name:  "Sam",
    state: sleeping,
  }
}

// Barber-goroutine
// Checks for the customers
// Sleeps - wait for the wakers to wake him up
func barber(b1 *Barber, wr chan *Customer, wakers chan
*Customer) {
  for {
    b1.Lock()
    defer b1.Unlock()
    b1.state = checking
    b1.customer = nil

    // checking waiting room
    fmt.Printf("Checking the waiting room: %d\n", len(wr))
    time.Sleep(time.Millisecond * 100)
    select {
    case c1 := <-wr:
      HairCut(c1, b1)
      b1.Unlock()
    default: // Waiting room is empty
      fmt.Printf("Sleeping Barber - %s\n", b1.customer)
      b1.state = sleeping
      b1.customer = nil
      b1.Unlock()
      c1 := <-wakers
      b1.Lock()
      fmt.Printf("Woken by %s\n", c1)
      HairCut(c1, b1)
      b1.Unlock()
    }
  }
}

func HairCut(c1 *Customer, b1 *Barber) {
  b1.state = cutting
  b1.customer = c1
  b1.Unlock()
  fmt.Printf("Cutting %s hair\n", c1)
  time.Sleep(time.Millisecond * 100)
  b1.Lock()
```

```
  wg.Done()
  b1.customer = nil
}


// customer-goroutine
// just fizzles out if it's full, otherwise customer
// is passed along to channel handling it's haircut etc
func customer(c1 *Customer, b1 *Barber, wr chan<-
*Customer, wakers chan<- *Customer) {
  // arrive
  time.Sleep(time.Millisecond * 50)
  // Check on barber
  B1.Lock()
  fmt.Printf("The Customer %s checks %s barber | room: %d,
w %d - customer: %s\n",
    c1, stateLog[b1.state], len(wr), len(wakers),
b1.customer)
  switch b1.state {
  case sleeping:
    select {
    case wakers <- c1:
    default:
      select {
      case wr <- c1:
      default:
        wg.Done()
      }
    }
  case cutting:
    select {
    case wr <- c1:
    default: // Full waiting room, and leave shop
      wg.Done()
    }
  case checking:
    panic("Customer shouldn't check for Barber when Barber
is Checking the waiting room")
  }
  b1.Unlock()
}

func main() {
  b1 := NewBarber()
  b1.name = "Jocky"
  WaitingRoom := make(chan *Customer, 5) // 5-chairs
  Wakers := make(chan *Customer, 1)      // Only-one waker
at time
  go barber(b1, WaitingRoom, Wakers)
```

```
    time.Sleep(time.Millisecond * 100)
    wg = new(sync.WaitGroup)
    n := 10
    wg.Add(10)
    // Spawn customers
    for i := 0; i < n; i++ {
      time.Sleep(time.Millisecond * 50)
      c1 := new(Customer)
      go customer(c1, b1, WaitingRoom, Wakers)
    }

    wg.Wait()
    fmt.Println("No more customers for day")
}
```

Example of a Producer-Consumer Problem

The problem depicts the producer and the consumer processes sharing a fixed-size buffer that serves as a queue. The producer's role is to generate data, store it in the buffer, and then restart. Simultaneously, the consumer consumes the data (i.e., removes it from the buffer) one piece at a time. The issue is ensuring that the producer does not attempt to add data to a full buffer and that the consumer does not attempt to remove data from an empty buffer. If the buffer is complete, the producer's approach is to either sleep or delete data.

When the consumer takes an item from the buffer, the producer is notified, and the buffer is refilled. If the buffer is empty, the consumer can go to sleep. The next time the producer inserts data into the buffer, the sleeping consumer is awakened.

```
package main

import (
  "flag"
  "fmt"
  "log"
  "os"
  "runtime"
  "runtime/pprof"
)
```

```go
type Consumer struct {
  msgs *chan int
}

// NewConsumer creates a Consumer
func NewConsumer(msgs *chan int) *Consumer {
  return &Consumer{msgs: msgs}
}

// consume reads the msgs channel
func (c1 *Consumer) consume() {
  fmt.Println("consume: Started")
  for {
    msg := <-*c1.msgs
    fmt.Println("consume: Received:", msg)
  }
}

// Producer-definition
type Producer struct {
  msgs *chan int
  done *chan bool
}

// NewProducer creates Producer
func NewProducer(msgs *chan int, done *chan bool) *Producer
{
  return &Producer{msgs: msgs, done: done}
}

// produce generates and sends messages over the msgs
channel
func (p1 *Producer) produce(max int) {
  fmt.Println("produce: Started")
  for i := 0; i < max; i++ {
    fmt.Println("produce: Sending ", i)
    *p1.msgs <- i
  }
  *p1.done <- true // signal when done
  fmt.Println("produce: Done")
}

func main() {
  // profile flags
  cpuprofile := flag.String("cpuprofile", "", "write cpu
profile to 'file'")
  memprofile := flag.String("memprofile", "", "write memory
profile to 'file'")
```

```go
    // get the maximum number of messages from the flags
    max := flag.Int("n", 5, "defines number of messages")

    flag.Parse()

    // utilize max num of the cores available
    runtime.GOMAXPROCS(runtime.NumCPU())

    // CPU Profile
    if *cpuprofile != "" {
      f, err := os.Create(*cpuprofile)
      if err != nil {
        log.Fatal("couldn't create CPU profile: ", err)
      }
      if err := pprof.StartCPUProfile(f); err != nil {
        log.Fatal("couldn't start CPU profile: ", err)
      }
      defer pprof.StopCPUProfile()
    }

  var msgs = make(chan int)   // channel for message
transmission
  var done = make(chan bool) // channel for controlling
when production is completed

    // Start goroutine for Produce.produce
    go NewProducer(&msgs, &done).produce(*max)

    // Start goroutine for the Consumer.consume
    go NewConsumer(&msgs).consume()

    // Finish the program when production is done
    <-done

    // Memory Profile
    if *memprofile != "" {
      f, err := os.Create(*memprofile)
      if err != nil {
        log.Fatal("couldn't create memory profile: ", err)
      }
      runtime.GC() // get up-to-date statistics
      if err := pprof.WriteHeapProfile(f); err != nil {
        log.Fatal("could not write memory profile: ", err)
      }
      f.Close()
    }
}
```

Goroutines – CONCURRENCY IN GoLang

A Goroutine is a type of Go programming language feature. A Goroutine is a function or method in our program that runs independently and simultaneously with other Goroutines. In other terms, a Goroutine is any constantly running activity in the Go programming language. A Goroutine can be compared to a fine thread. The cost of creating Goroutines is relatively minimal when compared to the thread. Every program contains at least one Goroutine, known as the main Goroutine. All Goroutines are subordinate to the main Goroutines; if the main Goroutine stops, all goroutines in the program terminate. Goroutine is constantly at work in the background.

Concurrency boosts performance by making use of several processing cores. The API support in Go allows programmers to build parallel algorithms efficiently. Concurrency support is an optional feature in most mainstream programming languages. However, it comes standard with Go.

Go Concurrent Programming

Concurrent programming uses the many processor cores seen in most modern computers. The idea has been around for a long time, even when the single Core had one core. Many computer languages, including C/C++, Java, and others, use many threads to achieve some concurrency.

A single thread is a small set of instructions scheduled to be executed sequentially. We may think of it as a task within a larger enterprise.

Issues with Multithreading

Multithreaded applications are challenging to debug as well as create and maintain. Furthermore, it is not always possible to divide every process into several threads to make it as performant as concurrent programming. Multithreading has its own set of costs. The environment handles several functions, including inter-process communication and shared memory access. The developers here are free to concentrate on the task at hand instead of being weighed down by the details of parallel processing.

Keeping these factors in mind, another method of multiprocessing is to rely entirely on the operating system. In this instance, the developer must manage the challenges of inter-process communication or the cost of shared-memory concurrency. This strategy is quite versatile in performance, but it is also pretty easy to do wrong.

How to Create a Goroutine

We may create our own Goroutine by simply prefixing the function or method call with the go keyword, as seen in the syntax below:

```
func name(){
// statement
}
// using the go keyword as the prefix of a function
call
go name()
```

Example:

```
// Program to illustrate the concept of Goroutine
package main
import "fmt"
func display(str string) {
    for g := 0; g < 5; g++ {
        fmt.Println(str)
    }
}
func main() {
    // Calling-Goroutine
    go display("Welcomehome")
    // Calling-normal-function
    display("Helloeveryone")
}
```

MULTIPLE Goroutines

In our program, a Goroutine is a function or procedure that runs independently and simultaneously with other Goroutines. In other terms, a Goroutine is any continuously running activity in the Go programming language. We may have several goroutines in a single program in the Go computer language. We may create a goroutine by prefixing the function or method call with the go keyword, as seen below:

```
func name(){
// statement(s)
}
```

```
// using the go keyword as the prefix of your function
call
go name()
```

Example:

```
// Program to demonstrate the Multiple Goroutines
package main
import (
    "fmt"
    "time"
)
// For goroutine 1
func Aname() {
    arr1 := [4]string{"Shreya", "Disha", "Kartik",
"Mira"}
    for t1 := 0; t1 <= 3; t1++ {
        time.Sleep(160 * time.Millisecond)
        fmt.Printf("%s\n", arr1[t1])
    }
}
// For goroutine 2
func Aid() {
    arr2 := [4]int{500, 102, 209, 901}
    for t2 := 0; t2 <= 3; t2++ {
        time.Sleep(500 * time.Millisecond)
        fmt.Printf("%d\n", arr2[tk2])
    }
}
// main-function
func main() {
    fmt.Println("!Main Go-routine Start!")
    // calling-Goroutine 1
    go Aname()
    // calling-Goroutine 2
    go Aid()
    time.Sleep(3100 * time.Millisecond)
    fmt.Println("\n!Main Go-routine End!")
}
```

What Is the Difference between Parallelism and Concurrency?

Sr. No.	Concurrency	Parallelism
1.	Concurrency is the problem of simultaneously conducting and managing numerous computations.	Parallelism is the job of conducting numerous calculations at the same time.
2.	Concurrency is achieved by the interleaving of processes on the central processing unit (CPU), also known as context switching.	While it is accomplished through the use of several central processing units (CPUs).
3.	Concurrency can be accomplished by utilizing a single processing unit.	While this is not accomplished with a single processing unit, it necessitates the use of numerous processing units.
4.	Concurrency increases the quantity of work that is completed simultaneously.	While increasing the system's throughput and processing performance.
5.	Concurrency deals with many things at the same time.	While it does several things at the same time.
6.	The non-deterministic control flow technique is referred to as concurrency.	While the method is deterministic control flow.
7.	Debugging with concurrency is difficult.	While debugging is difficult, it is simpler than concurrency.

Goroutines Provide Several Advantages over Threads

When compared to threads, Goroutines are incredibly inexpensive. They only have a few kb in stack size and may expand and decrease to meet the application's demands, whereas threads require a specific and set stack size.

Goroutines are multiplexed to a smaller number of operating system threads. There may be just one thread in a program with thousands of Goroutines. If any Goroutine in that thread becomes stuck, such as when waiting for user input, another OS thread is started, and the other Goroutines are shifted to the new OS thread. All of this is handled by the runtime, and we as programmers are abstracted from these technical nuances and provided with an explicit API for working with concurrency.

Goroutines interact using channels. Channels are designed to prevent race problems when accessing shared memory with Goroutines. Compare channels to a conduit via which Goroutines interact.

COMMUNICATE TO SHARE MEMORY

Traditional threading models (such as those used in Java, C++, and Python) require the programmer to interact across threads via shared memory. Locks are typically used to safeguard shared data structures, and threads will compete for such locks to access the data. In some circumstances, using thread-safe data structures like Python's Queue makes this easier.

Concurrency primitives in Go, such as goroutines and channels, offer an attractive and unique way of constructing concurrent software. Instead of employing explicit locks to manage access to shared data, Go supports the use of channels to transfer data references across goroutines. This method assures that only one goroutine has access to the data at any one moment. The idea is summed up in the document Effective Go:

Instead of communicating by sharing memory, communicate by sharing memory.

Take, for example, a program that polls a list of URLs. In a conventional threading context, data may be structured as follows:

```
type Resource struct {
   url        string
   polling    bool
   lastPolled int64
}

type Resources struct {
   data []*Resource
   lock *sync.Mutex
}
```

After that, a Poller function (several of which would execute in distinct threads) may look like this:

```
func Poller(res *Resources) {
  for {
      // get least recently-polled Resource
      // and mark it as being polled
      res.lock.Lock()
      var r1 *Resource
      for _, v1 := range res.data {
          if v1.polling {
              continue
          }
          if r1 == nil || v1.lastPolled < r1.lastPolled {
              r1 = v1
          }
      }
```

```
    if r1 != nil {
        r1.polling = true
    }
    res.lock.Unlock()
    if r1 == nil {
        continue
    }

    // poll URL
    // update Resource's polling and lastPolled
    res.lock.Lock()
    r1.polling = false
    r1.lastPolled = time.Nanoseconds()
    res.lock.Unlock()
    }
}
```

This function is around a page long and requires additional information to be completed. It doesn't even include the URL polling logic (which would be a few lines), and it won't gracefully manage the depleted pool of resources.

Let's have a look at the same functionality utilizing the Go idiom. Poller is a function in this example that accepts Resources to be polled from an input channel and delivers them to an output channel when they are finished.

```
type Resource string

func Poller(in, out chan *Resource) {
    for r1 := range in {
        // poll URL

        // send processed Resources to out
        out <- r1
    }
}
```

The delicate logic from the previous example has vanished, and our Resource data structure no longer holds accounting data. In reality, all that's left are the essentials. This should give us an idea of how powerful these simple language features are.

HOW TO USE Goroutines TO ACCESS SHARED RESOURCES

Access Shared Resources Using Goroutines

In the previous section, we discussed what Goroutines are and how to utilize them in our project. However, we have not discussed any issues that may arise while utilizing Goroutines.

We know that Goroutines let the program operate concurrently, but we must utilize them with caution when accessing specific shared resources.

Assume one go thread is running to credit the amount to the account while another go thread is running in parallel to debit the amount from the account.

We have no control over how each Goroutine is executed. As a result, one thread might be performed instantly while another can be internally delayed.

So, suppose Thread 1 credits $100 to X account and Thread 2 debits $100 from X account, then what happens is they both access the identical starting value, which is assumed to be $500.

If Thread 2 is processed immediately and returns the current amount to $400, Thread 1 retains the reference to an initial value of $500 and executes on top of that, returning $600 to the account.

However, the real amount must be $500 since the $100 will be credited, and the $100 will be debited from the same account. Therefore, the total must be $500. This results in inconsistency while working with concurrency.

So, when one thread accesses a specific variable, all other threads should be blocked from altering or accessing the same resource.

Using Mutual Exclusion to Get Access to Shared Resources

This is the only way to access shared resources by employing Mutual Exclusion, often known as Mutex.

So, to implement or use this in our GoLang project, we must employ the sync package, which includes the Mutex type.

A Mutex is a lock that prevents two things from happening simultaneously. A mutual exclusion lock is a mechanism used to ensure that threads of execution have exclusive access to shared data. When one Goroutine obtains the mutual exclusion lock, the other Goroutines must wait for the lock to be released.

Let's have an example to show how to use Mutex in the GoLang project.

```go
package main

import (
    "fmt"
    "math/rand"
    "sync"
    "time"
)

var balance int

var mutex = &sync.Mutex{}

func credit() {
    for c := 0; c < 5; c++ {
        mutex.Lock()
        balance += 120
        time.Sleep(time.Duration(rand.Intn(100))
* time.Millisecond)
        fmt.Println("After crediting, balance:", balance)
        mutex.Unlock()
    }
}

func debit() {
    for c := 0; c < 5; c++ {
        mutex.Lock()
        balance -= 120
        time.Sleep(time.Duration(rand.Intn(100))
* time.Millisecond)
        fmt.Println("After debiting, balance:", balance)
        mutex.Unlock()
    }
}

func main() {
    balance = 220
    fmt.Println("Initial balance:", balance)

    go credit()
    go debit()

    fmt.Scanln()
}
```

The Mutex object's Lock() and Unlock() procedures allow you to mark the beginning and conclusion of a vital section and prevent several goroutines from accessing the same resource. So, while one Goroutine has the lock, the other Goroutine has no choice except to wait till Unlock() is called.

Using Atomic Counters to Get Access to Shared Resources

This is another method for making thread-safe modifications to shared variables using atomic counters, which allow us to do mathematical operations one goroutine at a time.

The atomic package contains low-level atomic memory primitives used to develop synchronization algorithms.

Instead of utilizing the Mutex object to ensure that the balance is accurately credited or debited, use the AddInt64() method from GoLang's sync/atomic package.

```
package main

import (
    "fmt"
    "math/rand"
    "sync"
    "sync/atomic"
    "time"
)

var balance int64

func credit() {
    for c := 0; c < 10; c++ {
        // adds 120 to balance atomically
        atomic.AddInt64(&balance, 100)
        time.Sleep(time.Duration(rand.Intn(120))
* time.Millisecond)
    }
}

func debit() {
    for c := 0; c < 5; c++ {
        // deducts -120 from balance atomically
        atomic.AddInt64(&balance, -120)
        time.Sleep(time.Duration(rand.Intn(120))
* time.Millisecond)
    }
}
```

```
func main() {
    balance = 220
    fmt.Println("Initial balance:", balance)

    go credit()
    go debit()

    fmt.Scanln()

    fmt.Println("Final Balance:", balance)
}
```

The AddInt64() method atomically adds a value to the variable we provided through the address using the & operator, then returns the changed value.

The AddInt64() method assures that no other thread may access or alter the variable while one thread is adding a value to it.

It behaves similarly to Mutex above but without the requirement for GoLang's Lock() and Unlock() methods.

So, these are the two methods for accessing shared resources in GoLang using Goroutines.

Concurrency Issues

- **Non-atomic:** Non-atomic operations that are interruptible by several processes might cause issues.

- **Non-atomic:** Non-atomic operations that are interruptible by several processes might cause issues.

- **Race conditions:** Race circumstances occur when the result is determined by who of multiple processes arrives at a place first.

- **Blocking:** Processes might become stuck while waiting for resources. A procedure might be stalled for an extended time while waiting for input from a terminal. This would be highly undesirable if the procedure is needed to update specific data regularly.

- **Starvation:** Starvation happens when a process cannot get service to progress.

- **Deadlock:** Deadlock happens when two processes are stalled, and neither can continue to operate.

Concurrency Disadvantages

- It is necessary to secure several apps from one another.
- It is mandatory to use extra techniques to coordinate several apps.
- Switching between apps necessitates additional performance overheads and complexity in operating systems.
- Running too many programs concurrently might result in substantially decreased performance.

Benefits of Concurrency

- **Many programs are running:** It allows us to run multiple apps simultaneously.
- **Improved resource usage:** It allows resources that are not being used by one program to be utilized by another.
- **Improved average response time:** Without concurrency, each application is completed before starting the next one.
- **Better performance:** It helps the operating system to perform better. When one application utilizes the CPU and another only uses the disk drive, the time it takes to complete both applications simultaneously is less than the time it takes to run each application sequentially.

Problems with Concurrency

- **Sharing global resources:** It is challenging to share global resources safely. If two processes both utilize a global variable and both do read and write operations on that variable, the order in which those operations are performed is essential.
- **Optimal resource allocation:** It is difficult for the operating system to manage resource allocation optimally.[1]

---

[1] https://www.geeksforgeeks.org/concurrency-in-operating-system/

- **Locating programming mistakes:** Finding a programming fault is challenging since reports are seldom repeatable.

- **Locking the channel:** It may be wasteful for the operating system to simply lock the channel, preventing other processes from using it.

This chapter covered concurrency or parallelism, GoRoutines, and shared resources with its relevant examples.

CHAPTER 5

GoLang for JavaScript Developers

IN THIS CHAPTER

➢ Flow control

➢ Types

➢ Modules and packages

➢ Error handling

➢ Comparing keywords and syntax

➢ Functions

We discussed handling concurrency in the last chapter, and in this chapter, we will explore flow control, types, modules, and packages. Furthermore, we will cover error handling and keyword and function comparison.

FLOW CONTROL

There is just one loop in the Go programming language, and it is a for loop. A for loop in GoLang is a type of repetition control structure that enables us to create a loop that will run a set number of times. In the

DOI: 10.1201/9781003309055-5

Go programming language, this for loop is used in a variety of ways, including:

1. **As basic as possible for loop:** It is similar to what we see in other programming languages, such as C, C++, C#, Java, etc.

   Syntax:

   ```
   for initialization; condition; post{
           // statements
   }
   ```

   Here,
   The initialization statement is optional and is executed before the for loop starts. An introductory statement, such as variable declarations, increment or assignment instructions, or function calls, always includes an initialization statement.

   The condition statement includes a boolean expression evaluated at the beginning of each loop iteration. If the conditional statement's value is true, the loop runs.

   The post statement follows the for loop body. The condition statement is re-evaluated after the post statement; if the conditional statement's value is false, the loop is ended.

   Example:

   ```
   // Program to show the use of simple for loop
   package main
   import "fmt"
   // main-function
   func main() {
       // for loop
       // This loop starts when d = 0
       // executes till d<5 condition is true
       // post statement is d++
       for d := 0; d < 5; d++{
         fmt.Printf("hello-everyone\n")
       }
   }
   ```

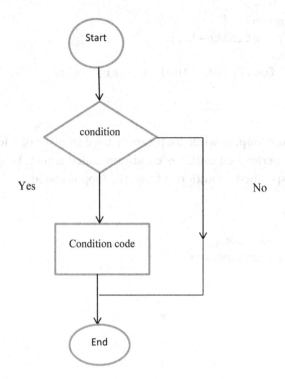

For loop in GoLang.

2. **For loop as infinite loop:** A for loop may be used as an endless loop by removing all three expressions from it. When a user does not add a condition statement in a for loop, the condition statement is assumed to be true, and the loop enters an infinite loop.

Syntax:

```
for
{
    // Statements
}
```

Example:

```
// Program to show the use of an infinite loop
package main
    import "fmt"
// main-function
```

```
func main() {
    // infinite-loop
    for {
        fmt.Printf("Hello-everyone\n")
    }
}
```

3. **while for loop:** A while loop can be used in place of a for loop. This loop is performed until the condition stated is met. When the value of the specified condition is false, the loop is ended.

Syntax:

```
for condition{
    // statements
}
```

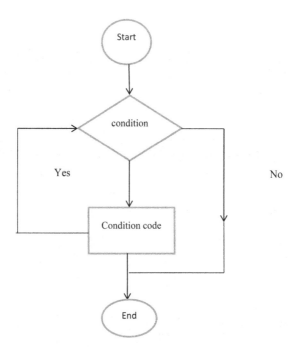

While loop in GoLang.

Example:

```
// Program to demonstrate for loop as while Loop
package main
```

```
import "fmt"
// main-function
func main() {
    // while loop for loop executes till
    // d < 3 condition is true
    d:= 0
    for d < 3 {
        d += 2
    }
    fmt.Println(d)
}
```

4. **Simple range in for loop:** The range can also be used to create a loop.

Syntax:

```
for c, d:= range rvariable{
    // statements
}
```

The iteration values are saved in the variables c and d. Iteration variables are another name for them.

The second variable, d, is optional.

The range expression is evaluated once before the loop begins.

Example:

```
// A program that demonstrates the use of a basic
range loop
package main
import "fmt"
// main-function
func main() {
    // Here rvariable is array
    rvariable:= []string{"HEW", "Hey",
"Heyeveryoneworld"}
    // c and d stores value of rvariable
    // c store index number of the individual
string and
    // d store individual string of given array
    for c, d:= range rvariable {
        fmt.Println(c, d)
    }
}
```

5. **Using a for loop for strings:** A for loop can run over the Unicode code points in a text.

Syntax:

```
for index, chr:= range str{
    // Statement..
}
```

Example:

```
// A program to demonstrate the use of a for loop
with a string
package main
import "fmt"
// main-function
func main() {
    // String as range in for loop
    for c, d:= range "CcdXY" {
        fmt.Printf("The Index number of %U is
%d\n", d, c)
    }
}
```

6. **For maps:** A for loop can iterate through the key and value pairs in the map.

Syntax:

```
for key, value := range map {
    // Statement..
}
```

Example:

```
// Maps are used in this program to demonstrate
the use of loops.
package main
import "fmt"
// main-function
func main() {
    // using-maps
    mmap := map[int]string{
        22:"Piiks",
```

```
        33:"POP",
        44:"PiiksofPiiks",
    }
    for key, value:= range mmap {
        fmt.Println(key, value)
    }
}
```

7. **For channel:** A for loop can cycle over the channel's successive data until the channel is terminated.

Syntax:

```
for item := range Chnl {
    // statement..
}
```

Example:

```
// A code to demonstrate the use of a loop using
channel
package main
import "fmt"
// main-function
func main() {
    // using-channel
    chnl := make(chan int)
    go func(){
        chnl <- 200
        chnl <- 2000
        chnl <- 20000
        chnl <- 200000
        close(chnl)
    }()
    for d:= range chnl {
        fmt.Println(d)
    }
}
```

Loop Control Statements in Go

Loop control statements alter the program's execution in the Go programming language. When the specified loop's execution exits its scope, the objects generated within the scope are also destroyed. The Go programming language offers three types of loop control statements:

- Break

- Goto

- Continue

Break Statement

The break statement is used to end the loop or statement it presents. If they are present, the control is then passed to the statements that follow the break statement. If the break statement is included in the nested loop, it only stops the loops that contain the break statement.

```
// Go program to show the
// use of break statement
package main

import "fmt"

// Main function
func main() {
    for c:=0; c<5; c++{
    fmt.Println(c)

    // For loop breaks when the value of c = 4
    if c == 4{
        break;
    }
    }
}
```

Goto Statement

This statement is used in the program to transfer control to the labeled statement. The label serves as valid identification and is inserted immediately before the statement from which control is transferred. Programmers rarely use Goto statements because they make tracking the program's control flow harder.

```
// Go program to show the
// use of goto statement
package main
```

```
import "fmt"

func main() {
    var y int = 0

    // for loop work as a while loop
    Lable1: for y < 9 {
        if y == 6 {

            // using the goto statement
            y = y + 1;
            goto Lable1
        }
        fmt.Printf("value is: %d\n", y);
        y++;
    }
}
```

Continue Statement

This statement is used to ignore the execution portion of the loop if a given condition is met. The control is then returned to the beginning of the loop. It skips the following statements and proceeds with the next loop iteration.

```
// Go program to illustrate
// the use of continue statement
package main

import "fmt"

func main() {
    var y int = 0

    // for loop work as a while loop
    for y < 9 {
        if y == 5 {

            // skip two iterations
            y = y + 2;
            continue;
        }
        fmt.Printf("value is: %d\n", y);
        y++;
    }
}
```

TYPES

Basic Types

Data types specify the data types that can store in a valid Go variable. The Go language divides types into various categories, which are as follows:

- Basic types contain numbers, strings, and booleans.

- Aggregate types contain arrays and structs.

- Examples of reference types are pointers, slices, maps, functions, and channels.

- The interface type.

This section will go through the fundamental data types in the Go programming language. The Basic Data Types are even further split into three subcategories, as follows:

- Numbers

- Booleans

- Strings

Numbers

In Go, numbers are divided into three subcategories, which are as follows:

- **Integers:** The Go programming language supports both signed and unsigned numbers in four different sizes, as shown in the following table. Signed integers are indicated by int, whereas unsigned integers are denoted by uint.

Data Type	Description
int8	8-bit signed integer
int16	16-bit signed integer
int32	32-bit signed integer
int64	64-bit signed integer
uint8	8-bit unsigned integer
uint16	16-bit unsigned integer
uint32	32-bit unsigned integer
uint64	64-bit unsigned integer
Int	In and uint have the same size, either 32 or 64 bits

(Continued)

Data Type	Description
Uint	In and uint have the same size, either 32 or 64 bits
Rune	It is the same as int32 and represents Unicode code points
Byte	It is an abbreviation for uint8
Uintptr	It is an unsigned integer type. It does not have a defined width, but it can hold all of the bits of a pointer value

Example:

```go
// Integers are used in this program to
demonstrate their use
package main
import "fmt"
func main() {
    // 8bit unsigned int using
    var X uint8 = 221
    fmt.Println(X, X-3)
    // Using the 16bit signed int
    var Y int16 = 32676
    fmt.Println(Y+2, Y-2)
}
```

- **Floating-point numbers:** Floating-point numbers in Go are categorized into two categories, as shown in the following table:

Data Type	Description
float32	32 bit IEEE 754 floating-point number
float64	64 bit IEEE 754 floating-point number

Example:

```go
// illustrate the use of floating-point numbers
package main
import "fmt"
func main()
{
    c := 22.46
    d := 35.88
    // Subtract of two floating-point number
    e := d-c
    // Display the result
    fmt.Printf("The Result is: %f", e)
```

```
    // Display the type of c variable
    fmt.Printf("\nThe type of e is : %T", e)
}
```

- **Complex numbers:** The complex numbers are separated into two portions in the following table. These complex integers also include float32 and float64. The built-in function generates a complex number from its imaginary and real components, while the built-in imaginary and real functions remove those components.

Data Type	Description
complex64	Complex numbers have float32 as both a real and an imaginary component.
complex128	Complex numbers have float64 as both a real and an imaginary component.

Example:

```
// Illustrate use of the complex numbers
package main
import "fmt"
func main() {
    var c complex128 = complex(17, 2)
    var d complex64 = complex(9, 2)
    fmt.Println(c)
    fmt.Println(d)
    // Display the type
    fmt.Printf("The type of c is %T and "+
            "the type of d is %T", c, d)
}
```

Booleans

The boolean data type only represents two values: true or false. Boolean values are neither inherently nor explicitly changed to any other type.

Example:

```
// A program that demonstrates the use of Boolean
package main
```

```go
import "fmt"
func main() {
    // variables
    strng1 := "PiiksofPiiks"
    strng2:= "piiksofpiiks"
    strng3:= "PiiksofPiiks"
    result1:= strng1 == strng2
    result2:= strng1 == strng3
        // Display the result
    fmt.Println( result1)
    fmt.Println( result2)
    // Display type of the
    // result1 and result2
    fmt.Printf("The type of result1 is %T and "+
                    "the type of result2 is %T",
                            result1, result2)

}
```

Strings

A string data type comprises a sequence of Unicode code points. In other words, a string is a collection of immutable bytes, which means that it cannot change once it is produced. A string can contain any human-readable data, including zero-value bytes.

Example:

```go
// A program that demonstrates the use of strings.
package main
import "fmt"
func main()
{
    // strng variable stores strings
    strng := "PiiksofPiiks"
    // Display length of the string
    fmt.Printf("The Length of the string is:%d",
                                len(strng))
    // Display the string
    fmt.Printf("\nthe String is: %s", strng)
    // Display the type of strng variable
    fmt.Printf("\nType of strng is: %T", strng)
}
```

Type Conversion

T(v) is a function that converts the value v to the type T. Here are some numerical conversions:

```
var c int = 43
var d float64 = float64(i)
var e uint = uint(f)
```

Or, to put it another way:

```
c := 43
d := float64(i)
e := uint(f)
```

Go assignment between objects of different kinds necessitates an explicit conversion, which means you must explicitly change types whenever you send a variable to a function that expects another type.

Type Assertion

We can use type assertion if you have a value and wish to convert it to another or a specified type (in the case of an interface). A type assertion takes a value and attempts to construct another version in the explicit type supplied.

In the following example, the timeMap function accepts a value and, if it can be represented as a map of interfaces{} keyed by strings, injects a new entry named "updated at" with the current time value.

```
package main

import (
  "fmt"
  "time"
)

func timeMap(y interface{}) {
  d, ok := c.(map[string]interface{})
  if ok {
    d["updated_at"] = time.Now()
  }
}
```

```
func main() {
  foo := map[string]interface{}{
    "Matt": 43,
  }
  timeMap(foo)
  fmt.Println(foo)
}
```

It is not necessary to perform the type assertion on an empty interface. It's frequently utilized when you have a function that takes a parameter of a specific interface, but the inner function code operates differently depending on the object type. Here's an illustration:

```
package main

import "fmt"

type Stringer interface {
  String() string
}

type fakeString struct {
  content string
}

// function used to implement Stringer interface
func (k *fakeString) String() string {
  return k.content
}

func printString(value interface{}) {
  switch str := value.(type) {
  case string:
    fmt.Println(str)
  case Stringer:
    fmt.Println(str.String())
  }
}

func main() {
  k := &fakeString{"Ceci n'est pas un string"}
  printString(k)
  printString("Hello, Everyone")

}
```

Another example is when determining whether an error is of a specific type:

```
if err != nil {
    if msqlerr, ok := err.(*mysql.MySQLError); ok && msqlerr.
Number == 1062 {
        log.Println("We got MySQL duplicate:(")
    } else {
        return err
    }
}
```

Structs

A struct is a group of fields/properties. New types can be defined as structs or interfaces. If we come from an object-oriented background, think of a struct as a lightweight class that allows for composition but not inheritance.

We do not need to declare getters and setters on struct fields because they are automatically accessible. However, only exported (capitalized) fields may be accessed outside a package.

```
package main

import (
  "fmt"
  "time"
)

type Bootcamp struct {
  // Latitude of event
  Lat float64
  // Longitude of event
  Lon float64
  // Date of event
  Date time.Time
}

func main() {
  fmt.Println(Bootcamp{
    Lat:  34.012837,
    Lon:  -118.495339,
    Date: time.Now(),
  })
}
```

By listing the values of its fields, a struct literal assigns a freshly allocated struct value. Using the "Name:" syntax, we may list only a subset of fields (the order of named fields is irrelevant when using this syntax). The & prefix creates a reference to a newly allocated struct.

Structure literals are declared as follows:

```
package main

import "fmt"

type Point struct {
  C, D int
}

var (
  e = Point{1, 2}  // has type Point
  f = &Point{1, 2} // has type *Point
  g = Point{X: 1}  // D:0 is implicit
  h = Point{}      // X:0 and D:0
)

func main() {
  fmt.Println(e, f, g, h)
}
```

Using the dot notation to access fields:

```
package main

import (
  "fmt"
  "time"
)

type Bootcamp struct {
  Lat, Lon float64
  Date     time.Time
}

func main() {
  event := Bootcamp{
    Lat: 34.012837,
    Lon: -118.495339,
  }
  event.Date = time.Now()
```

```
fmt.Printf("Event on %s, location (%f, %f)",
    event.Date, event.Lat, event.Lon)
}
```

Initializing

The new expression in Go allows us to allocate a zeroed variable of the specified type and return a pointer to it.

```
c := new(int)
```

A struct literal is a typical approach to "initialize" a variable holding a struct or a reference to one. Another possibility is to write a constructor. This is often done when the zero value is insufficient, and we need to provide specific default field values, for example.

It is worth noting that the following formulations, which use new and an empty struct literal, are similar and result in the same type of allocation/ initialization:

```
package main

import (
    "fmt"
)

type Bootcamp struct {
    Lat float64
    Lon float64
}

func main() {
    c := new(Bootcamp)
    d := &Bootcamp{}
    fmt.Println(*c == *d)
}
```

Composition vs. Inheritance

Many of us come from an OOP background and are accustomed to inheritance, which Go does not provide. Instead, we must consider composition and interfaces.

The Go team created a brief yet informative section on this subject.

Composition (or embedding) is a well-known concept among most OOP programmers, and Go supports it; here's an example of a problem it solves:

```go
package main

import "fmt"

type User struct {
    Id        int
    Name      string
    Location  string
}

type Players struct {
    Id        int
    Name      string
    Location  string
    GameId    int
}

func main() {
    p1 := Players{}
    p1.Id = 28
    p1.Name = "Katt"
    p1.Location = "CA"
    p1.GameId = 70414
    fmt.Printf("%+v", p1)
}
```

The preceding example illustrates a common OOP difficulty; our Player struct contains the same attributes as the User struct, including a GameId field. It's not a big thing to have to duplicate the field names, but we can make it easier by assembling our struct.

```go
type User struct {
    Id            int
    Name, Location string
}

type Players struct {
    User
    GameId int
}
```

We have two options for initializing a new variable of type Player. To set the fields, use the dot notation:

```go
package main

import "fmt"

type User struct {
    Id               int
    Name, Location string
}

type Players struct {
    User
    GameId int
}

func main() {
    p1 := Players{}
    p1.Id = 28
    p1.Name = "Katt"
    p1.Location = "CA"
    p1.GameId = 70414
    fmt.Printf("%+v", p1)
}  .
```

Another possibility is to use a struct literal:

```go
package main

import "fmt"

type User struct {
    Id               int
    Name, Location string
}

type Players struct {
    User
    GameId int
}

func main() {
    p1 := Players{
```

```
    User{Id: 28, Name: "Katt", Location: "CA"},
    70414,
  }
  fmt.Printf(
    "Id: %d, Name: %s, Location: %s, Game id: %d\n",
    p1.Id, p1.Name, p1.Location, p1.GameId)
  // Directly set field defined on the Player struct
  p1.Id = 16
  fmt.Printf("%+v", p1)
}
```

We can't merely pass the composed fields when using a struct literal with an implicit composition. Instead, we must supply the types that make up the struct. Once configured, the fields are immediately accessible.

Because our struct is made up of another struct, the User struct's functions are likewise accessible to the Player. Let us develop a way to demonstrate that behavior:

```
package main

import "fmt"

type User struct {
  Id             int
  Name, Location string
}

func (u *User) Greetings() string {
  return fmt.Sprintf("Hello %s from %s",
    u.Name, u.Location)
}

type Players struct {
  User
  GameId int
}

func main() {
  p1 := Players{}
  p1.Id = 28
  p1.Name = "Katt"
  p1.Location = "CA"
  fmt.Println(p1.Greetings())
}
```

As we can see, this is a pretty powerful approach to designing data structures, but it becomes much more intriguing when viewed through the lens of interfaces.[1] By combining one of our structures with one that implements a specific interface, our structure implements the interface automatically.

Here's another example; this time, we'll look at creating a Job struct that can also function as a logger.

Here's how it's done explicitly:

```go
package main

import (
    "log"
    "os"
)

type Job struct {
    Command string
    Logger  *log.Logger
}

func main() {
    job := &Job{"demo", log.New(os.Stderr, "Job: ", log.Ldate)}
    // same as job := &Job{Command: "demo",
    // Logger: log.New(os.Stderr, "Job: ", log.Ldate)}
    job.Logger.Print("test")
}
```

Our Job struct contains a Logger field, which is a reference to another type (log.Logger)

We set the logger when we create our value so that we may call its Print function later by chaining the calls: a job.Logger.Print()

However, Go allows us to go much farther by employing implicit composition. We can forgo establishing the field for our logger because all methods are now accessible via a reference to the log. Our struct has loggers available:

```go
package main

import (
    "log"
    "os"
)
```

---

[1] https://www.GoLangbootcamp.com/book/types#sec-initializing_values

```
type Job struct {
  Command string
  *log.Logger
}

func main() {
  job := &Job{"demo", log.New(os.Stderr, "Job: ", log.Ldate)}
  job.Print("starting-now..")
}
```

We must still set the logger, which is frequently an excellent reason to use a constructor (custom constructors are used when we need to set a structure before utilizing a value). What's excellent about implicit composition is that it allows us to simply and inexpensively make our structs implement interfaces. Assume we have a function that accepts variables and implements an interface with the Print method by adding *log.Logger to our struct (and properly initializing it), our struct is now implementing the interface without the need for us to write any new methods.

HOW DO YOU MAKE MODULES IN GoLang?

Since 1.11, Go has featured support for versioned modules, as described here, with the original prototype known as vgo. The idea of modules was first initiated in Go to address the issue of dependencies inside our Go programs. Several packages are gathered and concatenated to build a module, which is saved in a file with a go.mod file at its root in a tree-like structure.[2]

Note: To work with Go modules, you must update the version of Go on your system to the most recent version.

Let's look at how to make modules in GoLang now. To build a module, first create a directory and then use the following commands to navigate within it:

```
mkdir go_modules
cd go_modules
```

Use the following command to set the current directory as the root of the module, which will allow us to handle dependencies:

```
go mod init go_modules
```

---

[2] https://www.geeksforgeeks.org/how-to-create-modules-in-GoLang/

Because we are operating outside of the $GOPATH/src module, we must specifically supply the module name during startup.

We can now see if the go.mod file was produced and, if so, what its contents are.

The following step is to write a basic Go file containing the following code:

```go
// file inside current module
package gfg_go

import("fmt")

func initialiser() string {

    fmt.Printf("In gfg_go package. \n")

    // returns current module
    // and package name
    return_string := "Module : go_modules."
    return return_string

}
```

We can additionally create another Go file with the following code to test the function as mentioned above:

```go
package gfg_go
import (
    "testing"
    "fmt"
    "strings"
)

// function to test if original
// go program is working
func TestFunction(test *testing.T) {

    test_string1 := "go_modules"

    // calling function from
    // previous go file
    res := strings.Split(initialiser(), ":")
```

```
// removing spaces and line-ending
// punctuation before comparing
test_string2 := strings.Trim(res[1], ". ")

if test_string1 == test_string2 {
        fmt.Printf("Successful!\n")

} else {
        // this prints error message if
        // strings don't match
        test.Errorf("Error!\n")
}

}
```

We should observe that our test builds passed after executing the go test command.

Adding Dependencies to the Go Module

To add dependencies to our module, we will use the require() function along with the module's version:

```
module go_modules

go 1.14

require github.com/rs/zerolog v1.14.3
```

PACKAGE MANAGEMENT USING Go MODULES

Package management is a critical component of every project setup. To enhance developer delivery time, we rely substantially on effective package management at Halodoc. With a standardized package manager across projects, our developers can set up any project once familiar with the tech stack.

A package manager is used to build the environment by obtaining, updating, or deleting project dependencies. It can download or update the package, often from a remote host, by determining the precise version of the package. Go modules is one of the package managers available in Go for dealing with dependencies.

What Exactly Is the Go Module?

A Module is a collection of Go packages placed in a file tree under the $GOPATH/pkg folder, with a go.mod file at the root. This file defines the module's path, your project's import path, and its dependency requirements, which are the other modules required for a successful build.

As of Go 1.11, the go command (go build, go run, and go test) automatically examines and adds dependencies needed for imports if the current directory or any parent directory contains a go.mod file. Host projects outside of the $GOPATH/src folder.

Go Modules add two additional files to a Go project:

- go.mod defines the name of a module, its dependencies, and its minimal versions.

- go.sum is a dependency lock file that is created automatically.

Both files are situated at the project's root level.

Initially, we used Go Dep as our Go package management at Halodoc. Since the deprecation of Dep in 2020, we have opted to migrate to Go modules, as it has become the official recommendation for dependencies and is widely used in the Go ecosystem.

The majority of the Go Dep features are available on Go Modules:

- The Go module, like Dep, may place dependencies in a/vendor directory, allowing different projects to rely on various versions of the same packages.

- Go Modules is a built-in functionality; no extra tools, such as go dep, are required.

- Allow and encourage that projects be hosted outside of the $GOPATH.

Check for dependencies automatically while building, running, or testing the Go Module & Dep command comparison:

Command	Go Modules	Go Dep
Initiate project	go mod init	dep init
Add dependency	go get <libsName>	dep ensure -add <libsName>
Install in vendor	go, mod vendor	dep ensure
Remove unused modules	go mod tidy	-

Starting Out
Module Initializing
To begin, we must start the module within your project:

```
$ cd gitlab.com/go-module-project #project directory
$ go mod init
```

Inside, a go.mod file with the name of our project directory as the module and the version of Go we are using will be produced.

Setting Up Dependencies
After initializing the go.mod file, we may use the go get command to get specified versions of modules. Example:

```
$ go get -u github.com/gin-gonic/gin
```

The package manager will check for and download the dependency's most recent tag. Download all child dependencies required if the -u parameter is used. The go.sum file will be added to our project after a dependency for the project has been downloaded. The contents of the go.mod file are changed to indicate all of the dependencies that have been downloaded in their latest versions.

There will be times when we are creating code in our Go project, and the dependencies have not been downloaded by the go get command but are mentioned as an import statement. To confirm this, run/build our project, which will automatically check for and download suitable versions of the dependencies depending on our code.

```
$ go build
```

We may also just download the missing dependencies and not run/build our project:

```
$ go mod download
```

The go build/go run command, by default, also performs the go mod download command.

Eliminating Unnecessary Dependencies
The go mod clean command will examine the go.mod file for any unneeded dependencies to get rid of reliance. To demonstrate, delete the

Go code that utilizes the github.com/gin-gonic/gin module stated above during go get.

```
$ go mod tidy -v
```

The program will produce the result shown below, and any unneeded dependencies in the go.mod and go.sum files are deleted.

```
$ go mod tidy -v
```

Updating a Dependency Version

During development, you may need to upgrade the module version we're using to a particular branch or tag version. This can be accomplished through command, as demonstrated by the following examples:

Description	Command
Install the latest tag version	go get github.com/gin-gonic/gin
Install specific tag version	go get github.com/gin-gonic/gin@v1.6.2
Install a specific branch	go get github.com/gin-gonic/gin@master
Install specific commit	go get github.com/gin-gonic/gin@1bdf86b

We may also alter the go.mod file and then run go mod download.

ERROR HANDLING

Errors suggest that something is wrong with the software. Assume we are attempting to open a file that does not exist in the file system. This is an aberrant condition, and an error indicates it.

In Go, errors are just values. The built-in error type is used to express errors. Later in this course, we'll learn more about the error type.

Error-values are kept in variables, supplied as parameters to functions, returned from functions, and so on, much like any other built-in type, such as int, float64, etc.

Let's begin with an example program that attempts to open a file that does not exist.

```
package main

import (
    "fmt"
    "os"
)
```

```
func main() {
    f, err := os.Open("/test.txt")
    if err != nil {
        fmt.Println(err)
        return
    }
    fmt.Println(f.Name(), "open-successfully")
}
```

We attempt to open the file /test.txt (which will not exist in the playground). The os package's Open function has the below given signature:

```
func Open(name string) (file *File, err error)
```

If the file is opened successfully, the Open method will return the file handler, and the error value will be nil. If an error occurs when opening the file, a non-nil error is returned.

If a function or method delivers an error, it is often the final value returned by the function. As a result, the Open function returns err as to the final value.

In Go, the natural approach to handling errors compares the returned error to nil. A nil value implies that no error happened, but a non-nil value indicates that an error occurred. We check to see if the error is not nil in this situation. If it is not nil, we simply print an error message and exit the main function.

When we run this code, it will print:

```
open /test.txt: No such file or directory
```

Error Type Representation

Let's look at how the built-in error type is defined. Error is a kind of interface with the following definition:

```
type error interface {
    Error() string
}
```

It only has one method with the signature Error() string. As an error, any type that implements this interface can be used. This function returns an error explanation.

When printing the error, the fmt.Println function internally uses the Error() string method to obtain the error information.

Various Approaches to Getting More Information from an Error

Now that we've established that error is an interface type let's look at how we may get more information about an error.

In the preceding example, we just printed the error explanation. What if we needed the exact path to the file that triggered the error? Parsing the error string is one technique to acquire this. This was the end result of our program.

```
open /test.txt: No such file or directory
```

We can analyze this error message to obtain the file path "/test.txt" of the file that produced the issue. However, this is a crude method. In subsequent versions of Go, the error description might change at any time, causing our code to fail.

But do you think there is a more efficient way to obtain the file name? Yes, it is possible, and the Go standard library employs various methods to convey additional information about mistakes. Let's take a look at them one at a time.

1. **Ascertaining the underlying struct type and obtaining further information from the struct fields**

   If we carefully read the description for the Open function, we will notice that it returns an error of type *PathError. PathError is a struct type, and its standard library implementation is as follows:

```
type PathError struct {
   Op    string
   Path string
   Err   error
}

func (e1 *PathError) Error() string { return e1.Op +
" " + e1.Path + ": " + e1.Err.Error() }
```

We can see from the code above that *PathError implements the error interface by declaring the Error() string function. This function returns the operation, path, and actual error concatenation. As a result, we received the error notice,

```
open /test.txt: No such file or directory.
```

PathError struct's Path field contains the file's path that generated the error. Let's change the code we built before to print the path.

```
package main
import (
    "fmt"
    "os"
)
func main() {
    f, err := os.Open("test.txt")
    if err != nil {
        if pErr, ok := err.(*os.PathError); ok {
            fmt.Println("Failed to open file at path",
pErr.Path)
            return
        }
        fmt.Println("Generic-error", err)
        return
    }
    fmt.Println(f.Name(), "open-successfully")
}
```

In the above application, we first verify in line 8 whether the error is not nil, and then in line 9, we use type assertion to extract the underlying value of the error interface. If we're unfamiliar with type assertion, we recommend reading https://GoLangbot.com/interfaces-part-1. In line 11, we print the path using pErr.Path. This software generates,

```
Failed to open the file at path /test.txt
```

Suppose the underlying issue is not of the type *os.PathError, the control will proceed to line 13, producing a generic error message.

2. **Asserting the underlying struct type and obtaining further information via methods**

   The second option for obtaining further information from an error is to assert the underlying type and obtain additional information by calling methods on the struct type.

   Let's look at the given example to grasp this better.

   The DNSError struct type is defined in the standard library as follows:

   ```go
   type DNSError struct {
       ....
   }

   func (e *DNSError) Error() string {
       ....
   }
   func (e *DNSError) Timeout() bool {
       ....
   }
   func (e *DNSError) Temporary() bool {
       ....
   }
   ```

The DNSError struct includes two methods: Timeout() bool and Temporary() bool, both of which return a boolean value indicating whether the issue is due to a timeout or is temporary.

Write a program that asserts the *DNSError type and uses these methods to ascertain if the problem is temporary or due to a timeout.[3]

```go
package main
import (
    "fmt"
    "net"
)
func main() {
    addr, err := net.LookupHost("GoLangbot123.com")
    if err != nil {
        if dnsErr, ok := err.(*net.DNSError); ok {
            if dnsErr.Timeout() {
                fmt.Println("operation timed-out")
                return
            }
```

---

[3] https://GoLangbot.com/error-handling/

```
        if dnsErr.Temporary() {
            fmt.Println("temporary-error")
            return
        }
        fmt.Println("Generic DNS-error", err)
        return
    }
    fmt.Println("Generic-error", err)
    return
    }
    fmt.Println(addr)
}
```

In line 7 of the program above, we attempt to obtain the IP address of an invalid domain name GoLangbot123.com. In line 9, we retrieve the error's underlying value by assuming it to type *net.DNSError. Then, in lines 10 and 14, we check to see if the problem is due to a timeout or if it is temporary.

The error is neither transitory nor caused by a timeout in our scenario. Hence, the program will output.

```
Generic DNS error lookup GoLangbot123.com: no such
host
```

If the error had been transient or due to a timeout, the accompanying if statement will run, and we can handle it appropriately.

3. **Direct comparison**

The third method for obtaining more information about an error is to compare it with a variable of type error directly. Let's look at an example to see how this works.

The filepath package's Glob function returns the names of all files that match a pattern. When the pattern is malformed, this method returns the error ErrBadPattern.

ErrBadPattern is a global variable defined in the filepath package.

```
var ErrBadPattern = errors.New("syntax error in the
pattern")
```

To generate a new mistake, use errors.New()

When a pattern is malformed, the Glob function returns ErrBadPattern.

Let's develop a little program to detect this issue.

```
package main
import (
    "fmt"
    "path/filepath"
)
func main() {
    files, err := filepath.Glob("[")
    if err != nil {
        if err == filepath.ErrBadPattern {
            fmt.Println("Bad pattern-error:", err)
            return
        }
        fmt.Println("Generic-error:", err)
        return
    }
    fmt.Println("matched-files", files)
}
```

We look for files with the pattern [which is a flawed pattern]. We check to see whether the error isn't nil. To learn more about the issue, we immediately compare it to filepath. In line 9, there is an ErrBadPattern. If the requirement is met, the mistake is caused by a faulty pattern. This program will print,

```
Bad pattern error: syntax error in the pattern
```

Don't Ignore Errors

Never, ever disregard a mistake. Ignoring mistakes invite difficulties. Let me rework the example, ignoring the error-handling code, to show the names of all files that fit a pattern.

```
package main
import (
    "fmt"
```

```
    "path/filepath"
)
func main() {
    files, _ := filepath.Glob("[")
    fmt.Println("matched-files", files)
}
```

We already know that the pattern is incorrect from the prior case. In line 7, we used the blank identifier to disregard the error provided by the Glob function. In line 8, we just print the matched files. This program will print,

```
matched files []
```

Because we disregarded the error, the result shows that no files fit the pattern, but the pattern itself is incorrect. As a result, never overlook mistakes.

IN GoLang, THERE ARE SEVERAL TECHNIQUES TO COMPARE STRINGS

The string in Go is an immutable chain of arbitrary bytes encoded using UTF-8 encoding. We have two options for comparing strings to each other.

Making Use of Comparison Operators

Go strings allow comparison operators such as ==, !=, >=, <=, <, >. The == and != operators are used to determine if the provided strings are equal, while the >=, <=, <, > operators are used to determining the lexical order. The outcomes of these operators are of the Boolean type, which means that if the condition is met, it will return true; otherwise, it will return false.

First Example:

```
// program to illustrate the concept
// of == and != operator with the strings
package main

import "fmt"

// Main-function
func main() {
```

```go
    // Creating, initializing the strings
    // using the shorthand declaration
    str1 := "Peeks"
    str2 := "Peek"
    str3 := "PeeksforPeeks"
    str4 := "Peeks"

    // Checking string are equal
    // or not using == operator
    result1 := str1 == str2
    result2 := str2 == str3
    result3 := str3 == str4
    result4 := str1 == str4

    fmt.Println("Result 1: ", result1)
    fmt.Println("Result 2: ", result2)
    fmt.Println("Result 3: ", result3)
    fmt.Println("Result 4: ", result4)

    // Checking string are not equal
    // using != operator
    result5 := str1 != str2
    result6 := str2 != str3
    result7 := str3 != str4
    result8 := str1 != str4

    fmt.Println("\nResult 5: ", result5)
    fmt.Println("Result 6: ", result6)
    fmt.Println("Result 7: ", result7)
    fmt.Println("Result 8: ", result8)

}
```

Second Example:

```go
// program to illustrate the concept
// of comparison operator with the strings
package main

import "fmt"

// Main-function
func main() {
```

```
// Creating, initializing
// slice of string using
// the shorthand declaration
myslice := []string{"Peeks", "Peeks",
                "pfp", "PFP", "for"}

fmt.Println("Slice: ", myslice)

// Using comparison operator
result1 := "PFP" > "Peeks"
fmt.Println("Result 1: ", result1)

result2 := "PFP" < "Peeks"
fmt.Println("Result 2: ", result2)

result3 := "Peeks" >= "for"
fmt.Println("Result 3: ", result3)

result4 := "Peeks" <= "for"
fmt.Println("Result 4: ", result4)

result5 := "Peeks" == "Peeks"
fmt.Println("Result 5: ", result5)

result6 := "Peeks" != "for"
fmt.Println("Result 6: ", result6)

}
```

Using the Compare() Method

We may also compare two strings using the strings package's built-in function Compare(). After comparing two texts lexicographically, this method produces an integer value. The values returned are as follows:

- Return 0, if str1 == str2.

- Return 1, if str1 > str2.

- Return -1, if str1 < str2.

Syntax:

```
func Compare(str1, str2 string) int
```

Example:

```
// program to illustrate how to compare
// string using the compare() function
package main

import (
    "fmt"
    "strings"
)

func main() {

    // Comparing string using the Compare function
    fmt.Println(strings.Compare("pfp", "Peeks"))

    fmt.Println(strings.Compare("PeeksforPeeks",
                                "PeeksforPeeks"))

    fmt.Println(strings.Compare("Peeks", " PFP"))

    fmt.Println(strings.Compare("PeeKS", "PeeKs"))

}
```

FUNCTIONS IN Go

Functions are frequently coding blocks or statements in a program that allow the user to reuse the same code, saving memory and time, and, most importantly, increasing code readability. A function is, in essence, a collection of statements that together perform a particular task and provide the result to the caller. A function can also complete a job without returning any results.

Function Declaration

A function declaration is a technique for creating a function.

Syntax:

```
func function_name (Parameter-list) (Return-type) {
    // function-body
}
```

The declaration of the function includes the following:

- **func:** In the Go computer language, it is a keyword that is used to describe a function.

- **function_name:** This is the name of the function.

- **Parameter-list:** It provides the name and type of function parameters in the parameterlist.

- **Return-type:** This is an optional parameter that specifies the types of values that the function returns. If we want to use return type in our function, we must include a return statement.

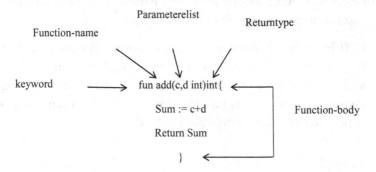

Function Calling

When a client needs to run a function, they invoke or call it. The function's capabilities must be provided to be used. As shown in the example below, we have an area () function with two parameters. We refer to this function by its name, area(23, 12), with two parameters in the main function.

```
// Program to show the
// use of function
package main
import "fmt"
// area() is used to find the
// area of the rectangle
// area() function two parameters,
// i.e, length, width
func area(length, width int)int{
    arr := length* width
    return arr
}
```

```
// main-function
func main() {
    // Display area of the rectangle with
    // method calling
    fmt.Printf("Area of rectangle is : %d",
area(23, 12))
}
```

Function Arguments

In Go, the arguments sent to a function are known as real parameters, but the parameters received by a function are known as formal parameters.

The Go language utilizes the call by value mechanism by default to pass parameters in a function. For providing parameters to our function, the Go programming language gives two options:

- **Call by value:** The values of actual parameters are passed to the function's formal parameters in this method of parameter passing, and the two types of parameters are retained in separate memory regions. As a result, any modifications made within functions do not appear in the caller's actual parameters.

  Example:

  ```
  // Program to demonstrate the
  // concept of call by value
  package main
  import "fmt"
  // the function which swap values
  func swap(c, d int)int{
      var o int
      o= c
      c=d
      d=o
      return o
  }
  // main-function
  func main() {
    var x int = 27
    var y int = 40
    fmt.Printf("x = %d and y = %d", x, y)
    // call by values
    swap(x, y)
  ```

```
    fmt.Printf("\n x = %d and y = %d",x, y)
}
```

- **Call by reference:** Because the actual and formal parameters both point to the same place, any changes made within the function are mirrored in the caller's parameter list.

Example:

```
// Program to show the
// the concept of call by reference
package main
import "fmt"
// function which swap the values
func swap(c, d *int)int{
    var o int
    o = *d
    *c = *d
    *d = o
    return o
}
// main-function
func main() {
var x int = 20
 var y int = 10
 fmt.Printf("x = %d and y = %d", x, y)
// call by reference
 swap(&x, &y)
    fmt.Printf("\n x = %d and y = %d", x, y)
}
```

FUNCTION RETURNING MULTIPLE VALUES

In the Go computer language, the return statement permits us to return multiple values from a function. In other terms, a single return statement in a function might return various values. The return values have the same type as the parameters in the parameter list.

Syntax:

```
func function_name(parameter_list)(returntype_list){
    // code
}
```

Example:

```
// program to show how a function may return
several values
package main
import "fmt"
// myfunc return three values of the int type
func myfunc(c, d int)(int, int, int ){
    return c - d, c * d, c + d
}
// main-Method
func main() {
    // return values are assigned into the
different variables
    var myvar1, myvar2, myvar3 = myfunc(41, 22)
    // Displayvalues
    fmt.Printf("Result is: %d", myvar1 )
    fmt.Printf("\nResult is: %d", myvar2)
    fmt.Printf("\nResult is: %d", myvar3)
}
```

Giving Names to the Return Values

Return values in the Go computer language can be given names. In our code, we may also utilize variable names like this. There is no necessity to include a return statement with these identifiers since the Go compiler will recognize that they must return data. This is referred to as a bare return. Using a simple return eliminates duplication in our code.

Syntax:

```
func function_name(para1, para2 int)(name1 int,
name2 int){
    // code
}
```

Example:

```
// show how to give names to return the values
package main
import "fmt"
// myfunc return two values of int type
// here return the value name is rectangle & square
```

```
func myfunc(c, d int)( rectangle int, square int ){
    rectangle = c*d
    square = c*c
    return
}
func main() {
    // return values are assigned into the two
different variables
    var area1, area2 = myfunc(14, 18)
    // Display-values
    fmt.Printf("The Area of rectangle is: %d", area1 )
    fmt.Printf("\nThe Area of square is: %d", area2)

}
```

VARIADIC FUNCTIONS

A variadic function takes a variable set of variables to invoke. In other words, the variadic function will accept zero or more arguments from the user.fmt. Printf is an example of a variadic function; it takes one fixed parameter at the beginning and can take any number of arguments afterward.

Syntax:

```
function function_name(para1, para2...type)type{
// code..
}
```

Example:

```
// Program to show the
// concept of variadic function
package main
import(
    "fmt"
    "strings"
)
// Variadic function to join string
func joinstr(element...string)string{
    return strings.Join(element, "-")
}
func main() {
```

```
// zero-argument
fmt.Println(joinstr())
// multiple-arguments
fmt.Println(joinstr("Heyyy", "HEW"))
fmt.Println(joinstr("Heyyy", "Everybody",
"World"))
fmt.Println(joinstr("H", "E", "Y", "Y", "Y"))
}
```

ANONYMOUS FUNCTION

The Go scripting language has an anonymous function. An anonymous function lacks a name. When it is necessary to write an inline function, an anonymous function can create a closure in Go. Anonymous functions are also known as function literals.

Syntax:

```
func(parameter_list)(return_type){
// code
// Use return-statement if returntype are given
// if return_type is not given, then do not
// use the return statement
return
}()
```

Example:

```
// Program to show how to create anonymous
function
package main
import "fmt"
func main() {
    // anonymous-function
    func(){
        fmt.Println("Welcome to Home")
    }()
}
```

GoLang main AND init FUNCTIONS

The Go programming language has two unique methods: main() and init().

main() Function

In Go, the main package is a one-of-a-kind package that contains exe-cutable programs, such as the main() function. The main() function is a one-of-a-kind function that acts as the executable program's starting point. It takes no parameters and returns none. There is no need to invoke the main() method directly because Go executes it for you, and every executable program must include a single main package and the main() function.

Example:

```
// Program to illustrate the concept of main()
function
// Declaration of the main package
package main
// Importing-packages
import (
    "fmt"
    "sort"
    "strings"
    "time"
)
// Main-function
func main() {
    // Sorting given slice
    str := []int{455, 39, 223, 29, 86, 38, 427, 29}
    sort.Ints(str)
    fmt.Println("Sorted slice: ", str)
    // Finding-index
    fmt.Println("The Index value is: ", strings.
Index("Hello", "ks"))
    // Finding-time
    fmt.Println("Time is: ", time.Now().Unix())
}
```

init() Function

Like the main function, the init() function accepts no parameters and returns nothing. This function is included in every package and is called when the package is loaded for the first time. Because this function is declared implicitly, we can't use it anywhere else. In the same application, we can build many init() functions and will execute them in the order in which they are built. Init() functions can be inserted anywhere in the program and are called in the order of the lexical file name. And statements are allowed if the init() function is used, but please remember that the init() method is executed before the main() function call, so it is not dependent on the main() function.

Example:

```
// Program to show the
// tconcept of init() function
// Declaration of the main package
package main
// importing-package
import "fmt"
// multiple init()-function
func init() {
    fmt.Println("Welcome home")
}
func init() {
    fmt.Println("Hello everybody ")
}
// main-function
func main() {
    fmt.Println("Welcome to class")
}
```

This chapter covered flow control, types, modules, and packages in GoLang. Moreover, we discussed error handling, comparing keywords, and functions.

CHAPTER 6

Code Optimization

IN THIS CHAPTER

➤ Optimization tips

➤ Writing secure code

➤ Best coding practices

➤ Security and hardening ideas

We covered functions, types, modules, packages, and error handling in the last chapter. This chapter will go through code optimization.

A PATTERN FOR OPTIMIZING Go

- Step 1: Enable pprof
  What exactly is pprof: Pprof is the standard method for profiling go applications included with go. The pprof package may disclose memory and CPU consumption across our program over HTTP and the running command line and contention information.

  To activate pprof, follow these steps: We may enable pprof in our application by including the line import_"net/http/pprof" and running the default http server. Another alternative, which we use at Splunk to explicitly restrict where the handler is connected, is to enable particular pprof endpoints in our code using something like the following.

DOI: 10.1201/9781003309055-6

```
import "github.com/gorilla/mux"
import "net/http/pprof"
var handler *mux.Router
// .....
handler.PathPrefix("/debug/pprof/profile")
.HandlerFunc(pprof.Profile)
handler.PathPrefix("/debug/pprof/heap")
.HandlerFunc(pprof.Heap)
```

- Step 2: Look for Anything to Optimize
  What should be done:

```
curl http://ingest58:6060/debug/pprof/profile > /tmp/
ingest.profile
go tool pprof ingest /tmp/ingest.profile
(pprof) top7
```

What this accomplishes: To see the output of pprof, Go includes a local pprof tool. The/debug/pprof/profile endpoint will gather a 30-second profile. Above, I save the output to a local file, then run pprof on the stored output. Note that the last parameter of pprof might be a URL rather than a local file. The command top7 displays the top seven CPU-intensive tasks.

Result:

```
12910ms of 24020ms total (56.79%)
 Dropped 481 nodes (cum <= 120.10ms)
 Showing top 30 nodes out of 275 (cum >= 160ms)
      flat  flat%   sum%       cum   cum%
    1110ms  4.62%  4.62%    2360ms  9.83%  runtime
.mallocgc
     940ms  3.91%  8.53%    1450ms  6.04%  runtime
.scanobject
     830ms  3.46% 11.99%     830ms  3.46%  runtime
.futex
     800ms  3.33% 15.32%     800ms  3.33%  runtime
.mSpan_Sweep.func1
     750ms  3.12% 18.44%     750ms  3.12%  runtime
.cmpbody
     720ms  3.00% 21.44%     720ms  3.00%  runtime.xchg
     580ms  2.41% 23.86%     580ms  2.41%  runtime._
ExternalCode
```

This indicates that none of these functions are developed by us. Mallocgc, scanobject, and mSpan Sweep, on the other hand, all indicate CPU utilization during garbage collection. We could delve further into each of these functions, but instead of optimizing Go's garbage collector, it would be a better use of my time to improve my usage of Go's garbage collector. In this situation, object creation is on the heap.

- Step 3: Look at the Causes of GC
  What should be done:

```
curl http://ingest58:6060/debug/pprof/heap > /tmp/
heap.profile
go tool pprof -alloc_objects /tmp/ingest /tmp/heap.
profile
(pprof) top3
```

What this accomplishes: It's worth noting that the endpoint we download has a URL identical to the profiler above, but it ends in/ heap. This will provide us with a summary of the heap use on the computer. We save it again to a file for subsequent comparison. The -alloc objects argument displays the number of allocated objects throughout the application's lifetime.

Result:

```
4964437929 of 7534904879 total (68.87%)
 Dropped 541 nodes (cum <= 37674524)
 Showing top 10 nodes out of 133 (cum >= 321426216)
      flat  flat%  sum%        cum   cum%
 853721355 11.33% 11.33%  859078341 11.40%  github
.com/signalfuse/sfxgo/ingest/tsidcache/tsiddiskcache
.(*DiskKey).EncodeOld
 702927011  9.33% 20.66%  702927011  9.33%  reflect
.unsafe_New
```

This suggests that 11.33% of my object allocations occurred within the method EncodeOld of the object DiskKey, which was predicted.

Partition(), on the other hand, used 8.29% of my total allocations, which was unexpected given that it should only be doing simple math.

- Step 4: Determine Why Partitioner Is Using So Much Memory. What to Do

```
(pprof) list Partitioner.*Partition
```

What this does is output the source lines of the function we're interested in and count which statements generated heap allocations within the function. This is one of several commands available within pprof. Another handy one is peeking, which displays the callers and callees of functions. By entering "help" and playing with what we see, we can receive a comprehensive list.[1]

Result:

```
Total: 11323262665
  ROUTINE ========================= github.com/signalfuse/
sfxgo/ingest/bus/rawbus.(*Partitioner).Partition in /
opt/jenkins/workspace/ingest/gopath/src/github.com/
signalfuse/sfxgo/ingest/bus/rawbus/partitioner.go
  927405893  927405893 (flat, cum)  8.19% of Total
          .          .     64: if ringSize == 0 {
          .          .     65:  return 0, ErrUnsetRingSize
          .          .     66: }
          .          .     67: var b1 [8]byte
          .          .     68: binary.LittleEndian.
PutUint64(b1[:], uint64(message.Key.
(*partitionPickingKey).tsid))
  239971917  239971917     69: logherd.Debug2(log, "key",
message.Key, "numP", numPartitions, "Partitioning")
          .          .     70: murmHash := murmur3.
Sum32(b1[:])
          .          .     71:
          .          .     72: // 34026 => 66
          .          .     73: setBits := uint(16)
          .          .     74: setSize := uint32
(1 << setBits)
          .          .     75: shortHash := murmHash &
(setSize - 1)
```

---

[1] https://www.splunk.com/en_us/blog/devops/a-pattern-for-optimizing-go-2.html

```
          .         .     76: smallIndex := int32
 (shortHash) * int32(k.ringSize) / int32(setSize)
  687433976   687433976      77: logherd.Debug3(log,
 "smallIndex", smallIndex, "murmHash", murmHash,
 "shortHash", shortHash, "Sending to partition")
          .         .     78: return smallIndex, nil
          .         .     79:}
          .         .     80:
```

What this indicates is that: This demonstrates that executing debug logging causes variables to escape from the stack to the heap. We could delete those lines because this debug logging isn't technically necessary. But first, let us test this idea. The function "logherd.Debug2" is a wrapper that looks like the following and exists to reduce the memory overhead of logrus WithField instances when debug is disabled.

```
// Debug2 to logger 2 key/value pairs and
message.  Intended to save mem alloc that WithField
creates
func Debug2(l *logrus.Logger, key string, val
interface{}, key2 string, val2 interface{}, msg
string) {
  if l.Level >= logrus.DebugLevel {
      l.WithField(key, val).WithField(key2, val2)
.Debug(msg)
  }
}
```

- Step 5: Determine Why Log Statements Cause So Many Allocations
What should be done:

```
go build -gcflags='-m'.  2>&1 | grep partitioner.go
```

What this achieves is that the -m argument for a building will output to stderr the compiler's optimization decisions. This covers whether the compiler may allocate a variable on the stack or if it must relocate it to the heap. If the compiler cannot ensure that a reference to the variable is not found elsewhere, Go will relocate it to the heap.

Result:

```
./partitioner.go:63: &k1.ringSize escapes to heap
./partitioner.go:62: leaking param: k1
./partitioner.go:70: message.Key escapes to heap
./partitioner.go:62: leaking param content: message
./partitioner.go:70: numPartitions escapes to heap
./partitioner.go:77: smallIndex escapes to heap
./partitioner.go:77: murmHash escapes to heap
./partitioner.go:77: shortHash escapes to heap
./partitioner.go:68: (*Partitioner).Partition b
doesn't escape
./partitioner.go:71: (*Partitioner).Partition b
doesn't escape
```

What this implies is that the essential sections are on line 77, which shows that smallIndex, murmHash, and shortHash all escape to the heap. I'm producing more objects on the heap than we need since the compiler executes short-lived heap allocations.

- Step 6: Benchmark the Partition Function
  What we should write:

```
func BenchmarkPartition(b1 *testing.B) {
    r1 := rand.New(rand.NewSource(0))
    k1 := partitionPickingKey{}
    msg := sarama.ProducerMessage {
        Key: &k1,
    }
    p1 := Partitioner{
        ringSize: 1024,
        ringName: "quantizer.ring",
    }
    num_partitions := int32(1024)
    for c := 0; c < b1.N; c++ {
        k1.tsid = r1.Int63()
        part, err := p1.Partition(&msg, num_partitions)
        if err != nil {
            panic("Error-benchmarking")
        }
        if part < 0 || part >= num_partitions {
            panic("Bench-failure")
        }
    }
}
```

What it does: This benchmark simply produces B.N objects and performs a basic check on the return value to ensure that it has not been optimized away. When programmers embark on optimization hunts, creating benchmarks is a suggested "before" step to ensure we're heading on the right path.

- Step 7: Test Memory Allocations in the Partition Function
  What should be done:

```
go test -v -bench.  -run=_NONE_ -benchmem
BenchmarkPartition
```

This runs benchmarks that match the regex "." and -benchmem will also run benchmarks that measure heap use on average each iteration. By supplying _NONE_ to -run, we're instructing tests to execute unit tests with the "_NONE_" string inside them, which saves us some time. In other words, run all of the benchmarks but none of the unit tests.

Result:

```
PASS
BenchmarkPartition-8 10000000         202 ns/op       64
B/op      4 allocs/op
```

This indicates that my benchmark's loops took an average of 202ns and, more crucially, allocated four objects for each operation.

- Step 8: Get Rid of the Logging Statements
  What we should write:

```
@@ -66,7 +65,6 @@ func (kl *Partitioner)
Partition(message *sarama.ProducerMessage,
numPartitions i
        }
        var bl [8]byte
        binary.LittleEndian.PutUint64(bl[:],
uint64(message.Key.(*partitionPickingKey).tsid))
```

```
-        logherd.Debug2(log, "key", message.Key,
"numP", numPartitions, "Partitioning")
        murmHash := murmur3.Sum32(b1[:])
        // 34026 => 66
@@ -74,7 +72,6 @@ func (k *Partitioner)
Partition(message *sarama.ProducerMessage,
numPartitions i
        setSize := uint32(1 << setBits)
        shortHash := murmHash & (setSize - 1)
        smallIndex := int32(shortHash) * int32(k.
ringSize) / int32(setSize)
-        logherd.Debug3(log, "smallIndex", smallIndex,
"murmHash", murmHash, "shortHash", shortHash, "Sending
to partition")
        return smallIndex, nil
}
```

What this does: we removed the log lines as a workaround. They were inserted during testing/debugging and were never deleted. In this scenario, just eliminating the log lines is a straightforward approach.

- Step 9: Rerun the Build to See Whether the Variables Have Changed. Escape to the Heap
  What should be done:

```
go build -gcflags='-m'. 2>&1 | grep partitioner.go
```

Result:

```
./partitioner.go:62: &k1.ringSize escapes to heap
./partitioner.go:61: leaking param: k1
./partitioner.go:61: (*Partitioner).Partition message
doesn't escape
./partitioner.go:67: (*Partitioner).Partition b
doesn't escape
./partitioner.go:68: (*Partitioner).Partition b
doesn't escape
```

What this implies is that smallIndex, murmHash, and shortHash no longer provide messages indicating that they have escaped to the heap.

- Step 10: Rerun Benchmark to Look into New Allocations per Operation
  What should be done:

```
go test -v -bench.    -run=_NONE_ -benchmem
BenchmarkPartition
```

Result:

```
PASS
BenchmarkPartition-8 30000000            40.5 ns/op
0 B/op          0 allocs/op
ok    github.com/signalfuse/sfxgo/ingest/bus/rawbus
1.267s
```

This implies that each operation now takes only 40ns, and there are no allocations per operation. This is the essential element for us because we attempted to optimize heap consumption.

Why Is Code Optimization Necessary?

While writing code, we constantly judge and choose between solutions that may appear similar at first glance. Later, it is frequently discovered that confident choices result in a more efficient program than others; thus, a hunt for best coding practices and optimization approaches naturally occurs. We consider the entire development process as an optimization issue to solve.

Although optimization challenges are not the only ones that developers face daily (there are other choices and searching issues), optimization is the work that probably embraces the many stages of web development the most.

Code optimization can occur at several levels, depending on how near the optimization is to machine code. We can only conduct higher-level optimizations in web development because assembly- or runtime-level optimizations are not a choice, but there are still numerous options.

We can optimize our programs at the architectural level with better design patterns and the source code level with best coding practices and suitable tools. We can also increase our team's performance by incorporating coding style guides into our workflow.

Whatever approach we choose, there is one rule of thumb that every code optimization effort must follow: we must always carry out the optimization in a way that does not affect the meaning of the code.

The benefits of code optimization rise in tandem with the size of our project, and because even small projects may develop into huge ones over time, learning excellent code optimization skills nearly always yields demonstrable beneficial effects.

Code Base That Is Cleaner

As a project evolves and additional developers begin to work on it, duplications and overlaps generally occur sooner or later, and we suddenly find we don't understand what's going on.

One of the pillars of good software development is adhering to the DRY (Don't Repeat Yourself) philosophy. A well-structured, highly optimized code base that allows us to reuse the same pieces several times is always sleeker and tidier, making it easier to comprehend and work with.

Improved Consistency

Consistency is like cleaning; no one sees it when it's done well, but when neglected, the entire home looks sloppy, and we find ourselves in disarray.

Accomplishing perfect consistency is difficult since guaranteeing backward compatibility can hinder progress, but paying attention to employing clear coding principles, compatible APIs, and consistent standards can undoubtedly alleviate the suffering.

Maintaining code consistency in mind is especially crucial when dealing with legacy code or more significant projects with multiple developers.

Pages That Load Faster

Buying a quicker automobile is analogous to optimizing code. Consequently, our code runs faster, and our site or application uses less memory than previously. Although the optimization process may take more time and money, the end result is a better experience for both developers and end-users.

Faster code means faster website load times, which is essential in search engine optimization and conversion marketing. According to research, "almost half of the online visitors anticipate a site to load in 2 seconds or less, and they are likely to exit a site that isn't loaded within 3 seconds" thus, speed is not something we can afford to neglect.

Improved Code Readability
Code readability is a crucial part of code maintenance. Untidy code with ad hoc formatting is difficult to read and, as a result, difficult to understand, especially for engineers who are new to a project.

We may avoid the agony of dealing with indecipherable code by employing code optimization strategies such as:

- Consistent formatting, including logical use of indentation, whitespace, and vertical spacing.

- Eliminating excessive noise, such as self-explanatory, obvious comments.

More Efficient Refactoring
In web development, we regularly inherit code from someone else and rapidly realize that it is far from optimum, whether in structure, performance, or maintainability. The same thing might happen with past projects we built when we had considerably fewer programming skills.

In other circumstances, the aims of an otherwise excellent project shift with time, and we must focus on other aspects of the program than before.

We refer to refactoring when we update (clean up) current code to optimize it without changing its functionality. Refactoring must be done with caution since, if done incorrectly, we might quickly end up with a codebase that is even less optimum than the original.

Easier to Understand Debugging
Debugging consumes a substantial percentage of the web development workflow and is sometimes laborious or even intimidating activity. It's difficult enough to debug our code, but it's even more challenging to spot faults in someone else's, especially if it's a never-ending code that only utilizes functions.

Architectural patterns and smart design, such as using objects and distinct modules and clear coding principles, may help with debugging.

Enhanced Workflow
Many web development projects are managed by remote or distributed teams, such as open-source communities. One of the most challenging aspects of managing such a process is making communication effective enough for team members to understand each other readily and not explain settings continuously.

Best practices and style guidelines that are agreed upon may bridge the gap between people from diverse backgrounds, not to mention the regular communication challenges that most online projects have between design and development teams.

Code optimization is also workflow optimization since if team members speak the same language and have the same stated goals, they will be able to work together much more quickly.

Code Upkeep Is Now Easier

Although constructing something from the ground up is more fun than maintaining preexisting code, we still need to undertake ongoing code maintenance from time to time. Working with existing systems may also provide new perspectives on code optimization because it is a unique experience than early optimizations in a new project.

We are already at a point in software maintenance where we can detect actual speed and efficiency issues and deal with real users rather than hypothetical use cases.

Although code maintenance is sometimes overlooked in developer circles, it can be rewarding if we follow best practices such as utilizing dependable version control, dependency management, staging and testing platforms, and adequately documenting our work.

Improved Feature Development

Constant innovation is essential for keeping relevant in our business since if we haven't shown anything new to our audience in a while, we will swiftly fall behind. When working with a well-optimized, clean code base, we can typically extend and add new features to a program faster.

The Ultimate Guide to GoLang Performance Optimization

GoLang is a popular language for cloud-based and server-side applications. Artificial intelligence, machine learning, and data science are among the fastest expanding fields, and you already know that GoLang is a popular programming language for developing such applications. This blog article provides tried-and-true strategies for improving GoLang performance.

GoLang Performance Hints That Have Been Proven and Tested

Optimization of Resource Efficiency

Product owners may increase the performance of their apps by optimizing resource use. Some portions of our program require more resources than others, and you must identify these red flags in our application program. It might be the CPU, the bandwidth, or the RAM.

Optimization of Latency in GoLang

We must identify the bottlenecks in our software here. The purpose is to increase Go performance optimization in the latency of a particular function. The latency of GoLang is automatically increased when the resource efficiency of our application improves. Improved latency, on the other hand, may need greater resource use. However, to work on both program bottlenecks and hot spots simultaneously, we must be aware of both.

Efficiency of Algorithms

A program can do the same task in various methods with variable magnitudes. By using algorithm optimization, we will get maximum performance in our application. Continue reading our article to meet and overcome the three efficiencies mentioned above (latency, resource, and algorithm) in our GoLang application. It is a hand-picked list compiled with the assistance of our knowledgeable Go engineers.

When we hire a GoLang developer from us, we will receive all of the experience required to create an application for our users.

Patterns of GoLang Application Performance

We must utilize third-party tools and built-in packages for optimization to improve the performance of our GoLang application. Our program compiler will rarely be able to optimize our Go program code independently. As a result, we've compiled a list of best-practice guidelines that serve as industry benchmarks. Each piece of advice is essential since it is specific to our application type and requirements. We can select one of these GoLang performance patterns based on our app logic and load.

Use Goroutines Sparingly

Goroutines, also cost-efficient, distinguish GoLang as a worthwhile programming language.

However, goroutines have a considerable memory footprint, which impacts the speed of our project. In general, Go coders build limitless goroutines with no regard for when they will leave. As a result, we recommend that we only start a goroutine if we know when it exists.

CPU Work Should Parallelize

Synchronization takes a long time, and if we can parallelize our work by leveraging available cores, we will undoubtedly improve the speed of our Go program. This step will linearly accelerate the execution of our program.

Asynchronous I/O Operations

Network transactions and file input/output operations are the most prevalent bottlenecks. To improve the speed of our GoLang application, we may make individual I/O operations asynchronous. As a result, similar activities can execute in parallel, reducing downstream latency. To synchronize several I/O operations, use sync.WaitGroup.

Keep an Eye on Our Timeouts

I/O operations often take a long time, resulting in latency. To avoid this, avoid initiating any I/O job without knowing how long it would take. Before putting a timeout on each network request, we should start utilizing SetDeadline, SetReadDeadline, and SetWriteDeadline.

Memory Should Not Allocate in Hot Spots

When we create new items, the system uses memory and CPU cycles, causing latency to increase. It keeps the garbage collector busy, which is not a good indication, especially in high-traffic areas. As a result, we should reuse objects and utilize sync wherever feasible.

Make Use of Lock-Free Algorithms

Avoid synchronization since it creates racing scenarios and contentions. Avoid mutex to increase performance and latency. For several famous data structures, there are numerous lock-free methods available.

Prefer Read-Only Locks

Our goroutines must wait long because we assume full locks on large, synchronized objects. We should utilize read-only locks to avoid this kind of issue.

Reduce or Eliminate the Use of 'cgo'

cgo allows Go applications to access C libraries. The cgo function, on the other hand, has a significant overhead. It drains threads in the same way as blocking I/O does during operation. We should never call C code in the middle of a tight loop. We recommend that we avoid using cgo for the optimum performance of our GoLang application.

Make Use of Buffered I/O

Accessing unique items necessitates disk operations, which reduces program efficiency. Using buffered input/output can significantly enhance our app's performance since it will have to read and write more significant data blocks.

Use Binary Instead

Text file formats PostgreSQL supports both binary and text forms. Binary, on the other hand, is significantly quicker than text. When converting from network byte order, the processing is only necessary when utilizing the binary form. As a result, the binary format is more efficient for transmission than the text format for the PostgreSQL server.

StringBuffer and StringBuilder Are Preferable

The system allocates a new string using the "+" and "+=" operators on each assignment. We should utilize StringBuffer and StringBuilder to address this inefficiency for faster program execution.

Make Use of Regular Expressions

Some apps may utilize the same regular expression several times, and compiling the regular expression before each usage will make our app inefficient. As a result, built regular expressions are used for repeated matching.

Slices Should Preallocate

When our demand exceeds the present capacity, the Go language automatically allocates memory. When the array travels to a new place, the system provides double memory during reallocation. To reduce memory waste and wasteful trash collection, we should preallocate the slices wherever feasible.

Select Protocol Buffers and MessagePack as Our Options

Because they employ reflection, JSON and Gob are a little hesitant. Instead, Protocol Buffers and MessagePack should be used.

For Maps, Use int Rather Than a String

If our application uses Maps, we prefer int keys over string keys. Customize our business demands with a top-tier GoLang development firm.

GoLang FOR SECURE CODING

Stuck in a Rut with Manual Security

Many Go developers use popular frameworks like Revel, Martini, and Gin Gonic to provide efficient back-end APIs. These APIs are often used in conjunction with various clients, such as web clients or mobile applications, which connect with the back end using REST or gRPC.

In contrast to other languages' monolithic structures, Go programs frequently divide themselves into microservices or groupings of smaller microliths. The reliance on security knowledge required to recognize significant flaws that require remediation situations when the program and its logic are abused is a prevalent difficulty in building apps.

Teams can threat-model a specific application or use automated methods to detect common security risks using some programming languages. However, the Go language's weak static typing destroys many data-flow tools, and the popularity of NoSQL databases affects what most security teams should be looking for (not SQL injection).

Although static analyzers like staticcheck and gosec can be utilized, the bulk of these issues corresponds to quality-level tests, comparable to the IntelliJ Code Inspections currently accessible within integrated development environments (IDEs). These legacy application scanning solutions generate a high percentage of false positives, but they also miss undiscovered dangers.

With Go, There Is a Need for Integrated, Automated Security

To increase the security of Go apps, organizations must adopt a new strategy. A contemporary and automated application security strategy should focus on two forms of risk:

- Open-source flaws occur when a program depends on a vulnerable library.

- Custom-code vulnerabilities occur when an otherwise secure program assembles otherwise secure code unusual and hazardous.

Integrated analysis (also known as instrumentation) provides a new level of security for Go programs. Contrast Security is the first to provide Go instrumentation without requiring source code changes. Contrast's method embeds sensors inside the program, allowing it to monitor data as it moves through it and discover and inform teams of vulnerabilities in real-time.

Unlike static code analysis or blind analyzers, which fuzz test REST/gRPC entry points, integrated analyzers operate inside the application to watch what's going on and discover how code is accessing vulnerable channels. For example, suppose data is sent to a SQL query without validation. In that case, the sensor can indicate that the path was insecure even if no one was actively looking for security problems.

This form of comprehensive, automated application security detection facilitates the discovery of various significant concerns (without requiring that a developer be fully trained in application security). This includes OWASP Top Ten security risks like path traversal, allowing attackers to control their access to various files on a file system. It also addresses injection attacks (the top risk on the most recent OWAP list). Unauthorized code is put into a program to change databases, access file systems, or penetrate programs.

How Does Instrument-Based Security Work in the Go Pipeline?

Developers utilize the Contrast Go tool instead of the Go compiler during the build process to effortlessly add instrumentation to their test pipeline. As a result of this, two things occur:

- A scanner collects all direct and transitive dependencies to determine whether the Go program uses vulnerable libraries. When a new Common Vulnerabilities and Exposures (CVEs) is identified in a library, whether now or later, this inventory promptly determines which apps are affected and notifies the security team.

- The Contrast Go program embeds interactive application security testing sensors into the application binary, providing specific security detection and monitoring during runtime. Contrast may now analyze the application's security posture in real-time as it runs.

Teams can determine whether to upgrade any dependencies before promoting quality assurance to prevent known CVEs.

Teams can deploy the Contrast security-aware binaries to test environments throughout the testing process. They may then use the app usually, carrying out any relevant use cases of interest to the team. Dedicated security testing is unneeded at this stage because Contrast identifies and alerts the security team of vulnerability detections, removing the guesswork. Any security concerns discovered can then be prioritized by teams.

Contrast Go currently offers just IAST sensors for assessing code during the build and test processes. In keeping with the Contrast Application Security Platform's whole software development life cycle, future Contrast Go features will include runtime application protection and observability to safeguard Go apps in production.

Contrast Goes Above and Beyond with Modern Application Security

Teams wishing to improve the security of their Go apps may now utilize the industry's first interactive Go application security analyzer. With the inclusion of the Contrast Go agent in the Contrast Application Security Platform, security flaws in Go code may be detected automatically. Contrast Go incorporates sensors into the application's binary, allowing Contrast to monitor and immediately discover security flaws. There is no need for separate security checks; the Contrast agent integrated into the program provides a direct evaluation of the application during runtime.

This update is handy for firms looking to safeguard their APIs. The Contrast Go agent uses composition analysis to find known vulnerabilities in third-party libraries and integrated analysis to find undiscovered vulnerabilities in API runtime. As soon as a new, previously undisclosed vulnerability is detected, the Contrast DevSecOps Control Center displays which apps are vulnerable.

Until today, there has been no better security alternative for Go apps. The Contrast Go agent identifies just the critical vulnerabilities while making it quick and straightforward for developers to resolve problems on their own. Contrast provides security teams with far more speed and efficiency than older application security products through integration and automation.

Go Security Best Practices

The popularity of GoLang has grown over time. Docker, Kubernetes, and Terraform have placed significant bets on this programming language. Go has lately become the de facto standard for developing command-line tools.

However, the absence of vulnerabilities does not imply that the programming language is entirely safe. Humans can design unsafe apps if certain practices are not followed. For example, by following OWASP's secure coding guidelines, we can figure out how to implement these practices while using Go.[2] That's precisely what we're going to do this time. We'll go through practices to keep in mind when working using Go in this piece.

Verify the Input Entries

Validating user entries is essential for functionality and avoiding attackers who give us invasive data that might harm the system. Furthermore, we assist users in using the application with greater confidence by preventing them from making dumb and common blunders. For example, we may block a user from deleting several records simultaneously.

We may use native Go packages like strconv to handle string conversions to different data types to validate user input. For complicated validations, Go also supports regular expressions using regexp. Even while Go prefers native libraries, there are third-party packages such as validator. Validator makes it easier to provide validations for structs or specific fields. For example, the following code checks to see if the User struct includes a valid email address:

```
package main

import (
  "fmt"

  "gopkg.in/go-playground/validator.v9"
)

type User struct {
  Email string 'json:"email" validate:"required,email"'
  Name  string 'json:"name" validate:"required"'
}

func main() {
  v1 := validator.New()
  a1 := User{
    Email: "a1",
  }

  err := v1.Struct(a1)

  for _, el := range err.(validator.ValidationErrors) {
    fmt.Println(el)
  }
}
```

---

[2] https://blog.sqreen.com/top-6-security-best-practices-for-go/

Make Use of HTML Templates

Cross-site scripting, or XSS, is a significant and prevalent vulnerability. This vulnerability entails the attacker being able to insert malicious code into the app to change the output. A JavaScript code, for example, maybe sent as part of a URL's query string. The JavaScript code might be performed when the program returns the user's value. As a result, we must be aware of this and sanitize user input as a developer.

The package html/template in Go is used to encode what the program will return to the user. So, instead of the browser executing an input like script>alert("We've Been Hacked!");/script>, displaying an alert message, we could encode the input, and the app would handle the input as if it were a standard HTML code written in the browser. An HTTP server that returns an HTML template will appear as follows:

```
package main
import (
  "html/template"
  "net/http"
)
func handler(w http.ResponseWriter, r *http.Request) {
  param1 := r.URL.Query().Get("param1")
  tmpl := template.New("heyyy")
  tmpl, _ = tmpl.Parse('{{define "T"}}{{.}}{{end}}')
  tmpl.ExecuteTemplate(w, "T", param1)
}
func main() {
  http.HandleFunc("/", handler)
  http.ListenAndServe(":8080", nil)
}
```

However, third-party libraries are available when constructing web apps in Go. For example, the Gorilla web toolkit contains libraries to assist developers with tasks such as encoding authentication cookie information. Nosurf is another HTTP package that aids in preventing cross-site request forgery.

Protect Ourselves against SQL Injections

If we've been a developer for a while, you've probably heard about SQL injections, which are still ranked first on OWASP's Top 10 list. However, we should keep a few considerations in mind when using Go. The first step is to ensure that the user who connects to the database has limited rights.

As discussed in the previous section, it's also good to sanitize the user's input or escape special characters using the HTMLEscapeString method from the HTML template package.

The most important piece of code we'd need to add, though, is the usage of parameterized queries. On the go, we prepare a statement on the DB rather than in a connection. Here's an instance of how parameterized queries are used:

```
customerName := r.URL.Query().Get("name")
db.Exec("UPDATE creditcards SET name=? WHERE customerId=?",
customerName, 123, 70)
```

But what if the database engine doesn't support prepared statements? What if it has an impact on query performance? We can use the db.Query() method, but we must first sanitize the user's input, as shown in earlier sections. Other third-party libraries are available to prevent SQL injections, such as sqlmap.

Despite our best efforts, vulnerabilities occasionally sneak through or reach our apps via third parties. Consider using an application security management platform like Sqreen to defend our web apps against essential threats like SQL injections.

Encrypt Any Sensitive Data

A challenging string to read, such as in base-64 format, does not imply that the concealed value is hidden. We'll need a technique to encrypt data so that attackers can't simply decipher it. Database passwords, user passwords, and even social security numbers are examples of information we want to encrypt.

OWASP recommends a few encryption algorithms, including bcrypt, PDKDF2, Argon2, and scrypt. Fortunately, a Go package offers strong encryption implementations, such as crypto, for encrypting data. For example, consider the following code as an example of how to utilize bcrypt:

```
package main

import (
  "database/sql"
```

```
    "context"
    "fmt"

    "GoLang.org/x/crypto/bcrypt"
)

func main() {
    ctx := context.Background()
    email := []byte("rohan.doe@somedomain.com")
    password := []byte("47;u5:B(95m72;Xq")

    hashedPassword, err := bcrypt.GenerateFromPassword
(password, bcrypt.DefaultCost)
    if err != nil {
        panic(err)
    }

    stmt, err := db.PrepareContext(ctx, "INSERT INTO accounts
SET hash=?, email=?")
    if err != nil {
        panic(err)
    }
    result, err := stmt.ExecContext(ctx, hashedPassword,
email)
    if err != nil {
        panic(err)
    }
}
```

Remember that we must still use caution while transmitting information across services. We don't want to send the user's information in plain text. It makes no difference if the program encrypts user inputs before storing the data. Assume that someone on the Internet is sniffing our traffic and recording our system's request records. An attacker might use this information to cross-reference it with data from other systems.

Make HTTPS Communication Mandatory

Nowadays, most browsers need HTTPS to be enabled on all websites. If the site isn't utilizing HTTPS, Chrome, for example, will display a notice in the address bar. As a policy, an Infosec team might require in-transit encryption for communication between services. To secure an in-transit connection in the system, it is not enough to have the app listening on port 443. To prevent attackers from lowering the protocol to HTTP, we must also employ correct certificates and enforce HTTPS.

Here is some code for a web application that uses and enforces the HTTPS protocol:

```go
package main

import (
    "crypto/tls"
    "log"
    "net/http"
)

func main() {
    mux := http.NewServeMux()
    mux.HandleFunc("/", func(w http.ResponseWriter, req
*http.Request) {
        wl.Header().Add("Strict-Transport-Security",
"max-age=53072000; includeSubDomains")
        wl.Write([]byte("This is server example.\n"))
    })
    cfg := &tls.Config{
        MinVersion:              tls.VersionTLS12,
        CurvePreferences:        []tls.CurveID{tls.
CurveP521, tls.CurveP384, tls.CurveP256},
        PreferServerCipherSuites: true,
        CipherSuites: []uint16{
            tls.TLS_ECDHE_RSA_WITH_AES_256_GCM_SHA384,
            tls.TLS_ECDHE_RSA_WITH_AES_256_CBC_SHA,
            tls.TLS_RSA_WITH_AES_256_GCM_SHA384,
            tls.TLS_RSA_WITH_AES_256_CBC_SHA,
        },
    }
    srv := &http.Server{
        Addr:         ":443",
        Handler:      mux,
        TLSConfig:    cfg,
        TLSNextProto: make(map[string]func(*http.Server,
*tls.Conn, http.Handler), 0),
    }
    log.Fatal(srv.ListenAndServeTLS("tls.crt", "tls.key"))
}
```

It's worth noting that the app will be listening on port 443. The line that enforces the HTTPS setting is as follows:

```go
w.Header().Add("Strict-Transport-Security", "max-age=53072000;
includeSubDomains")
```

We may also wish to include the server name in the TLS settings, as seen below:

```
config := &tls.Config{ServerName: "ourSiteOrServiceName"}
```

Even if our web app is solely used for internal communication, implementing in-transit encryption is always a smart idea. Consider the possibility that an attacker may sniff your internal traffic for whatever reason. It's always smart to raise the challenge bar for potential future attacks wherever feasible.

Be Cautious of Mistakes and Logs

Last but not least, error handling and logging are essential features to have in our Go projects.

To successfully debug in production, instrument our apps appropriately. However, we must use caution when displaying problems to consumers. We don't want users to know what went wrong. Attackers may use this information to deduce which services and technologies they utilize. Furthermore, keep in mind that, while logs are helpful, they must be kept somewhere. In addition, if logs get into the wrong hands, they are used to develop an impending assault on the system.

So the first thing we should know or remember is that there are no exceptions in Go. This implies we'd have to handle errors differently in other languages. The standard is as follows:

```
if err != nil {
   // handle error
}
```

In addition, Go provides a native library for working with logs. The most straightforward basic code is as follows:

```
package main

import (
   "log"
)
```

```
func main() {
  log.Print("Logging in the Go")
}
```

However, there are third-party logging libraries available. Logrus, glog, and loggo are a few examples. Here's a little bit of logrus code:

```
package main

import (
  "os"
  log "github.com/sirupsen/logrus"
)

func main() {
  file, err := os.OpenFile("info.log", os.O_CREATE|os.
O_APPEND, 0644)
  if err != nil {
    log.Fatal(err)
  }

  defer file.Close()

  log.SetOutput(file)
  log.SetFormatter(&log.JSONFormatter{})
  log.SetLevel(log.WarnLevel)

  log.WithFields(log.Fields{
    "animal": "fish",
    "size":   20,
  }).Info("A group of fish emerges from the ocean")
}
```

Finally, ensure that we follow all preceding guidelines, such as encryption and sanitization of the data we enter into the logs.

BEST PRACTICES FOR GoLang

Go, the programming language is a few that includes built-in concurrency and was designed with a specific purpose. As a result, all programmers who have just begun studying Go will benefit from this list of recommended practices, so let's get started.

This list is organized into groups based on functionality.

Syntax

Go is a compiled static language. This means that there are some ground rules that we must follow. This will help reduce confusion while working in a large team when each group must build its code and verify it is compatible with the others.

Assign Datatypes to Newly Created Variables

It appears to be pretty simple to utilize the walrus operator (:=) for everything. However, when your code is in the thousands of line areas, it may get complicated for other teams and us, especially if there is an issue to trace back. It also has an exquisite appearance:

```
func main(){
    var c int = 2022
    //do-something
    }
```

Do Not Declare a Variable or Import a Package That We Do Not Require

In specific IDEs, Go automatically eliminates unnecessary variables and packages, whereas it gives an error otherwise. This can be perplexing for novices and is frequently frustrating when troubleshooting. The comment tags are the easiest solution to fix this problem:

```
//this is a single line comment
/*this is a
multiline comment*/
```

Follow Proper Naming Conventions

A good name is consistent, simple, and easy to remember.

- In Go, use MixedCase for all names. Do not utilize underscores in the same way that Python does.

- Acronyms should be written in all capital letters.

- Keep local variables to a minimum. Common variables, such as an index or a loop parameter, can be represented by a single letter.

Make Use of Comments to Help in Knowledge Transfer
When many programmers are working on the same piece of code. It is usual practice to provide a brief explanation in the source code that includes the name of the module, its purpose, and the author's name. It is also reasonable to explain within a complex piece of code.

Simple, Readable, and Maintainable Code
Avoid Nesting by Dealing with Mistakes First
It is best to check for a nil error at the program's start. This simplifies the code and decreases the reader's workload.

Avoid Utility Repeats
Go has "utility types" that have been optimized to execute certain duties, such as binWriter, which may reduce a 20-line code with repeats to 12 lines:

```
if w1.err = binary.Write(w1.w1, binary.LittleEndian, v1);
w1.err == nil {
  w1.size += int64(binary.Size(v1))
}

//little Endian is a font. nothing exotic.
```

To Address Exceptional Circumstances, Use the Type Switch
A switch statement is a condensed version of an if-else expression. It executes the first case whose value matches the condition phrase.

The switch in Go is similar to those in C, C++, Java, JavaScript, and PHP, except Go only runs the selected case, not all subsequent cases. Go provides the break statement required at the end of each case required in those languages. Another notable difference is that Go's switch cases do not have to be constants, and the values included do not have to be integers.

```
func (struct_name) Write(v1 input) {
  if err != nil { //error-handling-first
    return
  }
  switch x1 := v1.(type) {
  case string:
    //do-something
```

```
case int:
    //do some other-thing
default:
    //yet another-thing
    }
  }
}
```

Go Code Organization
Let's look at how a perfect Go program/package code is structured.

- Necessary code, such as license information, build tags, and package documentation, is placed first.

- The Import statements follow, with similar groupings separated by blank lines.

- The rest of the code should be given in a logical order, beginning with the most important types and finishing with utility functions.

It is best practice for programmers developing Go packages to break the code into multiple shorter files such as separate code and tests because the test programs are built at runtime. Also, when several files are in a package, it is customary to generate a doc.go file containing the package documentation.

Also, when utilizing go routines, terminate the channel after our function using that channel is complete to avoid leaking.

For Use in CI/CD Workflows

Continuous Integration and Continuous Delivery are abbreviations for Continuous Integration and Continuous Delivery in a product development environment. And with GoLang, it's pretty simple to practice CI/CD with the same efficiency level. The route to excellent CI/CD is obvious now that JFrog has contributed a public Go registry, and Artifactory has native support for GoLang.

Make Use of Go Modules
It is a widely used approach for handling versioned dependencies. We can import this Go module among other dependencies in our code:

```
import (
    "fmt"
    "io/ioutil"
    "net/http"
    "os"

// Public Go Module for the logging
    log "github.com/sirupsen/logrus"
)
```

The module functions may then be referenced in our GoLang code as follows:

```
// Send text to log
log.Printf("Heyy Log!")
```

Ensure Immutability and Availability Using GOPROXY

Each Docker image is created once and then promoted through several staging repositories. In this manner, we can ensure that what was tested is precisely what is sent to production.

Once we've established our GoLang dependencies as formed modules, we may make them immutable by establishing a GOPROXY. As a result, we can always ensure what a specific version of a module includes, ensuring that our builds are always reproducible.

This chapter covered a pattern for code optimization, optimization tips, security best practices, and best practices for GoLang. Moreover, we also covered secure code in GoLang.

CHAPTER 7

GoLang Tutorials and Projects

> ➤ Creating a QR code in GoLang

> ➤ Creating an HTTP client

> ➤ Working with APIs in GoLang

The previous chapter discusses code optimization, securing code, and coding practices. This chapter will discuss creating OR code, creating an HTTP client, and working with API.

WEB APPLICATION TO GENERATE QR Code IN GoLang

A Quick Response (QR) code is a two-dimensional graphical code employed for its quick reading and excellent storage capacity. This graphical code consists of black modules in a square pattern on a white background. Use any data to encode the information (e.g., binary, alphanumeric, or Kanji symbols).

The simplest example of a web application for creating barcodes. A third-party bar-code package contains the algorithm or internal logic for generating bar codes. This example demonstrates how to utilize a package and develop a web application.

DOI: 10.1201/9781003309055-7

Install the Necessary Package

Use the Barcode package to generate a variety of barcodes. We may install this package on our git bash terminal by using the following command:

```
go get github.com/boombuler/barcode
```

Development

Main.go Source Code

The main function starts with a call to http.HandleFunc instructs the http package to use homeHandler to handle all requests to the web root ("/"). homeHandler is a function of the type http.HandlerFunc. Its parameters are an http.ResponseWriter and an http.Request.

ViewCodeHandler is a function that allows visitors to examine a created QR-code on a new page. It will handle URLs that begin with "/generator/," the template for the function. The contents of generator.html will be read by ParseFiles and returned as a *template.

```go
package main

import (
    "image/png"
    "net/http"
    "text/template"

    "github.com/boombuler/barcode"
    "github.com/boombuler/barcode/qr"
)

type Page struct {
    Title string
}

func main() {
    http.HandleFunc("/", homeHandler)
    http.HandleFunc("/generator/", viewCodeHandler)
    http.ListenAndServe(":8080", nil)
}

func homeHandler(w1 http.ResponseWriter, r1 *http.Request)
{
    p1 := Page{Title: "QR-Code-Generator"}
```

```
   t1, _ := template.ParseFiles("generator.html")
   t1.Execute(w1, p1)
}

func viewCodeHandler(w1 http.ResponseWriter, r1 *http.
Request) {
   dataString := r1.FormValue("dataString")

   qrCode, _ := qr.Encode(dataString, qr.L, qr.Auto)
   qrCode, _ = barcode.Scale(qrCode, 512, 512)

   png.Encode(w, qrCode)
}
```

The FormValue function returns the value of the dataString input field, which is used to produce the QR code with the Encode method.

Generator.html Source Code
The HTML form is contained in a template file.

```
<h1>{{.Title}}</h1>
<div>Enter string we want to QRCode.</div>
<form action="generator/" method=post>
    <input type="text" name="dataString">
    <input type="submit" value="Submit">
</form>
```

Implementation

Using the command line or putty, execute the run command "Go ahead and run main.go".

SETTING UP THE Go HTTP CLIENT

When developing apps that interface with external services/products, we require a standardized method for establishing an intelligible relationship on both sides. APIs are used to facilitate and establish communication between the client and server.

In this session, we'll teach how to configure and create a connection between client and server and send HTTP requests to endpoints offered by other projects to supply resources to our application. Making request calls to an API entails sending an HTTP(s) request to a web server, as specified in the API's documentation.

The client is the host (e.g., the browser) that sends a request to a web server in the form of a URL for a particular service or data and receives a response. The server is a distant computer that accepts and processes requests before returning the necessary response data over the HTTP/HTTPS protocol.

HTTP Client in GoLang

In the net/http package, the Go standard library offers good support for HTTP clients. Throughout this section, we'll look at all of the configurations required for a Go application to perform HTTP/HTTPS queries to external sites.

To establish an HTTP client, we'll utilize the basic Go client from the net/http package by simply defining a variable of type http.Client.

```go
// go/src/http-client/main.go
package main
import (
    "fmt"
    "io/ioutil"
    "net/http"
    "time"
)
func main() {
    cl := http.Client{Timeout: time.Duration(2) * time
.Second}
    resp, err := cl.Get("https://go.dev/")
    if err != nil {
        fmt.Printf("Error %s", err)
        return
    }
    defer resp.Body.Close()
    body, err := ioutil.ReadAll(resp.Body)

    if err != nil {
      fmt.Printf("Error %s", err)
      return
    }

    fmt.Printf("Body : %s", body)
}
```

We may define and pass particular parameters when constructing an HTTP client to set up the client-server relationship.

We supplied a Timeout field of type time in the above code sample. Duration. When a client establishes an HTTP connection to the server, the server may take some time to reply to the request. This option allows us to set the maximum amount of time we should wait for a response from the server.

Specify other fields within http.Client:

- **Transport (type http.RoundTripper):** This modifies how HTTP requests are processed and performed within our code.

- **CheckedRedirect (function type func(req *Request, via []*Request):** In the event of a request redirection, we may utilize this field to build a function within our application to handle request redirections.

- **Jar (type CookieJar):** We may use this field to include cookies in HTTP requests.

POST and GET Requests

We defined a GET request to a URL in the preceding code block, https://go.dev/. We sent a call to the webserver and assigned the response and a possible error value to the variables resp and err.

```
. . . .
  resp, err := cl.Get("https://go.dev/")

  if err != nil {
    fmt.Printf("Error %s", err)
    return
  }
. . . .
```

The code snippet above is identical to making a POST request to a URL. However, in this scenario, we must add the data we are providing alongside the POST request to the body of the request to the webserver.

```
. . . .
  postData := bytes.NewBuffer([]byte('{"post":"boom-boom
library"}'))
  resp, err := cl.Post("https://go.dev/", "application/json",
postData)
```

```
    if err != nil {
        fmt.Printf("Error %s", err)
        return
    }
    ....
```

In the above excerpt, we defined a new variable, postData (type *bytes. Buffer), to contain the data sent with the request. The postData were then supplied as a parameter to the cl.Post method, along with the URL and data type.

Why not just use a JSON string as postData? This is since this argument must implement the io.Reader interface.

Let's take a brief look at obtaining the response from resp: now that we've seen how to perform a GET or POST request.

```
    ....
    defer resp.Body.Close()
    body, err := ioutil.ReadAll(resp.Body)

    if err != nil {
        fmt.Printf("Error %s", err)
        return
    }

    fmt.Printf("Body : %s", body)
    ....
```

We scheduled a function call to resp.Body using the defer keyword. Once the function returns, close the resp.Body, which is a stream of data returned by request. This is a required component of the software to eliminate potential persistent connections to the server.

Adding Request Headers

Let's create methods for each server request form we wish to make. This may need more code, but it offers us the freedom to own our code. We can then easily attach the desired headers to the request.

```
// go/src/http-client/main.go
package main
```

```
import (
    "fmt"
    "io/ioutil"
    "net/http"
    "time"
)

func main() {

    cs := http.Client{Timeout: time.Duration(2) * time.
Second}
    req, err := http.NewRequest("GET", "https://go.dev/",
nil)
    if err != nil {
        fmt.Printf("error %s", err)
        return
    }
    req.Header.Add("Accept", 'application/json')

    resp, err := cs.Do(req)
    if err != nil {
        fmt.Printf("Error %s", err)
        return
    }

    defer resp.Body.Close()
    body, err := ioutil.ReadAll(resp.Body)
    if err != nil {
        fmt.Printf("Error %s", err)
        return
    }

    fmt.Printf("Body : %s", body)
}
```

In the preceding code, we built a client and then specified a new request using the http.NewRequest function. We described the type of request we wanted using the parameters.

The function signature for http.Request is as follows:

```
(method, url string, body io.Reader) (*Request, error)
```

The first argument specifies the request's method. Then, in the second argument, we supply the URL and the body to store the data or nil in the case of a GET request because there is nobody to transmit.

Then, as seen below, we define the Header we wish to attach to the request:

```
req.Header.Add("Accepted", 'application/json')
```

Header fields are used to add and convey additional information about the request to the server. The HTTP 1/1 protocol includes numerous Header fields:

- The size (in bytes) of the message transmitted is defined as Content-Length. If no value is supplied, the default value is 2.

- The name and version of the application that submits the request are included in the User-Agent header. Curl/7.16.3, for example, if we use curl to make the request. If no value is supplied, Go-http-client/1.1 is used as the default.

- Authorization gives you the credentials you need to make a successful request. API keys, username/passwords, JWTs, and other credentials are used.

- Accept-Encoding defines the types of encoding that are permitted in the response. If no value is supplied, the default is gzipped.

- The Content-Type header specifies the type of material sent in the request to the server. If no value is supplied, the default is application/json.

- Accept determines which media types are permitted in the response.

A request's Header field implements the type map\[string\][]string, in which the keys are strings, and the values are slices of strings.

Our Requests Are Being Authorized

The HTTP Authorization request header can contain credentials used by the server to authenticate a user and grant access to protected resources.

```
....
req, err = http.NewRequest("GET", "https://www.xxxx.xxx", nil)
req.Header.Add("Accept", 'application/json')
```

```
req.Header.Add("Authorization", fmt.Sprintf("token %s",
os.Getenv("TOKEN"))
....
```

In the preceding code snippet, we used the os package in our application to get the access token. This is preferable to just obtaining the token. The Getenv function obtains and parses the environment variable TOKEN.

To send an environment variable to our program before starting it, we may add GITHUB_TOKEN=XXX to our go command, as seen below:

```
$ GITHUB_TOKEN=xxxxx go run main.go
```

WHAT IS THE GoLang REST API?

When working with websites, Representational State Transfer (REST) Application Programming Interface (API) gives user functionality. HTTP requests connect with REST APIs, allowing visitors to traverse a URL-based website. These URLs can return data that is kept as part of the API. Any updates to data or information are made by accessing the database associated with that API's URL. Most APIs nowadays will respond in the form of JSON.

Develop REST APIs readily in the GO programming language by establishing a basic server to process HTTP requests. First, in GoLang, create a .go file. Let's make three functions: Home(), handleReq(), and main():

- The Home() function automatically redirects the API to the Home() function's output.

- To process all URL requests, use the handleReq() method. This method will depend on URLs and calls to their corresponding functions. This function will match the URL path with a function that has been defined.

- The main() method is used to begin the API's execution.

```go
package main
// important libraries
import (
    "fmt"
    "log"
    "net/http"
)
// Home function
func Home()(w1 http.ResponseWriter, r1 *http.Request){
// This is what function will print.
    fmt.Fprintf(w, "Welcome to Home!")

}
// function to handle the requests
func handleReq() {
// will call the Home function by default.
    http.HandleFunc("/", Home)
    log.Fatal(http.ListenAndServe(":8200", nil))
}

func main() {
// starting the API
    handleReq()
}
```

Let's expand on this by adding another endpoint. We'll modify the code above to include a new function, return_contact().

```go
package main
// important-libraries
import (
    "fmt"
    "log"
    "net/http"
)
// Home-function
func Home()(w http.ResponseWriter, r *http.Request){
// This is what the function will print.
    fmt.Fprintf(w, "Welcome to Educative Home!")

}
func return_contact()(w http.ResponseWriter, r *http.
Request){
// This is what the function will print.
    fmt.Fprintf(w, "Email: support@educative.io")

}
```

```
// function to handle the requests
func handleReq() {
// will call the Home function by default.
    http.HandleFunc("/", Home)
    http.HandleFunc("/contact", return_contact)

    log.Fatal(http.ListenAndServe(":8200", nil))
}

func main() {
// starting API
    handleReq()
}
```

A user may now reach the endpoint contact by typing and inputting the URL:

```
http://localhost:8200/contact
```

Using GoLang to Consume a REST API

We will go through how to set up the Go project, the Go Modules utilized, and how to run the code.

Project Setup

```
mkdir GoLang-api
cd GoLang-api
go mod init github.com/cameronldroberts/GoLang-api
touch main.go
```

We're finally ready to get started with the coding. Open the GoLang-api project in our preferred editor and navigate to main.go, which contains the code.

Imports

First, we'll go over imports, which are how we bring in other Go modules. A module in Go is a grouping of one or more packages that contain related code. The following four will be used to access the API. Depending on the editor (and settings) we use, imports may be handled automatically, and we may not need to perform the next step of manually adding imports.

```
package main
import (
 "encoding/json"
 "fmt"
 "io/ioutil"
 "net/http"
)
```

Example of a Response
This is an example of a response from the API when we call it. We can transfer the structure of the JSON answer that we will get into a struct because we know its structure.

```
{
  "id": "XgVnOK6USnb",
  "jokes": "What did the calculator say to the student? We
can count on us",
  "status": 200
  }
```

Struct
Because the struct is quite simple, mapping from JSON to the struct below would not be too complex in this case.

```
type Response struct {
    ID      string 'json:"id"'
    Jokes   string 'json:"jokes"'
    Status int    'json:"status"'
  }
```

Code
Finally, a method invokes the API and processes the response. It is not recommended to place function logic within main() while working with Go because this is the entry point for our application. For the sake of this essay, we will put the code in main, however this is not recommended while programming in the real world.

```
func main() {
  fmt.Println("Calling API....")
  client := &http.Client{}
  req, err := http.NewRequest("GET", " http://www.
laughfactory.com/jokes/clean-jokes", nil)
  if err != nil {
    fmt.Print(err.Error())
  }
  req.Header.Add("Accept", "application/json")
  req.Header.Add("Content-Type", "application/json")
  resp, err := client.Do(req)
  if err != nil {
    fmt.Print(err.Error())
  }
 defer resp.Body.Close()
  bodyBytes, err := ioutil.ReadAll(resp.Body)
  if err != nil {
    fmt.Print(err.Error())
  }
 var responseObject Response
  json.Unmarshal(bodyBytes, &responseObject)
  fmt.Printf("API Response as a struct %+v\n",
responseObject)
 }
```

- First, we make an http client and an http request.

- We then add a few http headers to our request before sending it with "resp, err:= client.Do(req)".

- We read the response and then unmarshal it into our response structure.

- Finally, we print the result.

Run the Project
Use the following command to launch the project.

```
go run main.go
```

The main will be compiled and run as a result of this. Go ahead and file. If everything went correctly, we should have jokes written into our terminal. The output should look like this:

```
go run main.go
Calling API....
API Response as struct {ID:5h399pWLmyd Jokes:What did the
beaver say to the tree? It's been nice gnawing us.
Status:200}
```

Complete code:

```go
package main
import (
 "encoding/json"
 "fmt"
 "io/ioutil"
 "net/http"
)
type Response struct {
 ID      string 'json:"id"'
 Jokes    string 'json:"jokes"'
 Status int     'json:"status"'
}
func main() {
 fmt.Println("Calling API....")
client := &http.Client{}
 req, err := http.NewRequest("GET", " http://www
.laughfactory.com/jokes/clean-jokes", nil)
 if err != nil {
  fmt.Print(err.Error())
 }
 req.Header.Add("Accept", "application/json")
 req.Header.Add("Content-Type", "application/json")
 resp, err := client.Do(req)
 if err != nil {
  fmt.Print(err.Error())
 }
defer resp.Body.Close()
 bodyBytes, err := ioutil.ReadAll(resp.Body)
 if err != nil {
  fmt.Print(err.Error())
 }
var responseObject Response
 json.Unmarshal(bodyBytes, &responseObject)
 fmt.Printf("API Response as a struct %+v\n", responseObject)
}
```

In this chapter, we covered creating a QR code, creating an HTTP client, and working with APIs in GoLang.

Appraisal

Go is a general-purpose scripting language for system programming. It was developed by Rob Pike, Robert Griesemer, and Ken Thompson at Google in 2007. It is a statically typed programming language with syntax similar to C. It has garbage collection, type safety, dynamic typing, and sophisticated built-in types like variable-length arrays and key-value maps. It also contains an extensive standard library, and supports concurrent programming. Go was released in November 2009 and used in some of Google's production systems.

Packages are used in software design to handle dependencies efficiently. Go programming implementations employ a standard compile and link mechanism to generate executable binaries.

Go IS FAST

Go is a speedy scripting language. It is compiled to machine code and will automatically outperform interpreted or virtual runtime languages. Go apps compile rapidly as well, and the final binary is small. Our API delivers an 11.5 MB executable file in seconds.

EASY TO UNDERSTAND

Go's syntax is short compared to other languages, making it easy to learn. We can recall most of it, so we don't need to spend much time looking it up. It's also immaculate and easy to read. Non-Go programmers, especially those accustomed to C-style syntax, can usually read a Go program and comprehend what's going on.

DOI: 10.1201/9781003309055-8

STATIC TYPING

Go is a computer language that is strongly typed and statically typed. Integer, byte, and string are examples of primitive types. Another sort of structure is structure. Like any strongly typed language, the type system allows the compiler to catch entire classes of issues. Go has simple-to-use built-in types for lists and maps.

TYPES OF INTERFACES

In Go, interfaces exist, and any struct can implement an interface by simply implementing its methods. This helps you to decouple the dependencies in our code. Dependencies can then mock in tests. Using interfaces, we may create more modular, testable code. Go also has first-class functions, which helps us write more functional code.

STANDARD LIBRARY

Go includes an excellent standard library. It has handy built-in functions for working with primitive types. Packages make it easy to set up a web server, manage I/O, interface with encryption, and process raw data. JSON serialization and deserialization in the standard library are straightforward. Using "tags," we can add JSON field names directly next to struct fields.

EASIER CONCURRENCY MODEL

Concurrent programming is never simple, but Go makes it simpler than other programming languages. It is pretty simple to create a lightweight thread known as a "goroutine" and interact with it over a "channel." It is possible to design more complex patterns.

TOOLS FOR STATIC ANALYSIS

There are several sophisticated static analysis tools for Go. Gofmt, in particular, formats our code in the approved Go style. This can assist in normalizing many opposing viewpoints on a project and free up our team's time to focus on what the code is doing. Every build is run through gofmt, golint, and vetted, and if any warnings are found, the build fails.

GARBAGE COLLECTION

Memory management in Go was more straightforward than that in C and C++. Objects that have been dynamically allocated are destroyed. Because it does not support pointer arithmetic, Go makes using pointers safer. It also supports the use of value types.

TESTING ASSISTANCE

Testing support is included in the standard library. There is no need for reliance. If we have a code called example.go ahead and save our tests in a file named thing test.go, and then run "go test" Go will perform these tests rapidly.

WHAT'S THE NAME OF IT? IS IT GoLang or Go?

It's easy to hear the language referred to as both Go and GoLang, which might be confusing. We used to think they were names for other languages. However, GoLang is merely another name for Go, with the official name remaining unchanged.

The term GoLang comes from the domain name of the official Go website, GoLang.org. This is beneficial since "GoLang" is far more searchable on Google than "Go." As a result, it simplifies the life of those attempting to learn the programming language.

WHY SHOULD WE STUDY?

A Straightforward Learning Curve

Go is considered to be one of the most fundamental programming languages accessible. It's easy to pick up, especially if we're already familiar with another programming language.

Many Go developers who are confident in their teaching abilities say that they can educate a total novice on how to build an app in hours.

As per the 2020 StackOverflow Developer Survey, one of the main reasons Go climbed from 10th to 5th in popularity is its simplicity.

Excellent Documentation and a Vibrant Community

Go provides rich and straightforward documentation. The documentation may be found on the official website.

Aside from documentation, Go has a large and active community behind it, so we can always seek help if we get stuck.

Because the hashtag #GoLang is commonly used on Twitter, if we get stuck, we may tweet our inquiry with the hashtag attached.

We Can Do a Lot with Go

Go is a flexible programming language that may use for various web development, data research, cloud computing, and others.

If we want to work in cloud computing, we should study Go because it is supported by systems, such as Amazon Web Services, Google Cloud Platform, and Kubernetes.

Wages Are Appealing

As per the 2020 StackOverflow Developer Survey, Go professionals earn the third-highest median salary of $74,000, trailing only Perl and Scala.

This figure will rise more as Go develops in popularity and demand year after year. So, if we want to generate more money, we need to learn how to code in Go.

IS GoLang A SUITABLE CHOICE FOR STARTUPS?

All types of businesses use GoLang because of its scalability and performance. From startups to mid-level enterprises, every sort of organization may benefit from GoLang at a low cost. At the same time, huge corporations choose to use GoLang to manage massive, complicated projects.

IS THERE A FUTURE FOR GoLang in 2022?

In 2022, GoLang will be one of the most popular programming languages for back-end development. GoLang is superior to other programs because it is more lightweight and quicker than other languages.

WHICH METHOD IS THE MOST EFFECTIVE FOR INCREASING THE PERFORMANCE OF A GoLang APP?

Using many CPU cores is the greatest approach to boost the speed of your GoLang application. Goroutines are the finest feature for simply creating concurrency in a GoLang App.

WHEN COMPARED TO OTHER PROGRAMMING LANGUAGES, HOW QUICK IS GoLang?

GoLang is the quickest programming language in terms of performance and compilation time compared to other languages.

WHY IS GoLang SUPERIOR TO OTHER PROGRAMMING LANGUAGES?

With so many programming languages and frameworks available, determine which one is the best may difficult. This section will look at why

GoLang is superior to other popular programming languages like Python and Ruby. We'll talk about simplicity, concurrency support, performance, and much more!

GoLang's Definition

Google's GoLang programming language is an open-source project. It was designed to be a better choice for creating big programs, particularly those that require concurrency capabilities, such as channels and goroutines. GoLang can also compile code into the machine's native instruction set, allowing it to execute quicker than other languages.

BENEFITS OF USING GoLang INSTEAD OF OTHER PROGRAMMING LANGUAGES

The following advantages of GoLang over other programming languages entice developers to choose GoLang in project development.

- **Simplicity:** One of the primary reasons GoLang is superior to other programming languages is its simpler syntax. Go's syntax eliminates semicolons, curly brackets for control structures, and parentheses for function parameters, reducing what would otherwise be four characters to only two. This syntax and code writing simplicity make GoLang code easier to understand, allowing engineers to work faster and detect mistakes.

- **Quick Development:** GoLang significantly decreases development time with error checking, concurrency management, simplifying threads, and scalable goroutines.

- **Portability:** GoLang is portable because it can be compiled for any operating system and architecture. This differs from other languages, which must compile code into bytecode, which can only run on the platform on which it was produced.

- **Type Safety:** Go was built with rules governing how types must behave. So, if it encounters an issue due to those rules, you'll know what occurred and why without having to run additional tests or debug. It also has features like interfaces, which make developing complicated algorithms easier by eliminating part of the complexity.

WELL-KNOWN COMPANIES USE GoLang

Famous companies that use the GoLang Google Cloud Platform include:

- **Google Cloud Platform:** GoLang outperforms other programming languages and is the preferred language for their Kubernetes container orchestration system. This implies that it works with Node.js, Apache Mesos, and Docker containers, among many others.

- **Uber:** Uber's web app, developed in Phoenix on top of the Erlang VM running on the AWS Elastic Beanstalk infrastructure, is powered by GoLang. They also employ a bespoke scheduler implementation called Collective because go doesn't yet have strong support for concurrency at scale. Despite this constraint, GoLang has proved critical in allowing Uber's fast expansion over the last two years by scaling effectively and supporting modifications across tens or even hundreds of thousands of servers.

- **SoundCloud:** SoundCloud employs real-time static analysis, which is only feasible with GoLang. As a result, they opted to use GoLang in conjunction with Ruby on Rails. This makes it easy for consumers to receive immediate results for their searches. Eventually, SoundCloud's reliance grows steadily. Consequently, the organization currently employs six services and dozens of repositories that are entirely developed in GoLang.

WHAT KINDS OF PROJECTS CAN BE CREATED USING GoLang?

GoLang is superior to other programming languages for creating applications that must process large amounts of data at once.

GoLang may also be used as a scripting language with GoLang-written technologies, such as Docker, CoreOS, and Kubernetes. It works well for both small projects that require rapid iteration and bigger projects where it is critical to keep the code maintainable over time.

It makes no difference whether we're launching a firm utilizing containers like Uber, Google Cloud Platform, Red Hat OpenShift, or just deploying your own software without containerization. GoLang is superior to other programming languages and will aid in completing the task.

HOW DO WE MAKE A GoLang APPLICATION?

To begin, "hello" world looks like this:

```
$ echo "Hello Everyone" >hello-everyone
$ go run hello-everyone
```

There are three ways to utilize Go as our primary app development language; each has advantages and disadvantages but can get us up and running faster than other languages when working on small projects.

HOW IS GoLang SUPERIOR TO OTHER PROGRAMMING LANGUAGES?

Although GoLang is superior to other programming languages, it is a general-purpose programming language. Google introduced it in 2007 as an alternative to C++, Java, and Python. Thanks to its official Go compiler for Android, iOS, and Windows platforms, it may utilize on mobile devices.

Concurrency tools such as channels are also available in GoLang, making concurrent programming more accessible. These are ideal for working on numerous projects simultaneously without the need for sophisticated locking mechanisms, such as sync. WaitGroups and mutexes/locks are no longer supported (but they are still accessible).

Finally, GoLang is superior to other programming languages due to its speed. It is statically compiled, meaning there is no runtime compilation process after every line of code we write.

HOW DOES YAHOO MAKE USE OF GoLang?

Since 2013, Yahoo has used GoLang to run their search engine. One reason for development was that they want a programming language with high concurrency and dependability. But it was also the speed with which it builds programs that drew them in – less lost time between code updates being performed.

Also, because GoLang is superior to other programming languages, its popularity has grown over time, owing to the scarcity of alternatives, such as Python or Java. It may include properties, such as ease of development, asynchronous I/O, and parallelism (all without sacrificing performance).

HOW DOES GoLang COMPARE TO OTHER LANGUAGES?

GoLang is ideal for tasks that require a high level of concurrency. When faced with rising demands on their software systems from mobile, many firms suffer.

WHERE DOES GOOGLE USE GoLang?

Google uses GoLang to run its backend infrastructure and its iPhone translation app, Google Translate.

Dropbox is another Google product built with GoLang. Users may keep various files in the store and access them from any location and device.

GoLang's FUTURE

GoLang's future appears promising. The language will continue to be developed as developer demands evolve, and it will very certainly become more popular in the future years. As a result, if we don't want to fall behind, we should plan on learning it, as GoLang is superior to other programming languages.

WHAT ARE ITS STRENGTHS?

GoLang's strength is not just its speed (programs are built rapidly), but also its clean code with fewer mistakes owing to the lack of type checking, which allows for compiler optimizations. It provides great performance consistency since there are no checks across distinct system types, which might cause issues when actions combine numerous data sources.

WHERE DOES AMAZON USE GoLang?

One of the most active GoLang users is Amazon Web Services. The firm also published extensively on GoLang on its blog, found here. Amazon Web Services (AWS) Blog – General.

WHERE DOES NETFLIX MAKE USE OF GoLang?

Netflix uses GoLang in their API server and web application development since it outperforms other programming languages. They're also using it to make changes faster and with fewer code lines. As a consequence, they now have a more stable product that encourages better management.

WHAT ELSE IS IT USED FOR?

Many enterprises, like DigitalOcean, employ GoLang because of its quickness in answering requests and the flexibility to leverage Google Cloud Platform services via an SDK.

Groupon is also using it to construct extremely scalable website apps with minimal development effort across all of their geographies. Other firms including as also use this language.

Walmart Labs actively employs GoLang, even for production Expedia IT Engineers build 40% of new APIs in GoLang.

HOW IS GoLang SUPERIOR THAN OTHER PROGRAMMING LANGUAGES FOR BUSINESS?

GoLang is a compiled programming language. This indicates that the compiler generates an executable file (.exe) that may run without any additional procedures.

GoLang programs are often significantly quicker than those written in interpreted languages, such as Python, Ruby, or JavaScript. They do not need to be transformed before execution a process known as "interpretation."

This corresponds to lower latency for user-facing apps and a lower risk of defects while delivering new code updates, as opposed to dynamically typed languages (including PHP).

GoLang binaries are precompiled, so there is no need to wait for extra compilation periods. Furthermore, static type checking provides other benefits, such as greater testing coverage and stronger guarantees, which may be invaluable in big projects.

It's not only about speed and deployment for developers; making the language feel more "theirs" is also vital. GoLang has been marketed as being particularly easy to read with its simple syntax. This ensures that functions and code blocks are clearly separated. As a result, GoLang has become one of the most popular programming languages among programmers who have tried it.

OTHER ADVANTAGES OF USING GoLang

GoLang contains built-in concurrency and parallelism, unlike other languages, which require additional support.

GoLang provides much more than simply readability. The wording is basic, yet effective. It is incredibly portable, quick, and scalable with low developer effort, making GoLang an excellent choice for any project.

If we're searching for a Python or Java successor, Go is a great option. Because of all of its advantages, it is one of the finest programming languages for 2018.

GoLang is a computer language developed by Google that has become one of the most popular languages today. Therefore, it's no surprise that GoLang development professionals are in high demand.

It's also worth noting that, as an open-source language, GoLang is more stable than other languages. However, because of its simplicity and effectiveness, it can be utilized by anybody to construct their own apps and expand.

It is critical not just for corporations but also for people who wish to start their own enterprises. Because they do not require any kind of pricey software license or membership charge to get started with development. The combination of simplicity and effectiveness makes this a formidable weapon worth adding to your arsenal right now.

It removes the need to deal with Java. A more sophisticated language that necessitates the creation of extra code, which might slow down application performance. While Java may be excellent for corporate applications due to its extensive library, GoLang was created particularly for web app development, with no reliance on other languages like Python or Ruby.

HOW IS GoLang SUPERIOR THAN OTHER PROGRAMMING LANGUAGES FOR APP DEVELOPMENT?

It is less complex than JavaScript, yet it is strong enough to develop rich-media webpages and even gaming engines. Despite this, it is still compatible with all main developer tools, such as Google Maps API and Android Studio.

The GoLang compiler does not require runtime files. It implies that there will be no lengthy download waits before we begin our project. As a result, it enables speedier development and allows developers to devote more time to coding.

GoLang is one of the simplest programming languages to learn. Because its command-line parameters are minimal, its syntax is similar to those of other popular languages, such as Java or C++.

GoLang also provides type safety. It implies you won't have to spend as much time testing alternative code possibilities for faults. This saves a substantial amount of development time, allowing developers to allocate that time to other responsibilities.

In general, GoLang eliminates a lot of the headache of finding engineers who can work swiftly and efficiently. While remaining skilled enough to complete their tasks successfully without worrying about language mismatch among programmers.

While there may not be many firms that use GoLang yet. Google's success may be attributed to its rapid and simple syntax and the fact that it is a high-level language.

CREATING A WEBSITE

It's time to reconsider your attitude about GoLang. Investigate the factors contributing to GoLang's remarkable rise in popularity in recent years. Other computer languages, such as Python and Ruby, perform worse than GoLang. Because it can be compiled into native code, GoLang outperforms other programming languages. Google's Native Client toolchain, on the other hand, has no dependencies for standalone apps (NAC).

NAC's capability allows enterprises to search for lightning-fast outcomes from their programs. As a result, there is no bloat or extra baggage that is sometimes associated with other programming languages.

Because it does not require a runtime, Google's GoLang is faster than any other language. As a result, execution is substantially quicker than in Java or C++, and even faster in memory-constrained systems like embedded devices.

HOW DOES Go LINE UP AGAINST PYTHON?

- Python and Go both have a straightforward syntax and are supported by all major cloud providers first-party.

- Both Go and Python are simple to learn and straightforward to get started with for novices. Which is easier is debatable. Go is a simpler language that can be taught more quickly, but some people find it more difficult to get started than Python, which takes longer to master since there is more to understand.

- When compared to Python, Go is the new kid on the block, and it was built to be quick. Python is slower than Go. Much quicker.

- Python is popular in data science, whereas Go is ideal for system development.

- Python, as the senior language, has a larger library and community established around it.

- Python's dynamic typing may make it superior than Go for rapid prototyping.

- With Go, it may be easier to execute apps at scale. Google designed Go to address issues on a Google-sized scale, making it perfect for working on big concurrent applications. Concurrency, or the ability to run more than one program/task at the same time, is supported by Go. Python, meanwhile, does not.

IS Go AN OBJECT-ORIENTED PROGRAMMING LANGUAGE?

Both yes and no. There is no type hierarchy in Go, despite the fact that it contains types and functions and supports object-oriented programming. The idea of "interface" in Go offers a distinct approach that we feel is easier to use and more generic in certain aspects. There are various techniques to embed types in other types to give a similar – but not identical – to subclassing experience. Furthermore, Go methods are more broad than C++ or Java methods in that they may be written for any form of data, including built-in types, such as raw, "unboxed" integers. They are not limited to structs (classes).

Furthermore, the lack of a type hierarchy makes "things" in Go feel considerably lighter than in languages like C++ or Java.

Go took principles from procedural programming, functional programming, and object-oriented programming and combined them, while leaving out others, to develop its own distinct flavor of idiomatic programming style.

Enter structs Instead of Classes

Go does not have classes in the classic sense, but it does have struct types, which are far more powerful than their C counterpart. Struct types and their associated methods serve the same purpose as conventional classes, where the struct just contains the state and not the behavior, and the methods provide the behavior by enabling the state to be changed.

Encapsulation

One of the nicest aspects of Go is that capitalized fields, methods, and functions are all public. All other fields are unique to the package and are not exported. We can tell if anything is public or private with a single glance. There are no safeguards since there is no legacy.

Composition Outweighs Inheritance

This well-known notion, which is also addressed in the Gang of Four book, appears frequently in Go code.

We can include an unnamed (anonymous) field, which exposes the struct's fields and functions when declaring a struct. This is known as struct embedding.

Interfaces

Forget about Java and PHP-style interfaces. Interfaces in Go are considerably different, and one important aspect is that interfaces are met implicitly.

Interfaces are often relatively tiny, consisting of only one method. In idiomatic Go, we won't find extensive lists of methods.

Interfaces neatly provide polymorphism: by adopting an interface, we announce our readiness to embrace any kind of object that satisfies that interface.

Methods

Methods exist for types. They are specified outside of the type definition, using a syntax that may be familiar to JavaScript prototype method declarations.

Types Can Assign Methods

Methods can apply to any type, even simple data types. We cannot "enrich" the built-in basic types since methods may only add in the same package as the type is declared, but we can enrich any named type we build with a base type underlying representation.

Functions

Consider a standard object-oriented programming language, such as Java. How many times have we defined a class with static methods called "Utils"?

This is done to get around the idea that everything is an object and that function definition must contain within classes. This does not happen in Go since it contains functions. Not everything has to be an object or a method in the real world. Although "classes" and "objects" are beneficial, they cannot used for everything.

In Go, not everything is an object (and technically nothing is an object, although some people refer to type values and variables as "objects"), methods are functions connected with a type, but Go also permits functions to reside outside of an object, similar to C functions.

So, although Go supports methods, it also supports functions, including first-class functions (functions can store as struct fields, can pass as arguments to other functions, can return from a function or methods return value).

Less Bloat

Overall, the Go object-oriented programming approach is highly versatile and clear. Leaving classes and inheritance behind, we'll notice very little boilerplate, and instead of arguing over the ideal hierarchical structure for classes, which becomes difficult to modify, we'll have the ability to compose and decompose types as needed.

WHAT IS THE CAPABILITY OF GoLang?

Because Go is a general-purpose programming language, we may use it to create a variety of solutions. Furthermore, it has a slew of capabilities that help with the software development process, such as automated documentation and an embedded testing environment. Go, in addition to these development tools, expands the technological capabilities of its predecessors. For example, it has improved memory management, garbage collection, and concurrency support.

Creating Solutions Using Go

Although Go's authors designed the language to replace C, they also borrowed elements from other languages to improve Go's capabilities. Its source code readability and reusability, for example, are comparable to Python. It also performs well in networking and multi-server configurations. These characteristics make it an excellent platform for developing solutions ranging from web development to machine learning.

Applications for the Web

The intrinsic capabilities of GoLang to provide software developers with parallelism and scalability makes it quite well for web development projects. Go also outperforms dynamically typed languages like Python and PHP in terms of speed and performance. The GoLang community has also created a number of web app frameworks, including Beego, Martini, and Revel. These platforms have a number of basic capabilities that software developers may use to deliver projects more quickly and efficiently.

In addition to app frameworks, software developers may leverage Go's built-in features to create web apps. HTML, JSON, and HTTP are all part of the language's core codebase. We can use GoLang to develop a web server because it was designed by Google to satisfy their internal web infrastructure requirements. The actual benefit of using this technique is that the app and server share the same codebase, resulting in improved integration, scalability, and speed.

Development on the Server

Because of its concurrency, scalability, and speed, Go is an excellent language for developing server-side applications. Its implementation of goroutines deviates from the typical design of an Operating System thread required for each thread of operation. On the other hand, the goroutine oversees the interface between the code and the underlying server architecture. This method generates a natural non-blocking I/O paradigm, comparable to the methodology employed by Node.js. On the other hand, the Go callback system interacts with the scheduler automatically. Because of this architecture, each OS core may have a non-blocking I/O thread, making it much quicker and more scalable.

Go's static typing makes it a suitable language for server-side programming and its inherent non-blocking I/O features. Because the code is compiled into executable binaries before deployment, it does not require any runtime interpretation like JavaScript or Python. It is also simpler to deploy because the binary contains any code dependencies, eliminating the need to setup them in production.

Distributed Services

Concurrency is required for services dispersed across a network, such as those found in a microservices architecture. Because of Go's advantages in this area are well-suited for developing solutions that adhere to a distributed services model.

Using goroutines, software developers may provide the scalability required to manage several threads simultaneously. In addition to Go channels, this functionality creates the concurrency required for distributed network services. These Go code artifacts offer the communication object that allows goroutines to communicate information. In addition to maintaining the contact between goroutines, these objects offer the synchronization required for scalable event processing across dispersed network systems.

Cloud-Native Development

Because of its concurrency and networking features, Go has emerged as the language of cloud infrastructure. When we consider that Google built Go specifically for this reason, its features correspond nicely with the needs of cloud-native apps. Go's creators designed it for portability in addition to its built-in concurrency and networking features. These three characteristics make it a viable solution for developing cloud-based apps.

The mobility of GoLang is due to its cross-platform compatibility. We just need to write the code once using Go, and we can then deploy it wherever. Because we only need to handle one codebase, this feature makes maintainability significantly more realistic. If the software has to be changed, we simply need to make one modification and then build it for the appropriate deployment platform, whether Windows, Linux, or macOS. It also supports x86, ARM, and other specialized technologies like ppc64 and MIPS, so we may use it on services that use diverse CPU architectures.

Machine Learning

Go's adaptability as a general-purpose, cross-platform programming language allows software developers to utilize its machine learning capabilities. As a statically typed programming language, its binaries offer the speed and performance required for CPU-intensive, high computation computations. Its scalability, parallelism, and portability also provide data scientists with the flexibility to construct large-scale machine learning systems.

There are various machine learning libraries created in Go, in addition to its built-in functionality. Platforms, such as GoLearn, Gorgonia, and goml, are just a few examples. Using these technologies, software developers may integrate their code without relying on other libraries developed in a different programming language. Furthermore, because solution architects only need to handle a single Go codebase, this integration provides excellent portability and maintainability.

The Versatility of GoLang

Go's capabilities make it a versatile general-purpose programming language that can use to create a broad variety of applications. Its Goroutines, channels, and generated machine code binaries enable modern software solutions' scalability, concurrency, and portability. Go is a programming language that was developed in the cloud and was designed for speed. It can use to construct everything from web services and microservices to cloud-native apps and machine learning solutions.

Cheat Sheet

This cheat sheet offers some handy GoLang code snippets.

HEYYY EVERYONE

```
heyyy.go
package main

import "fmt"

func main() {
  message := greetMe("everyone")
  fmt.Println(message)
}

func greetMe(name string) string {
  return "Heyyy, " + name + "!"
}
```

Run:

```
$ go build
```

VARIABLES

Variable declaration:

```
var msg string
msg = "Heyyy"
```

```
Shortcut of above (Infers type)
msg := "Heyyy"
```

CONSTANTS

```
const Phi = 1.818
```

Constants can take the form of a character, string, boolean, or numeric value.

Basic Types
Strings

```
str := "Heyyy"
str := 'Multiline
string'
```

Strings are of the string type.

Numbers
Typical types:

```
num := 4          // int
num := 4.         // float64
num := 4 + 5i     // complex128
num := byte('a')  // byte (alias for uint8)
Other types
var u uint = 9          // uint (unsigned)
var p float32 = 32.7  // 32-bit float
```

Arrays

```
// var-numbers [5]int
numbers := [...]int{0, 0, 0, 0, 0}
```

Arrays are always the same size.

Slices

```
slice := []int{12, 32, 47}
slice := []byte("Heyyy")
```

Unlike arrays, slices have a variable size.

Pointers

```
func main () {
  x := *getPointer()
  fmt.Println("Value is", x)
}
```

```
func getPointer () (myPointer *int) {
  y := 134
  return &a
}

y:= new(int)
*y = 234
```

Pointers point to a variable's memory location. Go has been completely garbage-collected.

Type Conversions

```
x := 2
y := float64(x)
z := uint(x)
```

FLOW CONTROL

Conditional

```
if day == "saturday" || day == "sunday" {
  rest()
} else if day == "tuesday" && isTired() {
  groan()
} else {
  work()
}
```

Statements in if

```
if _, err := doThing(); err != nil {
  fmt.Println("Uh-oh")
}
```

In an if statement, a condition can be preceded by a statement before a;. Variables defined by the statement are only valid until the end of the if expression.

Switch

```
switch day {
  case "saturday":
    // cases do not "fall through" by default!
    fallthrough
```

```
  case "sunday":
    rest()

  default:
    work()
}
```

For Loop

```
for count := 0; count <= 20; count++ {
  fmt.Println("Counter is at", count)
}
```

For-Range Loop

```
entry := []string{"Jacky","Rohan","Lonas"}
for x, val := range entry {
  fmt.Printf("At position %d, character %s is
present\n", x, val)
}
```

While Loop

```
k := 0
a := 42
for k != a {
  k := guess()
}
```

FUNCTIONS

Lambdas

```
myfunc := func() bool {
  return a > 20000
}
```

Multiple Return Types

```
x, y := getMessage()
func getMessage() (x string, y string) {
  return "Hello", "Everyone"
}
```

Named Return Values

```go
func split(sum int) (a, b int) {
  a = sum * 41 / 19
  b = sum - a
  return
}
```

PACKAGES

Importing

```go
import "fmt"
import "math/rand"
import (
  "fmt"        // give fmt.Println
  "math/rand"  // give rand.Intn
)
```

Aliases

```go
import x "math/rand"

x.Intn()
```

Exporting Names

```go
func Heyyy () {
  ...
}
```

Packages

```go
package heyyy
```

CONCURRENCY

Goroutines

```go
func main() {
  // A "channel"
  ch := make(chan string)

  // Start the concurrent routines
  go push("Loe", ch)
```

```
    go push("Harry", ch)
    go push("Kurly", ch)

    // Read the 3 results
    // (Since our goroutines are concurrent,
    // the order isn't guaranteed)
    fmt.Println(<-ch, <-ch, <-ch)
}
```

```
func push(name string, ch chan string) {
    msg := "Hello, " + name
    ch <- msg
}
```

Buffered Channels

```
ch := make(chan int, 2)
ch <- 1
ch <- 2
ch <- 3

// fatal error:
// all goroutines are asleep - deadlock!
```

Closing Channels

```
Closes a channel
ch <- 1
ch <- 2
ch <- 3
close(ch)
```

Iterates across channel until it is closed.

```
for x := range ch {
    ...
}
```

```
Closed if ok == false
k, ok := <- ch
```

WaitGroup

```
import "sync"

func main() {
  var wg sync.WaitGroup

  for _, item := range itemList {
    // Increment the WaitGroup Counter
    wg.Add(1)
    go doOperation(&wg, item)
  }
  // Wait for the goroutines to finish
  wg.Wait()

}


func doOperation(wg *sync.WaitGroup, item string) {
  defer wg.Done()
  // do operation on the item
  // ....
}
```

ERROR CONTROL

Defer

```
func main() {
  defer fmt.Println("Done")
  fmt.Println("Working")
}
```

The implementation of a function is postponed until the surrounding function returns. Although the parameters are assessed instantly, the function call is not executed until later.

Deferring Functions

```
func main() {
  defer func() {
    fmt.Println("Done")
  }()
  fmt.Println("Working")
}
```

Defer blocks are better suited to lambdas.

```
func main() {
  var x = int64(0)
  defer func(x *int64) {
    fmt.Printf("& %v Unix Sec\n", *x)
  }(&x)
  fmt.Print("Done ")
  x = time.Now().Unix()
}
```

Unless we provide a reference to acquire the final value at the end of main, the defer func utilizes the current value of x.

STRUCTS

Defining

```
type Vertex struct {
  A int
  B int
}
```

```
func main() {
  v := Vertex{1, 2}
  v.A = 4
  fmt.Println(v.A, v.B)
}
```

Literals

```
v := Vertex{A: 1, B: 2}
// Field names can omitt
v := Vertex{1, 2}
// B is implicit
v := Vertex{A: 1}
```

Pointers to Structs

```
v := &Vertex{1, 2}
v.A = 2
```

Doing v.A is the same as doing (*v).A, when v is a pointer.

METHODS

Receivers

```go
type Vertex struct {
  A, B float64
}
func (v Vertex) Abs() float64 {
  return math.Sqrt(v.A * v.A + v.B * v.B)
}

v := Vertex{1, 2}
v.Abs()
```

Mutation

```go
func (v *Vertex) Scale(f float64) {
  v.A = v.A * f
  v.B = v.B * f
}

v := Vertex{6, 13}
v.Scale(0.5)
// 'v' is updated
```

Interfaces

Basic interface:

```go
type Shape interface {
  Area() float64
  Perimeter() float64
}
```

Struct

```go
type Rectangle struct {
  Length, Width float64
}
```

Methods

```go
func (k Rectangle) Area() float64 {
  return k.Length * k.Width
}
```

```go
func (k Rectangle) Perimeter() float64 {
  return 2 * (k.Length + k.Width)
}
```

Interface Example

```go
func main() {
  var k Shape = Rectangle{Length: 3, Width: 4}
  fmt.Printf("Type of k: %T, Area: %v, Perimeter:
%v.", k, k.Area(), k.Perimeter())
}
```

Bibliography

7 Types of Golang Operators – golangprograms.com. (n.d.). 7 Types of Golang Operators – Golangprograms.Com; www.golangprograms.com. Retrieved July 11, 2022, from https://www.golangprograms.com/go-language/operators.html

8 Key Reasons to Choose Go Programming Language for Cloud Infrastructure Projects | Xoriant. (n.d.). Xoriant; www.xoriant.com. Retrieved July 11, 2022, from https://www.xoriant.com/blog/product-engineering/go-programming-language-for-cloud-infrastructure-projects.html

A Pattern for Optimizing Go | Splunk. (2020, September 24). Splunk-Blogs; www.splunk.com. https://www.splunk.com/en_us/blog/devops/a-pattern-for-optimizing-go-2.html

A Practical Guide to Interfaces in Go (Golang) – golangbot.com. (2020, March 1). Go Tutorial – Learn Go from the Basics with Code Examples; golangbot.com. https://golangbot.com/interfaces-part-1/

Bodnar, J. (2022, April 25). *Go variable – working with variables in Golang*. Go Variable – Working with Variables in Golang; zetcode.com. https://zetcode.com/golang/variable/

Chapter 4. Arrays, slices, and maps · Go in Action. (n.d.). Chapter 4. Arrays, Slices, and Maps · Go in Action; livebook.manning.com. Retrieved July 11, 2022, from https://livebook.manning.com/book/go-in-action/chapter-4/22

Concurrency in Go | Engineering Education (EngEd) Program | Section. (n.d.). Engineering Education (EngEd) Program | Section; www.section.io. Retrieved July 11, 2022, from https://www.section.io/engineering-education/concurrency-in-go/#:~:text=In%20Go%2C%20concurrency%20works%20through,alongside%20other%20code%20or%20programs

Create a new project | GoLand. (2022, April 22). GoLand Help; www.jetbrains.com. https://www.jetbrains.com/help/go/create-new-go-project.html#download-go-sdk

Create an empty file in Golang – golangprograms.com. (n.d.). Create an Empty File in Golang – Golangprograms.Com; www.golangprograms.com. Retrieved July 11, 2022, from https://www.golangprograms.com/create-an-empty-file.html

DASC, T. is. (2020, July 11). *Seven Golang Features you must know about | by This is DASC | Medium*. Medium; medium.com. https://medium.com/@thisisdasc/seven-golang-features-you-must-know-about-944485d413fe

Error handling in Golang. (2021, May 4). Gabriel Tanner; gabrieltanner.org. https://gabrieltanner.org/blog/golang-error-handling-definitive-guide/

Fadatare, R. (n.d.). *Go (Golang) Read and Write File Example Tutorial.* Go (Golang) Read and Write File Example Tutorial; www.javaguides.net. Retrieved July 11, 2022, from https://www.javaguides.net/2021/05/go-golang-read-and-write-file-example.html

Forbes, E. (n.d.). *Reading And Writing To Files in Go | TutorialEdge.net.* TutorialEdge; tutorialedge.net. Retrieved July 11, 2022, from https://tutorialedge.net/golang/reading-writing-files-in-go/

Generate QR code with data in Golang | Golang Developer tips. (2021, October 25). Golang Developer Tips | See More. Do More...; godevtips.com. https://godevtips.com/en/2021/10/25/generate-qr-code-with-data-in-golang/

Getting started with Golang: A tutorial for beginners. (n.d.). Educative: Interactive Courses for Software Developers; www.educative.io. Retrieved July 11, 2022, from https://www.educative.io/blog/golang-tutorial

Go – Functions. (n.d.). Go – Functions; www.tutorialspoint.com. Retrieved July 11, 2022, from https://www.tutorialspoint.com/go/go_functions.htm

Go Basic Syntax Tutorial | KoderHQ. (n.d.). Go Basic Syntax Tutorial | KoderHQ; www.koderhq.com. Retrieved July 11, 2022, from https://www.koderhq.com/tutorial/go/syntax/

Go cheatsheet. (n.d.). Devhints.Io Cheatsheets; devhints.io. Retrieved July 11, 2022, from https://devhints.io/go

Go Packages (With Examples). (n.d.). Go Packages (With Examples); www.programiz.com. Retrieved July 11, 2022, from https://www.programiz.com/golang/packages

Go Programming Language (Introduction) – GeeksforGeeks. (2018, April 25). GeeksforGeeks; www.geeksforgeeks.org. https://www.geeksforgeeks.org/go-programming-language-introduction/

Go Syntax. (n.d.). Go Syntax; www.w3schools.com. Retrieved July 11, 2022, from https://www.w3schools.com/go/go_syntax.php

Go Variables and Constants. (n.d.). Go Variables and Constants; www.programiz.com. Retrieved July 11, 2022, from https://www.programiz.com/golang/variables-constants

Golang basics – writing unit tests. (2017, February 9). Alex Ellis' Blog; blog.alexellis.io. https://blog.alexellis.io/golang-writing-unit-tests/

Golang Maps – GeeksforGeeks. (2019, July 22). GeeksforGeeks; www.geeksforgeeks.org. https://www.geeksforgeeks.org/golang-maps/

Golang Tutorial: Learn Go Programming Language for Beginners. (2020, January 1). Guru99; www.guru99.com. https://www.guru99.com/google-go-tutorial.html

Guide on Go Programming Language. (2019, October 1). Appinventiv; appinventiv.com. https://appinventiv.com/blog/mini-guide-to-go-programming-language/

How to become a Golang developer: 6 step career guide. (n.d.). Educative: Interactive Courses for Software Developers; www.educative.io. Retrieved July 11, 2022, from https://www.educative.io/blog/become-golang-developer

How to Create an Empty File in Golang? – GeeksforGeeks. (2020, March 12). GeeksforGeeks; www.geeksforgeeks.org. https://www.geeksforgeeks.org/how-to-create-an-empty-file-in-golang/

How to Install Go on Windows? – GeeksforGeeks. (2019, June 28). GeeksforGeeks; www.geeksforgeeks.org. https://www.geeksforgeeks.org/how-to-install-go-on-windows/#:~:text=Downloading%20and%20Installing%20Go&text=Step%201%3A%20After%20downloading%2C%20unzip,you%20want%20to%20install%20this

Infante, W. (2021, September 24). *Golang Testing with TDD. Learning the basics of Go with a… | by William Infante | Medium.* Medium; williaminfante.medium.com. https://williaminfante.medium.com/golang-testing-with-tdd-e548d8be776

Interfaces in Golang – GeeksforGeeks. (2019, August 16). GeeksforGeeks; www.geeksforgeeks.org. https://www.geeksforgeeks.org/interfaces-in-golang/

Introduction to Functions in Golang | CalliCoder. (2018, March 29). CalliCoder; www.callicoder.com. https://www.callicoder.com/golang-functions/

Is Golang the Future? (n.d.). Is Golang the Future?; www.linkedin.com. Retrieved July 11, 2022, from https://www.linkedin.com/pulse/golang-future-georgia-luxton/

Keva Laya, S. E. (2022, February 7). *Is Golang Worth Learning.* Career Karma; careerkarma.com. https://careerkarma.com/blog/is-golang-worth-learning/#:~:text=Yes%2C%20Golang%20is%20still%20worth,the%20most%20loved%20languages%20list

Nagarajan, M. (2020, May 12). *Learning Go—Array, Slice, Map.* Medium; levelup.gitconnected.com. https://levelup.gitconnected.com/learning-go-array-slice-map-934eed320b1c

Nnakwue, A. (2022, January 14). *Exploring structs and interfaces in Go – LogRocket Blog.* LogRocket Blog; blog.logrocket.com. https://blog.logrocket.com/exploring-structs-interfaces-go/

Overview of testing package in Golang – GeeksforGeeks. (2020, August 21). GeeksforGeeks; www.geeksforgeeks.org. https://www.geeksforgeeks.org/overview-of-testing-package-in-golang/#:~:text=The%20testing%20package%20provides%20support,func%20TestXxx(*testing.T)

Packages in Golang – GeeksforGeeks. (2019, October 25). GeeksforGeeks; www.geeksforgeeks.org. https://www.geeksforgeeks.org/packages-in-golang/#:~:text=Packages%20are%20the%20most%20powerful,of%20the%20other%20package%20programs

Parr, K. (2021, September 13). *How to use pointers in Go – LogRocket Blog.* LogRocket Blog; blog.logrocket.com. https://blog.logrocket.com/how-to-use-pointers-in-go/

Reasons Why Golang is Better than other Programming Languages? (2021, May 7). Supersourcing; supersourcing.com. https://supersourcing.com/blog/reasons-why-golang-is-better-than-other-programming-languages/#:~:text=Golang%20is%20better%20than%20other%20programming%20languages%2C%20therefore%20it%20reduces,to%20save%20time%20and%20resources

Schurman, B. (2022, January 7). *Effective Error Handling in Golang – Earthly Blog*. Earthly Blog; earthly.dev. https://earthly.dev/blog/golang-errors/#:~: text=Error%20handling%20in%20Go%20is,catch%20methods%20to%20 handle%20them

Scully, E. (2020, August 6). *Go vs C++: A Complete Comparison | Career Karma*. Career Karma; careerkarma.com. https://careerkarma.com/blog/go-vs-c-plus-plus/#:~:text=Golang%20can%20boast%20speeds%20of,and%20 compiling%20pays%20off%20here

Structs in Go (Golang) | Detailed Tutorial with Examples | golangbot.com. (2020, May 1). Go Tutorial – Learn Go from the Basics with Code Examples; golangbot.com. https://golangbot.com/structs/

Talim, S. M. (2015, September 2). *What is the future for Go?. This year I had the privilege to... | by Satish Manohar Talim | Medium*. Medium; medium.com. https:// medium.com/@IndianGuru/what-is-the-future-for-go-e002b06a240b#: ~:text=Baron%20Schwartz%20%E2%80%94%20Go%20programmers%20 are,This%20will%20only%20increase

The 7 Best Ways to Learn Golang and Find Your Inner Gopher | Boot.dev. (2022, February 5). The 7 Best Ways to Learn Golang and Find Your Inner Gopher | Boot.Dev; blog.boot.dev. https://blog.boot.dev/golang/best-ways-to-learn-golang/#:~:text=Learn%20Go%20the%20free%20way&text=It's%20also%20 useful%20for%20experienced,code%20no%20matter%20their%20circumstance

Top 7 Reasons to Learn Golang – GeeksforGeeks. (2020, August 16). GeeksforGeeks; www.geeksforgeeks.org. https://www.geeksforgeeks.org/top-7-reasons-to-learn-golang/#:~:text=Easy%20to%20Learn,to%20get%20the%20task%20done

Tutu, A. (2017, February 7). *Writing Your First Program with Go | by AnnMargaret Tutu | Medium*. Medium; codeamt.medium.com. https://codeamt.medium. com/writing-your-first-program-with-go-79ee6a3c3b4d

Understanding Control Structures in Go | Developer.com. (2021, November 25). Developer.Com; www.developer.com. https://www.developer.com/languages/ control-structures-golang/

Understanding Pointers in Go | DigitalOcean. (2020, July 21). Understanding Pointers in Go | DigitalOcean; www.digitalocean.com. https://www.digital-ocean.com/community/conceptual_articles/understanding-pointers-in-go

Web Application to generate QR code in Go Programming Language – golangprograms.com. (n.d.). Web Application to Generate QR Code in Go Programming Language – Golangprograms.Com; www.golangprograms. com. Retrieved July 11, 2022, from https://www.golangprograms.com/web-application-to-generate-qr-code-in-golang.html

What is the Go Programming Language? (2020, May 1). SearchITOperations; www. techtarget.com. https://www.techtarget.com/searchitoperations/definition/ Go-programming-language#:~:text=Go%20(also%20called%20Golang% 20or,is%20statically%20typed%20and%20explicit

Your First Program — An Introduction to Programming in Go | Go Resources. (n.d.). Your First Program — An Introduction to Programming in Go | Go Resources; www.golang-book.com. Retrieved July 11, 2022, from https:// www.golang-book.com/books/intro/2

Index